PRAISE FOR
CREATIVITY AND
DATA MARKETING

"In a landscape weighed down by buzzwords and big concepts, Becky has crafted a thoughtful guide to navigating the art and science of data informed marketing. Too often the creative process of inspiration and design is divorced from the strategic practice of insight and analysis. This book is a much-needed bridge that models a new way of working while bringing these concepts alive through case studies and practical applications. A must-read for any modern marketer."
Mike Raffensperger, Head of Marketing, Amazon Live

"If you don't exclusively work with numbers, this is the least scary book on data that you could read. If you do work exclusively with numbers, this is the least scary book on data that you could share within your company to get everyone onto the same page. This book is every conversation you've wanted to have about data but weren't sure how to have. A comprehensive smorgasbord of the critical concepts, nuanced and undogmatic suggestions for how to apply them, and a handful of case studies that show the ideas in effect. For someone whose career has focused on finding humanity in numbers, it comes as no surprise that Becky's book puts her own humanity on full display in her explanation of numbers, where to find them and how they work their ways through companies. Data? Simple. Start here."
Mark Pollard, Founder of Mighty Jungle and Former Head of Strategy and Strategy Innovation at Big Spaceship, Saatchi & Saatchia and Leo Burnett

"At times journalistic and other times philosophical, Becky has written something I wish I had had during my early days in the entertainment industry. The book breaks down any misconceptions I had about data and even how I think about data and replaces them with new ways to think about things. She takes a feared topic like data and humanizes it. It's a must-read for anyone in the creative fields. An interesting and challenging book that can empower anyone who operates in a category, company or organization they consider creative. Becky helped provide a roadmap to review and reshape parts of my marketing organization to deliver on the power of data and insights. Her style and focus reflect a dedication to the spirit of experimentation to make things better and as a result has inspired and infused my department with that too."

Don Gold, CEO of start-up A Beautiful Perspective, Founder of UFCFit, Former VP of Entertainment, UFC

"This book mirrors design thinking through and through in its recommendation on how to make better marketing. This is one of many books, but it's the first of what I believe could be seminal texts on the use of data to drive marketing, new products and digital experiences. Big ideas, by nature, take a long time to work. They tackle the root, but to make effective change they take time. Becky has combined years'-worth of literature with a poetic perspective and a grounded sensibility of what's practical and distilled the debate on data and creativity in a way that's useful."

Vivian Rosenthal, Chief Founder in Residence of 30 Weeks, Google's incubator, and CEO of Snaps

"When you start humanizing the data beyond the transactions and purchase behaviour, true insight can be found. The principles that Becky outlines in this book have helped to reshape my data-heavy marketing organization to embrace creative experimentation. This experimentation has helped us create more effective and contextually relevant programs."

Monica Bloom, Global Vice President, Integrated Marketing at Getty Images

"The key battleground in marketing for the 21st century will be how creativity and data work together. Becky provides a vivid field guide to success. Advertising and media is an industry of people, and Becky focuses *how* this works – from players to process. Our industry has been *changed* by data; Becky covers philosophy, psychology, statistics and provides a look at how agency planners and creatives can better partner with brand clients to create relevant, engaging and business-driving work."

Paul Woolmington, Founder of Naked Communications, CEO

CREATIVITY AND DATA MARKETING

CREATIVITY AND DATA MARKETING

A practical guide to data innovation

KoganPage

First published in Great Britain and the United States in 2017 by Kogan Page Limited

2nd Floor, 45 Gee Street	c/o Martin P Hill Consulting	4737/23 Ansari Road
London	122 W 27th Street	Daryaganj
EC1V 3RS	New York, NY 10001	New Delhi 110002
United Kingdom	USA	India

© Becky Wang 2017

The right of Becky Wang to be identified as the author of this work has been asserted by her in accordance with the Copyright, Designs and Patents Act 1988.

ISBN   978 0 7494 7724 0
E-ISBN   978 0 7494 7725 7

British Library Cataloging-in-Publication Data

A CIP record for this book is available from the British Library.

Library of Congress Control Number

2016961116

Typeset by Integra Software Services, Pondicherry
Print production managed by Jellyfish
Printed and bound in Great Britain by CPI Group (UK) Ltd, Croydon CR0 4YY

CONTENTS

LIST OF ONLINE TOOLKITS

A primer on evolving research into insights

Software and data platforms for cultural trends

Open data sets for exploration

The creative brief quantified

The definitive guide to metrics, analytic methods, and vendors

Visit us at **www.koganpage.com/CDM**

ABOUT THE AUTHOR

Becky Wang is the CEO and a co-founder of Crossbeat (www.crossbeatny. com), a marketing agency and creative studio that operates at the intersection of creativity, data, and technology. The best way to predict the future, according to Abraham Lincoln, is to create it. Crossbeat is one of many boutique firms helping brands and start-ups invent and re-invent themselves digitally and creatively from the inside out, resulting in enterprise transformation and new products leveraging artificial intelligence, AR/VR, and massive interactive installations.

Prior to Crossbeat, Becky Wang co-launched Sunday Dinner, focused on helping brands and agencies figure out new ways to work together, where she managed a network of creative and digital companies and provided a layer of agency services including strategy, account, and production. Before that, she launched and grew Data Strategy at Droga5, where she was responsible for infusing the creative process with data, analytics, and new technology.

Prior to joining Droga5, Becky led the insights and analytics practice at Saatchi & Saatchi NY, where she built and validated the use of data and analytics in the creative development process and led the culture change to one of being data-informed. She served as the digital strategist on several brands including Olay, Trident, and General Mills.

Becky Wang has been featured in the *Huffington Post*, *Financial Times*, and Fast Company[1] for championing the role of the new type of hybrid planner with the quantitative, qualitative, and creative skills necessary to plan communications for today's technology-enabled content and media environment.

Becky has led the digital, brand, and data practices in the auto, CPG, financial, digital music, technology, and retail categories. She employs a number of best-in-class insight workshop methods, research practices, and big data techniques to underpin the brand, digital, and data strategy for a diverse set of clients including Toyota, P&G, General Mills, Sony, Stand Up to Cancer, AMC Networks, Gilt, Pepsi, Samsung, and more. She has served on the executive strategy team for Cannes Lion Award-winning work, including for Prudential.

Becky produced an independent film that premiered at the New York International Film Festival and Los Angeles United Film Festival and has been invited to speak both globally and in the United States at Culture:Tech UK, SXSW, OMMA Social, Social Media Summit, SANG, Voice of the Brand, NYK Brandwatch, Infopresse, and Internet Week.

Becky received a BA in English Literature with a Minor in Biostatistics. She is an iconoclast with a garnish of traditionalism and prefers to hear from all sorts of people via e-mail: bwang@crossbeatny.com or social media: @gnostica.

She loves to write, read, and dialogue. Feel free to send articles and strike up a conversation.

PREFACE

When I started my career, I did not think of myself as a data person. I thought of myself as an out-of-time journalist who, through social data, had the ability to gather more than a few stories about a community and weave a narrative based on my own understanding of how the world worked. Instead, I found I could read bits of a thousand stories and have my mind changed by the insight of many. It would allow me to tell a better, more truthful story. What I found was that by pursuing my interests in coding, strategy, analysis and storytelling, I could bridge a growing gap that needed to be filled to stay relevant and relatable.

I believe that explaining data analytics and data science around fundamental concepts can aid in developing task-oriented skills for all target audiences of this book, and facilitate communication between business, marketing and data stakeholders. It provides a shared vocabulary and enables both parties to understand each other better. It allows us to have a deeper discussion that can make a product successful and a team worth working with.

Data and creativity are ways of navigating decision making in these times of uncertainty. Continuous shocks to the market through lower and lower barriers to entry, the proliferation of devices and technology for consumers, and the 24/7 always-on programmes of marketing and media vying for our attention require a new framework for businesses, particularly marketing organizations, to help navigate. They require granular, sometimes real-time data and creativity to generate insights and to execute with swift, incisive action based on those insights. With each action, a new set of outcomes, decisions and results appears with data to help us course-correct in real time. Creativity increases our ability to respond quickly. Data increases our ability to respond with more assuredness.

This book is a study of how data and creativity work together to help marketers create and drive programmes to better understand why, how and what their customers choose, to deliver products and services that meet their needs, and to persuade by delivering the right message at the right time and place. When we marketers ask ourselves how data can be used in creative work, we must think beyond our traditional ideas of what 'data' and 'creative work' mean. Creative work is not simply a produced output that fits into channels, but rather a holistic platform that helps create a relationship with customers that transcends the transaction.

This book is meant to focus on the relationship between the two rather than forcing one discipline to work within the another. Originally titled *Creative Data Marketing*, the book was renamed *Creativity and Data in Marketing* to reflect the ever-growing influence that each has on marketing.

Who this book is for

Data and Creativity in Marketing is intended for three sorts of readers:

- Brand marketers and chief marketing officers building teams and processes to better work with data scientists, analysts and technologists implementing data platforms to serve marketing initiatives.
- Analysts, data scientists, and other data folks who want to better collaborate with marketing and business teams and make their practice approachable and understandable to other teams.
- Chief digital officers or innovation officers who need to internally organize to help lead the internal transformation in thinking and operations to support the available intelligence and knowledge locked in good data.

This is not a book for data scientists looking for algorithms or coding tips related to their discipline. Rather, this book is meant to help cross-disciplinary interactions amongst business, marketing, operations, technology and 'data' folks in order to foster dialogue and collaboration, as well as offer practical tips to implement programmes that deliver results.

This book is meant to explain principles in data analysis, statistics, and data science that reveal the WAY in which practitioners are taught to think about their craft and therefore how they approach problem solving. This book also talks about existing unspoken assumptions (also referred to as mental models in the remainder of the book) that shape marketing points of view so that data-driven colleagues can understand the broader aims of the marketing organization and what is important to their business and marketing colleagues. *Creativity and Data in Marketing* offers a practical set of guidelines to help navigate the landscape of vendors, partners and employees to build a digitally transformed organization that delivers results. This book also provides case studies from the point of view of all major stakeholders in the process of transformation of the marketing team into a strong team of data and creative players. From each perspective, we offer an overview of how they built their teams to support a successful marketing practice by illuminating a 'third way' of looking at problems – a combined creative and analytic approach to marketing and business problem solving.

Finally, this book is meant to provide marketing managers with a way to plan for the growth of their departments to integrate analytic and data thinking. This requires a marketer to be able to ask the RIGHT questions of their creative and data-oriented teams and set clear criteria to evaluate and measure the success of campaigns against the right metrics. One of my favourite presentations I referred to when researching the softer elements of the book such as team building and culture was by Rohan Gunatillake, titled 'You Are Not Your Work', which talked about mindfulness in business and in products.[2] I believe innovation and re-invention in any discipline require both a personal and interpersonal awareness to make them work.

As an agency co-founder, my job is not to sell creativity or insights, but to help solve business problems in smarter and relevant ways. I need co-conspirators on the client side who are willing to tackle uncertainty[3] and who are looking to believe that the power of creativity is 'just connecting things'[4] (thank you Steve Jobs).

This book is also intended to be useful in discussion and in day-to-day management and interactions between marketing, creative and data teams. The data concepts are introduced with proper names and descriptions of types of analysis performed using a range of business intelligence and data visualization tools (phrases sometimes used interchangeably). For example, the ability to group entities such as customers' behaviours, attributes or product purchases, known as clustering, is as important a concept as the ability to understand the bias introduced when only behaviours, attributes and purchases are entered into the clustering algorithm. In other words, other factors may also be important. That's why it's important, when discussing things like machine learning, predictive algorithms and recommendation engines, to understand the boundaries of what these techniques can do and that measures of success are not black and white, but often incremental improvements on where we were before.

The examples I've given in this book are all retail and/or B2C enterprises. There's a reason for that. Retail companies have led the digital revolution and have embraced creativity and data marketing to expand their reach. Consumer-facing businesses have had to deliver exceptional service and experience. As a result, design, marketing, consumer-first and retail-led businesses have done a great job of combining the power of data and creativity. What these retail and consumer brands can teach us is that old truisms like 'discounts boost sales' or that perception is reality aren't necessarily true. The reader may also notice that the examples in the book are from companies less than 25 years old, which coincides with the availability of the internet to the consumer, but also correlates with a cultural mindset about business, failure and progress.

I interviewed a wide range of companies beyond those that are high-lighted here, including companies in telecommunications, transportation, cable, logistics, and manufacturing. Many of these companies have written off their creativity and data marketing programmes as failures and have declined to be included in this book for fear of damaging their business reputation. In the course of my interviews and drafts, however, what I observed was that these programmes were not failures, but were very necessary steps in experimentation and innovation on the journey to a cohesive, next-generation marketing organization. What made these programmes 'failures' in their eyes was based on the criteria by which they defined failure and nothing else. In other words, only they them-selves have called it a failure. For example, one company I interviewed began their personalization programme by building a data infrastructure combining first- and third-party data to understand consumer preferences and actions for better upsell and content recommendation. Once the data management platform (DMP) was built, they applied analysis techniques to see what factors influenced purchase. The organization expected 'neat' segmentations that grouped people by age, location and types of services (such as men like sports, women like lifestyle content). In reality, they found a number of 'long-tail' consumer segments ('long-tail' refers to the 'tail' of a distribution graph that represents fewer customers existing in the distribution of different types of behaviour). The company wrote off the investment in this programme because they felt they could not MONETIZE these long-tail groups nor could they justify the additional investment in data and machine learning to discover the necessary relationships among factors that impact purchase and loyalty. In other words, success was dependent on the ability to use the outcomes in their established market-ing and business processes rather than a way to refine the approach toward personalization. Personalization, by definition, is meant to support smaller cohort groups, even if that is a group of one. By applying a traditional view of understanding consumers, the company lost an opportunity to invest in a programme that is now an expectation of any company dealing directly with consumers. The perceived 'failure' of the programme has made many of these companies reticent in sharing their stories. I respect their concerns, and hope that once they have achieved commercial success, these companies will be more forthcoming.

Other companies such as GE, IBM and Prudential are also exemplary leaders who have embraced innovation as a marketing function. Organizations like these have 'knowledge management' groups with a large amount of consumer data already. The introduction of big data has allowed them to augment their other business functions including marketing but also operations, sales and production. In these cases, the introduction of innovation (applied creativity), a title given to the design process of transformation, did not have to originate in marketing. Those types of case studies are best provided in the *Harvard Business Review* and other popular literature such as *The Silverlake Project: Transformation at IBM* by Roy A. Bauer *et al*[5] or *Good to Great* by Jim Collins.[6] Instead, this book focuses in on business transformation that begins in marketing through the use of both creativity and data. *Data and Creativity in Marketing* delves into the practice of combining data and creativity in marketing, as many of these organizations have transformed their businesses by providing a toolkit for innovation.

In a keynote presentation in New Mexico, Beth Comstock, former CMO and now president of innovation at GE, noted: 'Marketing must bring a different viewpoint to tough problems. The best marketers are the ones who have both the creativity and analytical skills in the right proportion.'

It's no longer a question of if or when, but a matter of how and what.

ACKNOWLEDGEMENTS

Frequency illusion was in full effect when writing this book. Once I embarked on this journey, I was suddenly receiving recommendations for experts to speak with, hearing about podcasts on the arduous process of writing, and seeing advertisements for writing apps like Ulysses. As it turns out, personalization and ad retargeting are working well with my personal data! However, I still credit luck, fortune, and a network of amazing individuals for the many introductions and connections that have been made in the process of writing this book.

Thanks to the following good people who lent me their time, their ears, their expertise, and occasionally their words for me to write (in no particular order).

Thank you to my family at Crossbeat, particularly my co-founder Dave Justus for embarking on the journey of putting our careers where our mouths were and LIVING this practice of data and creativity with me every day and staying generous, loyal, and true at the end of each day, as well as Amber, Hiye, Emma and Alex for being generous with their time and sense-making skills. That is very helpful to a rambler.

Thank you to lovely girlfriend Emma Wainwright for the late-night dance parties and gentle conversations when launching a business and writing a book at the same time seemed like too much to do. Thank you for making sure no one ate my sentences.

Thank you to my best friends Sadia Harper and Lila Feinberg for the endless texts, posts, emojis, wordplay, banter, bitmojis, selfies, and stories at 2 am while writing. #thestruggleisreal.

To all the great conversations, points of view and tremendous support from the following brilliant and generous pioneers in the space of innovation, data, and marketing:

Tony Hsieh, Patrick Martin, Graham Douglas, Tony Clement, Tye Rattenbury (who likely has the most quotes in the book), Denise Xifara and Luuk Derksen from Decoded, Liz Lukas, Jeff Cha, Monica Bloom, Claude Theoret, Beth Renninger, Karl Gneiting, Will McInnes for being suave, Dinah Alobeid for her enthusiasm, Jim Reynolds for his jovial ways, Josh Mackey for staying in touch and proving that Australians are the best drinkers, Will Sandwick for reminding me that I have something to teach, Sharon Klapka, Founder and

CEO of Adore Me, Morgan Hermand-Waiche, Paul Woolmington and Tricia Iboshi.

To the generous folks at Brandwatch for their encouragement and necessary reminders that smart, important and kind also apply to technology partners and data.

Special thank you to Frank Speiser (and Umair Mufti for connecting us) for being the smartest person I know in data and marketing.

I'd also like to thank people not attached to the book but who lit up the path of data and creativity for me: Ann O'Brien, Julie Flanders, Mark Pollard, Mike Jenkins, Dmytro Voytenko, Ruth Dover, Titu Andrescu, Jackie White, Jodee Rich, Travis Wallis, Priscilla Scala, Kimberly Aguilera, Danni Mohammed, Rosie Siman, Faris Yakob, George Swisher, Mike Palma and Vivian Rosenthal for encouraging me to make the author leap.

To Laura Ziskin, may she rest in peace, for teaching me the power of relationships in all creative projects.

To Saatchi & Saatchi for giving me credibility and all those frequent flier miles to talk about data and creativity.

To David Droga, Andrew Essex, Jonny Bauer and Maura McGreevy, all of whom helped me develop my point of view on creativity and data, for getting down and doing the work with me.

And of course, thank you to my first editor Susannah Lear, as well as Charlotte Owen and Jenny Volich at Kogan Page for believing in a first-time author who represents every possible outlier data on first-time authors – namely, pushing deadlines, talking about marketing first, and trying to change the book cover before the book was written. Thank you for your generosity.

Notes

1 Wang, Becky, 'Where data and creativity meet: confessions of a quant, Madison Avenue's "Hitman"', *Fast Company*, 6 May 2013 [online] http://www.fastcocreate.com/1682905/where-data-and-creativity-meet-confessions-of-a-quant-madison-avenues-hitman [accessed 1 May 2016]

2 Gunatillake, Rohan, 'You Are Not Your Work' presentation [online] http://99u.com/videos/51943/rohan-gunatillake-you-are-not-your-work?utm_source=99U&utm_campaign=df4463bfce-Weekly_10_25_2015&utm_medium=email&utm_term=0_bdabfaef00-df4463bfce-148459109 [accessed 1 May 2016]

3 Sacks, Danielle, 'The future of advertising', *Fast Company*, 17 November 2010 [online]http://www.fastcompany.com/1702130/future-advertising [accessed 1 May 2016]

4 De Wulf, Kristof, 'The future of creativity is connected', *Insites Consulting*, 4 June 2014 [online]http://www.insites-consulting.com/the-future-of-creativity-is-connected/ [accessed 1 May 2016]

5 Bauer, Roy A, Collar, Emilio and Tang, Victor (1993) *The Silverlake Project: Transformation at IBM,* Oxford University Press, London

6 Collins, James C (2001) *Good to Great: Why some companies make the leap – and others don't*, HarperBusiness, NY, USA

Big ideas that work: the promise of data and creativity

01

It's hard to believe that relative to practices like economics, production and business operations, marketing has been around for a very short time. Though the market of buyers and sellers has existed since the beginning of time, the practice of marketing did not come into being until the 1900s, when the industrial revolution made the process of producing goods faster and easier. Prior to this time, most disciplines that are now commonly associated with marketing were either assumed to fall within basic concepts of economics (eg price setting was viewed as a simple supply/demand issue), advertising (well developed by 1900), or in most cases, simply not yet explored (eg customer purchase behaviour, importance of distribution partners and influencer marketing).

Today, we now understand the deep relationship between the marketing of a product or service and the ideas of who we are and what we desire that are formed, propagated and reflected in media. Media's influence has now become inseparable from our behaviour and identities as human beings. According to Geoffrey Miller in *Spent:*

> Marketing is the systematic process to fulfil human desires by producing
> goods and services that people buy. It is that point where human nature
> meets the output of human innovation in the form of technology.[1]

Marketing, then, is something that has become a critical force in shaping how we think of ourselves, intimately tied to our consumption behaviour and yet trading in symbols, words, images and memes that also shape our interactions with one another. As a result, this definition of marketing and its goals now requires advertising (a component of marketing) to communicate value with more than just a list of features and benefits; it must do so using creativity to layer that communication with meaning with which consumers can personally identify. We require marketing to help deliver a product/service that has the right features – and today, characteristics such as being convenient, well-packaged and visually interesting are considered features themselves. To deliver this in the right form, marketing now needs new ways of gathering and parsing the research. We require marketing to help distribute and package these products. All of these new demands of marketing have created a complex consumer world and as such, now require new ways to help marketers navigate.

The history of marketing as a practice is a trail of applied (and discarded) philosophies transformed (and in some cases, just destroyed) by large technical, political, and cultural revolutions. Marketing itself has had its fair share of shifting popular practice and focus, from a time when the product was the focus of advertisements that trumpeted product features and quantified benefits, to the current vogue of customer-first messaging and branded content aimed at giving consumers advice on how to be better people with little mention of the product.

Packaged promotions, discount pricing, partnership marketing, vertical integration, e-commerce – all of these marketing innovations have been shaped by history including the Industrial Revolution, the export of American pop culture (and goods) into other parts of the world for propaganda purposes, the rise of mass media through TV, and the invention of the internet. The latest, and one that many predict to have the largest impact, is the rise of data and the power it will have to help marketers service the individual consumer through personalization, anticipation of needs and context recognition to truly be in the right place at the right time with the right message (and product).

To do this, marketers need to employ everything in their wheelhouse to support the systematic process of marketing. A savvy marketer today must have a creative sensibility to bring together many more disciplines than was once necessary – disciplines such as arts, humanities, science, mathematics, psychology and politics. Creativity, then, as defined in this book, is considered a uniquely human practice of seeing uncommon relationships amongst things – objects, ideas and people – and expressing these in the form of stories and interactions to generate emotional connection. Creativity is defined as a wholly human experience. This is an important distinction; while the attributes of creativity will be the same, the contents of that creativity will be shaped by technology and data. What we understand to be original or imaginative thinking will be shaped by the content of what we know – and the content is always shifting as a result of the influx of data, knowledge and insights that are coming in.

Creativity describes everything about the process of marketing that is uniquely human – it is the will, the curiosity, the north star that guides and moves forward the decision-making process in the messages, experiences, values and interactions we put out in the world about our brand to see how others will respond, participate and share with others.

Beau Lotto, a neuroscientist who has studied human perception, has shown that we don't see the real world – just our version of it:

> Since there is no inherent value in the incredibly complex patterns of light that fall onto our eyes, the brain tells itself stories, and it is these stories that are our perceptual and conceptual truths of the world that guide our behaviour.[2]

Specifically, Lotto's work aims 'to understand the principles by which the human brain encodes the meaning of sensory relationships that were previously useful – since the process of perception is, in fact, a manifestation of past experience.[3]

Creativity is a modern virtue. Right now, we are living in a creative boom. We now celebrate creativity in many forms. Platforms such as YouTube videos enable young stars on limited budgets; ideas like those created by advertising agencies shape culture and drive business results – see 'Real Beauty' (Dove), 'Like A Girl' (P&G) or 'We are Winners' (Adidas World Cup) – or highlight a core value/personality trait in leaders and entrepreneurs like Richard Branson, Steve Jobs, Oprah Winfrey, Beyoncé Knowles, and Tory Burch. According to a 2010 survey conducted by IBM's Institute for Business Values, CEOs' number one priority in terms of values they look for in their senior employees was 'creativity'.[4] Although 'execution' and 'engagement' were highly valued, 'creativity' is THE KEY to successful leadership in an increasingly complex world.'

The complexity of the world today has seen a number of driving factors: technology innovation, industrial revolution, and cultural evolution to name a few. The transformation of our lives as human beings and as consumers has been nothing short of revolutionary (four revolutions, in fact) but the idea of creativity as an output has stayed surprisingly consistent through the centuries. The understanding today of creativity as 'inspired output with impact' is one that holds, not just in culture, but in business as well. The outcome of 'inspired output with impact' is often customer attention, dollars and loyalty in a marketing context. Creativity, then, is used as a term to describe the process used by businesses to create those customer outcomes. Because the process is so different for different categories and companies, those on the outside (and sometimes even on the inside) of marketing often attribute (and wrongly so) the success of marketing on the 'inspired' part of creativity.[5]

In the promotional aspect of marketing, of which advertising is a large component, this allocation of success to 'inspired output' is even more explicitly connected and is a mindset encouraged by those working in the field. According to Leo Bogart, the American sociologist and marketing expert, 'The "great idea" in advertising is considered the realm of myth, to which measurements cannot apply.'[6] We can't be dismissive of the power of advertising and marketing to shape culture. In fact, I would argue that the goals of marketing now include that.

In more recent years, marketers have had to focus on market share that's made up of more than the total available market as defined by customer dollars. Marketers now need to grab a share of today's attention economy, which means that the competition is for a slice of the customer's time. And the market is now made up of a multitude of customer segments that have been broken down even further into the individual customer and his or her personal journey of awareness, purchase and loyalty. Why has this happened and what has it created?

1.1 The digital (and data) transformation of marketing

The practice of marketing has been transformed by three things. The first is the internet and the Web. With an ever-growing number of users, the Internet is central to the processes of globalization, cultural formations, social encounters and economic development for businesses. The barrier to entry in terms of production has never been lower. Companies now have the ability to reduce procurement costs through full price transparency, better supply chain management and higher inventory control – all through data and technology. For the consumer, this has opened up a plethora of choice in products and even in making a run at entrepreneurship. Fast fashion houses like Zara, Forever21 and H&M have turned the apparel industry 180 degrees by not only competing on price, but with an endless supply of fresh looks. As a result, supply has actually increased demand by giving access to a variety of companies not available before, offering a number of different products and services tailored to every customer's needs and wants.

The second transformation is the proliferation of devices. The increasing availability and uptake of internet-capable mobile devices is driving a surge in media consumption, and where there is consumption, there are producers to fill it. This has resulted in a near 24/7 media frenzy across hundreds of channels. Media consumption is no longer a one-way consumption of content but has become a many-to-many connection (as well as conversations and often transactions at the end of these conversations) resulting in networks formed around topics, interests and behaviours in marketplaces and platforms like eBay, Reddit, and Facebook.

The third breakthrough lies in sensor technology, increased computing power and the low cost of processors to transform objects beyond our phones into connected nodes that communicate around people. Devices and objects become connected to each other and the internet, and data has become the language for that connection – not in the form of 1s and 0s, but in the form of data about us and the world. There is cultural data from the billions of conversations happening every minute of every day in social channels. There is personal data from the services we use like Uber, electricity, digital music services like Spotify, or health fitness trackers like FitBit. There is behavioural data that streams from every search, check-in or share. But there's also ambient data that transmits location, temperature, time, connection type, access device and language based on sensors that don't even require our input as humans. What results then from all this information is not just a mountain of static, descriptive data, but an ever-increasing record of dynamic agents in real time. That's incredibly powerful information that can tell us a great deal about our preferences and behaviours as consumers.

The aspiration with data is massive. And it holds a lot of promise for creative marketing. The applications of data in marketing are at once realistic and utterly transformative relative to marketing's history, but there's a long road ahead of us in educating our marketing leaders on how to realize that value.

1.2 What is data (and where did it come from)?

To understand the role of data, we must start with what data is. Data is not simply numerical; it is a summary and encapsulation of information. What did information look like in the past? In the past, information was encoded as pictures and symbols. Archaeologists have uncovered clay tablets from as far back as 7,000 years ago using data to track and record growth of crops and herds in Mesopotamia. Today, we have round discs that can store 4 trillion times more information. Data has existed for centuries and has served humanity in different ways. What has always been informational is now turned into fodder for expertise and individual elements whose relationship can turn into human insight. Data is not simply numbers and mathematics, and it is broader than a practice of measurement and the communication of quantity, time and distance. Data is a collection of facts, such as numbers, words, measurements or observations, that can be either qualitative or quantitative in form.[7]

Data, then, can be packaged in small, organized forms that are friendly to human perception (a number) or accessible to human cognition (like an article written in a language understood by the reader). There are ways in which data can be packaged that are commonly accepted both by those packaging the data and those receiving the package, such as total, average, largest and smallest. For example, we know that there are nearly 7,000 taxi cabs in New York City to serve a population of 2 million people, that on average they pick up 150 people in an eight-hour shift, that the most cabs can be found in midtown driving the Upper East Side, and that the smallest amount are found in the neighbourhoods of Upper Manhattan.[8] Data, then, when packaged a specific way, can translate into something more meaningful to a person. The greater the emphasis on the relationship between data points (number of cabs in the Upper East Side vs. Upper Manhattan) or the conclusions that can be drawn from these data points (there are fewer people in Upper Manhattan), the more scope there is for creativity, and indeed bias. In fact, as human beings, we have taken in data from the time we were born. Some data is true for a majority (eg 'if I put my hand on the stove, it will hurt') while other data has been abstracted into stories that may hold less universal truth and more story-telling (eg 'I was scared by a clown when I was young, therefore clowns are scary'). We are, in fact, already comfortable with data and data sets.

This baseline definition of data can then help us begin to have a fresh relationship with what has become an overused buzz term – 'big data'. Big data is a term used to describe data sets that are so massive that they tax the capability of our existing computing and cognitive abilities to manage and manipulate. Data at this size doesn't become meaningless or something to be ignored just because our perception of or accessibility to the data requires additional tools beyond our eyes and brains. It is this power of data that helps marketers observe consumer behaviour that they neither think to ask about nor can do so politely.

Data has also made possible the emergence of new technologies such as the 'Internet of Things', sensors, self-driving cars and self-service business intelligence. It is also a trend amongst tens of thousands of Meetups to organize ordinary citizens around the practice of Citizen Data Science. This is the application of the 'Quantified Self' movement to the caches of open data now being made available by city, state and federal governments across the world. Machine learning, a newer term in the ever-growing lexi-con of data, has led to advancements that are now commonplace – like better search results – as well as deeply personal ones, like interpret-ing dreams or diagnosing ailments from a list of symptoms. Researchers have recently looked at the question of cancer and at the data around survival rates to determine whether cells are actually cancerous or not. Using a machine-learning algorithm, the machine was able to help identify 12 characteristics that help predict breast cancer from biopsied cells when previously only nine characteristics were identified by medical literature.[9]

It is clear that data is an innovation by which society is going to advance. And these practices being applied to science, economics and healthcare can also be applied to marketing when it comes to the myriad data sets we have at our disposal. When we have a large body of data, we can do things we could never do before. Therefore, data is meaningful not because of its size and type, but because it tells us something about the thing market-ers have always cared about: our actions, our beliefs and ourselves.

Data, particularly as it relates to marketing, generally describes product or human action or interaction. From a corporate perspective, this might be e-mails, computer logs, blogs, presentations or excel documents full of data in a combination of structured and unstructured formats about cost, culture, brand, category, consumer and HR. As consumer and audience members, every minute, we send 204 million e-mails, generate 1.8 million Facebook 'likes', send 278,000 tweets, and upload 200,000 photos to Facebook. Every click, purchase, like, is tracked by Google, Amazon, Facebook and 102 other vendors in the data ecosystem and is available (for a price). Products, in 2011, were tracked with 12 million RFID tags (radio frequency identification tags which capture data about product movement in the physical world). By 2021, that number is estimated to be 209 billion as the gap between the digital and physical worlds shrinks. In fact, products that were once analogue are now digital – books, magazines, music, grocery shopping and the retail experience.[10] Television networks are now converging with cable companies and networks to get closer to true TV watching population data rather than sample data on 2,000 homes. This includes a wide array of viewing habits, from channel selection to engagement with advertising to surfing habits. This data can now be fused with shopping data based on zip code information, to begin to understand the impact of TV media.

Companies like Intel, Bose, Sony and Microsoft are planning ways to 'win the living room' – a place where high-volume consumption of digital goods generates $91 billion in revenue per year.[11] To do this they are explor-ing data on preferences, location, behaviours and habits of consumers interacting with their favourite entertainment. Sophisticated customers, digital products and crowdsourced data and technology are driving enormous change in the marketplace and they are doing so through the adoption and use of technology that requires data to initiate action, sustain interaction and seamlessly move consumers to the next experience.

Marketers have also seen a rise in collaborative influence, from marketers to customers, and from customers to consumers, each of them sharing opinions, stories and information that all become data for one another and for marketers. Review sites like TripAdvisor, Facebook for Businesses and Foursquare provide quantitative scores and qualitative recommendations that help contextualize these scores. These massive data stores aggregate all reviews, but simple web extraction and MATLAB analysis can show ratings changes over time to help deliver even more value to consumers and marketers looking to understand drivers of growth (or decline). Companies like Gerson Lehrman Group connect institutional money managers with experts to share their opinions and expertise and aggregate these interviews online. In fact, this process piqued the interest and ire of the United States Securities Exchange Commission, who worried that aggregating disparate sources of expertise information that is harmless when siloed amongst many experts, can become dangerously close to dealing in insider information.

This reflects the state of today that could not have been predicted through anything but the pre-cognitive abilities of famous science fiction writers like Ray Bradbury, who ignited fears around electronic surveillance in his essays (most notably in 1950 with *The Martian Chronicles*),[12] Peter F Hamilton's *Commonwealth Saga*[13] that inspired with descriptions of self-driving cars, Isaac Asimov's predictive analysis of human behaviour in his *Foundation* series[14] or Philip K Dick's fantasies of targeted holographic advertising in *Minority Report*[15]. According to Esther Dyson, technology writer and futurist, in the near future, billions of objects will operate and interact with their own virtual identity.[16]

1.3 Data used for market research and products

In 2012, IBM published a series of in-depth interviews (IDIs) with 1,734 CMOs in 19 industries and spanning 64 countries to better understand how they could help their enterprises handle the fundamental shifts that were transforming their businesses.[17] The study revealed that the top four concerns had to do with data: the data explosion, social media, the proliferation of channels and devices, and shifting consumer demographics. The study codifies the very issues at hand when dealing with an increasingly digital world and the drivers of this data explosion.

A brief history of data for the purposes of research can provide context for the interwoven relationship between innovation and data. In 1663, John Graunt, the father of modern demography, tracked the birth and mortality records for London to help build a warning system for the bubonic plague. This analysis helped to estimate the actual population of London and to better understand the drivers of both childbirth and death. Franklin Delano Roosevelt enacted the New Deal, which required the tracking of nearly 26 million Americans and more than 3 million employers, to support one of its key pillars, the Social Security Act of 1937. IBM won the contract by developing a massive punch-card machine to help track this information. The Second World War drove the innovation around data processing in 1943, when the British were looking to decrypt the patterns in Nazi messages at a rate of 5,000 characters per second to reduce the time of the task from weeks to mere hours. The US Government built its first data centre in the 1960s to store all the tax returns and social security data in one place.

The birth of the internet, bankrolled by the US Defense Advancement Research Projects Agency (DARPA), introduced the infrastructure of the Web, and through the work of Tim Berners-Lee, it was brought to the public as the World Wide Web. This invention has served as the model by which information was made public by digital, searchable means. Karan Patel's 'Incremental Journey for the World Wide Web'[18] is a comprehensive survey of the evolution of the internet (and the data it generates). In the early days when it was mostly considered a read-only web, (aka Web 1.0), the goals of websites were to establish a presence and share information. From 1994 to 2004, the only available data was information on companies or on the individuals who created the company pages. Web 2.0 was the next evolution, known as the 'read-write web'.

Whereas Web 1.0 was uni-directional, Web 2.0's innovation allowed multi-directional communication and described much of the technology on the Web from the early 2000s to the late 2000s. Technologies that still play a large part of our lives now, including instant message, social networks, wikis and social commerce are all created upon the infrastructure of Web 2.0. A lot of data was generated here, and for much of that time (until very recently) this data was made public either for free or for a fee. Web 3.0 introduced the role of the machine to help us interpret and leverage all the

Figure 1.1   From Industry 1.0 to Industry 4.0 Adapted from the German Research Centre For Artficial Intelligence, 2011

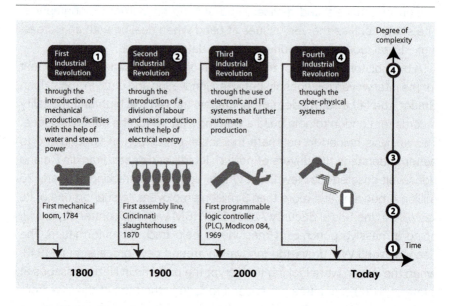

data generated from our read-write interactions. Known as the Semantic Web (or read-write-execute web), this period of Web evolution was the systematic, semantic tagging of content to convert information that can be located, interpreted and delivered by software. This layer of metadata helped companies like Google, Facebook and Apple monetize the content generated by companies and consumers online through advertising, virtual worlds and e-commerce.

In this period of the Web, which we are still in the midst of, the data generated has spawned metadata about data as well as aggregated summaries of the data. For example, in the context of online advertising, advertisers collect first-party data such as e-mail addresses and purchase history. On the other side, publishers also collect first-party data such as behaviours and user engagement with their media properties. The relationship between a multitude of advertisers and media properties has spawned the third-party data collectors who might pay a publisher to track activity on their site in a way that allows them to track that activity across a multitude of sites. This data isn't always accurate, but it is an attempt by the Semantic Web to create uniformity and standardization for a means of comparison.

In effect, big data has spawned even bigger data: Web 4.0, which is currently called 'the Web of Things'. Big data, metadata from the

Semantic Web, and advanced analytics and predictive machine learning algorithms will now allow the Web to 'read-write-execute-concurrency (execute simultaneously with other computers and programs)' so that it can develop intelligent systems such as personal assistants like Siri (another project funded by the government), or wearable technology like smart watches and devices with sensors that take location, weather and mood data to provide messages or product recommendations. This also includes advanced analytics with self-service discovery, where data is not only calculated into human-readable content, but is visualized in a way to explain itself to the non-technical, non-data-savvy person. This explanation of data in the context of digital technologies (web, sensors, interfaces) shows how data is already a currency that unpins many of our technological advances and extends much further than the way most marketers use data now.

The journey from Web 1.0 to 4.0 also underpins the changes that are happening within industries. The Industrial Revolution[19] mechanized the manufacturing and production of goods and services with the aid of water and steam. Industry 2.0 was a period of revolution through the introduction of the division of labour and the mass production that came about with the use of electrical energy. This in turn brought about a change in marketing, particularly as it related to promotion and pricing. Industry 3.0, which has been underpinned by the evolution of the Web as well as other IT and electronic innovation, has not only allowed the automation of production, but levelled the playing field in terms of placement and our very definition of product/service. Industry as we know it today is now being changed by Web 4.0 – a technology with its roots in communication and first embraced by marketing groups in business, but which is now shaping how product is actually made and consumed through the use of data to drive hardware products (colloquially known as 'Internet of Things', which refers to everyday objects that have network connectivity, thus allowing them to send and receive data).

With the emergence of this so-called 'Internet of Things', the binding of society through a web of inter-connected devices, almost every action and interaction will produce data. People, services and infrastructure will combine to create reams of information with significant personal, commercial and social value.

'Big data is the future because of the Internet of Things', remarks Curt Beckmann, chief technology officer at US data storage provider Brocade. 'In the future, there will be such a diverse array of devices and technology providing huge volumes and many layers of information.'[20]

Figure 1.2 Dealing with digital trends: web evolution

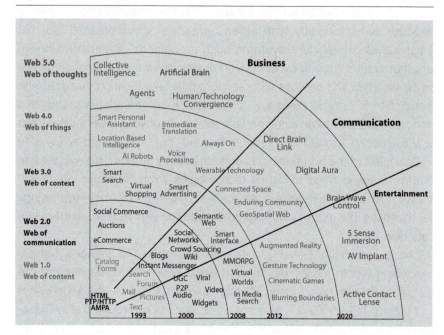

'You know, one FitBit tells you something about the individual wearing it but, when everyone is wearing them, it will create vast "meta-awareness"', says Beckmann, citing the popular fitness tracker brand, whose wristband devices monitor your movement via built-in GPS and motion sensors. 'Just as Google can use Big Data to estimate the spread of a flu virus based on global queries in its search engine, the information gained from the Internet of Things will be tremendously powerful.' These changes in industry have a major impact on marketing beyond communications. They provide a new way in which we can systematically meet the needs, desires and creative expression of ourselves as humans.

1.4 Data used for measurement

John Wanamaker's famous quote goes: 'I know that half of my advertising dollars are wasted... I just don't know which half.' In the early days of marketing promotion when advertising focused on pushing a product, the goal of measurement was framed in the context of product sales. Today, we don't live in a world where businesses are measuring sales, and sales alone. Because of fierce competition for audience attention and the tyranny of choice, we are fighting for people's attention first before we even begin to have a chance at their dollar (much less their loyalty). Complexity indeed has led to uncertainty because the pathways to the services and products we sell have, through the impact of technology and media, exponentially multiplied now that we live in an era of personalization where the consumer journey of one is what marketers must consider today.

The promise of data in helping to solve this problem of measurement has been well praised for nearly a decade now (since the start of digital advertising). Yet, a recent Forrester report claims that 43 per cent of marketers still don't know whether their marketing works. Millward Brown Digital found that 70 per cent of marketing executives would increase their spending on mobile, digital and social platforms if there were better ways to measure return on investment (ROI).[21] Only 23 per cent of B2C marketers polled said they were successful in tracking ROI on content marketing platforms. There's a lot that data has unlocked for us in terms of new creative approaches to communication, but we have yet to close the feedback loop of measurement.

Companies that use data and analytics well are twice as likely to have a top-quartile financial performance, five times more likely to make decisions 'much faster' than competition, three times more likely to execute decisions as intended, and twice as likely to use data very frequently when making decisions.[22] I believe we can apply these same metrics to the practice of marketing.

The marketer today has a dizzying array of tools and expertise at their disposal to help them in this quest. To illustrate just how many, there's a statistic from 2012's *Atlantic* that estimates there can be as many as 105 different vendors that collect data each time a consumer visits a company website.[23] And again, that's only on the collection side. There are many more partners and technologies to help generate insights from that data and transform the data into fuel and fodder for other forms of technologies and consumer experiences.

1.5 The data ecosystem in marketing: types of data

The ecosystem of marketing technology and data partners grows bigger each year. Since 2009, Terence Kawaja, founder and CEO of LUMAPartners, a strategic advisory firm focused at the intersection of media and technology, has provided an authoritative guide on the digital landscape from digital, social, video, to e-commerce.[24] Scott Brinker's

Chief Marketing Technologist blog, a well-known blog amongst the digital marketing community in the United States, created another categorization of marketing technology classification as well, but along functional lines rather than media formats.[25]

For the purposes of developing a general understanding, the best way to understand data and the ecosystem is to discuss the type of data available to the company – public vs. private, real time vs. historical, first party vs. third party, and other such distinctions. Depending on the marketing problem, there are many possible types of data sets that are worthy of exploration. The following are important factors to consider when sourcing data for the creative development process.

1.5.1 Public vs private

For a marketer, the debate between public and private data is not simply about protecting consumer rights around their personal information. Most marketers do not want to infringe on something as personal as someone's data. Public data, often referred to as syndicated data, follows a specific protocol for collection. It goes through a rigorous process of notice and choice that allows this data to be shared for commercial purposes.

As usage of these syndicated offerings such as social media grew, vendors created business models around amending and enhancing data through web extraction that could often identify anonymized originators of social conversations. Marketers began to raise data security and ownership questions. The market is now maturing rapidly into using a hybrid environment, where public data is being analysed using public cloud offerings, but its correlation with internal marketing data is conducted in a private cloud. Private clouds provide many of the benefits of public clouds, and yet offer the benefits of data and ownership protection.

1.5.2 Transaction-level vs. aggregate-level data

Transaction-level data is the most disaggregated form of storing information into 'data' form and it usually corresponds to the way the data was originally captured. Depending on the source (purchases, social posts, survey responses, e-mails), this information includes details of the transaction as well as unique identifiers to help identify each transaction. However, it's difficult to manage this volume of data despite the insights buried within. As a result, the transaction-level data can be 'rolled up' into aggregate data.

Aggregate data can include sales data, web analytics, social channel performance (using Facebook Insights or Twitter Analytics.) In general, the lower the level of aggregation, the more precise the summary. For example, those who liked a Facebook page over a year were 48 per cent male and 52 per cent female. We might lose some of the nuance that demonstrates which pieces of content were more helpful in converting the male audience. Or perhaps we'd like to see the churn from likes to non-likes in that time period.

Transaction-level 'first-party' data includes information that identifies a purchase pattern as one individual's. Of course, that individual's identity may be hidden while the 'key' to that person's identity lives on a third-party platform. That way, the only information the third-party platform has would be to link the name to a unique identifier and know nothing else about this person.

1.5.3 First-, second- and third-party data

First-party data refers to information that is collected by the company from their own customers or audiences. This can include data from consumer behaviours, actions or interests demonstrated across their website(s); customer data; subscription data; social data; or cross-platform data from mobile web or apps. It is often considered the most valuable, because it is available to only the company (which means that insight generation is unique).

Second-party data refers to customer sets that companies can share with other complementary companies, and extend the insights they've derived from their own customer engagement data to enrich customer profiles, stitch together cross-device identity, reach audiences at scale or help with ad targeting. Each company must maintain control of their data to maintain privacy requirements.

Third-party data is collected and aggregated by vendors across multiple websites or offline sources. This data has been used for nearly two decades and is plentiful, but the data is often based on inferences about intended behaviours rather than observations and facts derived through first-hand customer interactions.

1.5.4 Inferred vs. declared

Declared data is information that a consumer or audience member states about himself or herself. Often this is basic demographic data like age, gender, household income, interests and education. There is also inferred data, which is data collected and labelled to describe a characteristic or an outcome of data. For example, someone visiting a website for motorcycle enthusiasts may be separated into 'in a family', 'single', 'enthusiast' or 'dreamer' based on the content they select to read or a segmentation system that the DMP (data management platform) provider offers (often called modelled data). Of course, declared data isn't always completely accurate (as you recall, this is a response bias), but generally speaking, it gives a reliable reflection of your audience. The challenge, of course, is that you can't ask the consumer any and every question that comes to mind. That's why we have data that can be inferred. Modelled data relies on a data scientist or data analyst's interpretation of the data, which may be biased.

1.5.5 *Time series/freshness/historical data*

As we move toward a customer-focused experience in marketing supported through personalization, marketers must also pay attention to where customers are in the customer journey and whether their data accurately reflects the place in time that's relevant. There is nothing more mind-boggling and frustrating than making a purchase on Amazon.com and receiving retargeted ads AFTER the purchase. Customers often respond with a frustrated, 'I'm done! I'm sold! Why am I being re-sold on my $450 air purifier?' Time series data is also a way to further the conversation creatively. Consider Google's famous 'Parisian Love' ad where we follow the search entries by a young man as he finds love after a simple plan to study abroad in Paris that turns into sweet translations for a girl he's met that turns into a date which turns into love, marriage, and a how-to on assembling a crib. Time series data can help us with the sexier, predictive elements of creativity and data. The twin to time series data is historical data. There are a lot of considerations to storing and accessing historical data. For some cloud-based providers of analytics, this is often the driver of a price jump in order of magnitude, and for good reason. The ability to see before, during, and after events can help us begin the process of modelling factors. The final factor is 'freshness' of data, which refers to the time the data is recorded. Consider how, when we first created our profiles on Facebook, we entered our favourite bands, books and TV shows. Since then, in a survey of 1,000 social media users, only 13 per cent have updated their interests from the time they first set up their accounts.

1.5.6 Customer data

The most reliable and useful information about your customer is, well, your customer data. It's important to collect all the data you can. You may operate a B2B business where you might have access to individual sale data rather than B2C transaction data. Or, you might not have the market for a business that relies heavily on channel partners. For each of these types of customer data, I have included some considerations in data collection.

Purchase data is the transactions related to a consumer. This data should also include what products they buy, whether the product is new or not, how often they purchase, the date of the last purchase, and other factors in order to establish an understanding of the customer tempo. This can help determine areas of growth (people graduate from this product to another product), improve retention, and help provide guideposts for the creative ideation of what a customer might be like.

Demographic data is generally declared data. When combined with transaction data, we can apply cohort analysis to find generalized behaviour as well as outliers. This is important for marketers. For example, what assumptions about our customers can we challenge? Is there a growing group of people in another region that is entering into the purchase pool?

1.5.7 Product usage data

As products become digital, there is another path to purchase that meanders, mingles, and mixes into the traditional paths of purchase for an ever-evolving consumer journey. Product usage data might include support calls, consumer social media feedback, product stock unit numbers, purchase patterns based on online behaviour, and more. As marketers, if we can add value in exchange for giving us that information, we have an opportunity to understand the unique conditions that make our products or services shine.

1.5.8 Shopping data – clickstream data

This includes both click-stream data for e-commerce as well as data from groups like NPD or MRI who describe overall trends in retail shopping data. Clickstream data has obvious creative implications for the user experience on the commerce and marketing website. Clickstream data can also provide a view into consumer behaviour with technology and media.

By noting the 'geohash' location of the mobile device at the time of click, we can also see whether they are in the presence of other customers and friends. With the explosion of mobile apps by brands to deliver customized experiences, we can also see other information on the consumer's interaction with their devices as a whole. The importance of this data in the creative process lies in the virtual map it presents to help marketers understand the possibilities in a consumer's life. Did they use the Wi-Fi service, did they click back and forth between our app and another one, did they communicate with someone right after using our app, or just move onto another? Additionally, there is location data, device data, and other types of data related to the mobile, digital experience to be considered as well.

1.5.9 Shopping data – aggregated retail data

NPD/MRI often gather this data from the retailers themselves to create aggregate benchmarks, market size, and market valuation reports. This is critical in the use of data. Historically, this data was offered in report format by a number of research vendors including MRI's 'Survey of the American Consumer' and Experian-Simmons' 'National Consumer Study'. Once the domain of the media agency, these tools are now found in many creative agencies to help add data rigor to their strategic and creative capabilities. The beauty of these products is that they are offered in formats that are easy to use for non-technical people. Increasingly, from NPD to MRI, Experian to Audience Science, data is offered as a direct feed or as data application partners who layer their data into DMPs to build value-add solutions. Depending on the relative investment into data by your company, you can gain a number of insights from the packaged reports that are offered by many of these data and research groups.

By correlating this customer and consumer data between digital and non-digital advertisements (eg purchasing history, profile information, behaviour of customers on social media sites), companies can find patterns of behaviour for high-value customers.

This is an iterative process to link together, update, analyse, and make visual this data. In Chapters 5 and 6, we'll explore the ways in which a data scientist can work with business and reporting analysts in marketing to examine some of these initial relationships to help the CMO and the CIO/CTO make a case for access to data holistically for the benefit of all departments.

1.5.10 Conversation data

Customers contact companies in a number of ways and provide valuable data about shopping habits. Whether it be through call centre conversations, e-mails, web chats, forums, social media channels or blog commentary, these touchpoints offer a rich well of insight. Like any mining process, it requires identifying, extracting, storing, refining, and distributing data in such a way that it can be considered. For example, call centre calls can now be transcribed with nearly 95 per cent accuracy and coded for sentiment of caller and topic categories. Brandwatch, a social insights technology and services provider, can infer quite a bit of 'meaning' from social data, especially when blended and analysed alongside other datasets from CRM, web analytics, traditional survey and sales data. Topics such as purchase intent as well as segment conversations based on inferred demographics can be extracted when marketers and consumer insights professionals utilize these mixed data sets.[26] In one example, they were able to identify LGBT, African American, Millennial, and baby boomer segments to isolate patterns in conversation data to see what type of language they used to talk about their frustrations and aspirations as they related to financial planning and savings.

1.5.11 Social media data

In the early days of social media marketing, many marketers were using social media data to assess public opinion. It was the holy grail of data opportunity – free, ample, and giving voice to consumers who otherwise needed incentives to share their opinions. Our biases revealed themselves quickly. Response biases of respondents, access to the internet, channel selection based on preference rather than a demographic representation of the United States, and faulty sentiment analysis all brought the miracle of social media into the realm of the everyday. Social media is now a mainstay of customer communication – the everyday confers its privileges on the once-budding industry that way. Many of us still rely on social media to understand what's trending in the world; the metaphor of social media as a stream still remains intact.

What that means for marketers is that they must have the ability to tap into that stream of opinion and edited consciousness at any time and can, with the right support, turn it into a powerful well of consumer information to feed the creative process. Social media data is incredibly useful in detecting trends and patterns. Using it in conjunction with the

US Census Data, Barack Obama was able to declare a 'big data' victory over the Republican candidate Mitt Romney. Social media also helps us understand who the 'players' are in the realm of influence. This is critically important, as the proliferation of channels has made it hard for consumers to distinguish who to trust. Consumers are now moving in both directions – leaning on trusted names and faces for awareness and yet sceptical of benefits until researched for themselves.

Another important point about social media is the ever-changing nature of the analysis. Like people themselves, language evolves over time. Our desire to create a hierarchy of language, even from the bottom up, can lead us astray. For example, someone might talk about how much they love their Range Rover. People don't necessarily begin the conversation with, 'Do you want to talk automotive?' What they are talking about is their driving experience, which they might liken to swimming or sailing or flying. That doesn't mean that the speaker has these hobbies.

1.5.12 Public data

There is a wealth of information available for free. For larger companies, this may not necessarily be integrated into their data stack, but it's useful for marketers to leverage the data savvy of analysts, data strategists, and data scientists to better understand the world. WPCurve.com has curated an excellent list of free data sites, some of which are discussed below.

1.5.13 Census data

Census data is used to keep track of the population to help inform political needs. The process requires citizens to respond to a questionnaire with many questions. This massive undertaking provides information that is used by pollsters, marketers and retailers to understand their constituents and consumers.

1.5.14 Data.gov (United States), data.gov.uk (UK) and Open Data Portal (EU)

As an outcome of the open data initiative by the government, the federal government publishes standardized, formatted data on consumer habits, such as the Bureau of Labor and Statistics Consumer Diary. This is a fun resource that gives transaction-level data. Who knew that people buy bedding and sheets TWICE a year in the United States? In the UK, the national mapping authority Ordnance Authority created a map of Great Britain using the Open Data Portal for the popular video game Minecraft.

1.5.15 Location data: ESRI and ArcGIS Open Data

ESRI Maps is an international supplier of location information. This type of information is useful for all manner of businesses, including providing a centralized mapping function to better serve brick and mortar stores. For marketing purposes, companies can use mapping data to better target customers for social media, coupon optimization, and display advertising. For example, Coop Norge AS, a dominant retail market cooperative in Norway, used ESRI data to evaluate the existing stores' product mix and patronage patterns to review merchandising and marketing strategies.

1.5.16 Attitudinal data: Pew Center and the EU's JRC

The Pew Center is a non-partisan think tank that publishes attitudes of Americans (not necessarily the consumer). Each year, they publish reports about culturally impactful topics like Millennials, the internet, elections, and more.

The Joint Research Centre's (JRC) Research and Innovation Observatory (RIO) is a new initiative of the European Commission to monitor and analyse research and innovation developments at member country and levels to support better policy making in Europe.

The Horizon 2020 Policy Support Facility is a new instrument of the European Commission that gives member states and countries associated to Horizon 2020 practical support to design, implement and evaluate reforms that enhance the quality of their research and innovation investments, policies and systems.

1.5.17 Economic data: ICPSR, Eurostat, and ADB

The Interuniversity Consortium for Political and Social Research collects research from more than 800 universities, government, and non-profit agencies. More importantly, it has 8,000 research studies, including longitudinal academic studies like the University of Michigan Health and Retirement Study (HRS), which surveys a representative sample of approximately 20,000 Americans over the age of 50 every two years. Brands like Prudential, Visit Florida!(TM), Discovery Networks, and others have leveraged the in-depth interviews encoded as data to reveal much about American attitudes about retirement as it relates to assets, health, aging and financial plans.

Another vendor called Quandl provides a free, unlimited and unrestricted API for global economic data, including macroeconomic, demographic and social statistics. Quandl unifies free data from the World Bank, UN, Eurostat (specifically focused on providing statistics to the member EU companies), Asian Development Bank (ADB), Bureau of Economic Analysis (BEA) and other data publishers, in a single easy-to-use and powerful economic data API. They also offer other economic databases for additional cost from specialist data vendors, guaranteed to be accurate, comprehensive and up to date, via the same API.

1.5.18 API sources: Mashape

'Mashape' (www.mashape.com) is an API directory to aggregate free and for-fee API access. What is an API? APIs stands for 'Application Programming Interfaces' that savvy data analysts and data scientists can use to get access to data in a more structured form. APIs power many of our applications we use every day, like our productivity tools, games, social networks, and website apps. Data analysts can write in a common programming language to download, manipulate, and display data that is available globally. Examples of publishers, social networks, and online communities that offer API access to their data include the following:

1 The *New York Times* also offers an API to access their archives going back to 1851.
2 Reddit has a subreddit (community) that has aggregated a list of public domain data archives.
3 AWS offers datasets like web crawl data.
4 MSNBC.com offers anonymized views into their web data.

1.5.19 Web data such as Webscraper.io

This is a tool that helps extract data from websites. Keep in mind that while legal (since data is not considered original work for copyright, nor are the terms and conditions on most websites defensible in the United States and EU courts as of the publication date of this book), web scraping is a process. This is a great tool, however, for experimentation. If exploration looks good, consider licensing the information if used for more intensive purposes that require reliability like building a model or for business use.

Other countries including China have not specified these terms. In the EU, legislation is more focused on privacy than ownership of data in a public setting and has not specifically ruled in either case.

1.5.20 Benchmark data

Benchmark data is information collected from industry sources to determine how companies perform (especially best in class) relative to one another. For example, how do we know what is a well-performing website? Do the amount of traffic and percentage of people who click through the site compare equally, better, or worse than other similar websites?

There are a number of benchmark data vendors. Whether you use them as an analyst or as a data scientist, it's important to use reliable benchmark data. Comscore is an excellent partner; be sure to purchase both the desktop and mobile data to get a full read on site usage. Other benchmark data providers include AppFigures (which aggregates information on mobile apps), New Media Measure (a survey-based syndicated research provider on the attitudes of consumers as they relate to media and the internet), and Think with Google, which provides benchmarks and industry standards on media and marketing.

1.6 Data used for creative purposes

Content marketing as a sub-discipline of marketing is one result of the combined powers of creativity and data in marketing. It has driven many businesses forward, such as H&R Block, Virgin and Zappos. H&R Block, for example, has created a content strategy to support their marketing efforts despite the seasonality of their business in the United States (April 15!) By creating content that lives on local social media pages, they create content based on the number of times people visit their help pages on The Tax Institute, a branded content online publication. Virgin CMO Bob Fear described how the Virgin site transformed from a simple web portal to a source for content by having the content team working hand in hand with data scientists. Virgin started by creating an 'interest graph' (a phrase used to describe quantitatively the interests of a group) of site users based on search results, who and what they followed on social media, and the views they expressed online. The findings were then collated to inform what type of Virgin.com experience would serve the needs of distinct audiences: influencers, partners, existing customers and potential consumers. Entrepreneurship and music are two categories that one would readily associate with Virgin thanks to Richard Branson and his history in the music business, but Fear also discovered that space travel was one of the main conversation drivers around the brand. Zappos understands it must create a real connection by providing relevant information beyond their buying decisions. Zappos creates engaging content on YouTube, Pinterest, as well as their own digital magazine *Zappos Now*. Each piece of content is informed by detailed data on its customers.

Each of these brands now tells their brand story not as a single narrative, but by offering very customized stories, examples, information and advice about their products and their consumers in the context of the forum they are on. These pieces of content, either as tweets, videos, blogs or social media posts, rely on data in many ways: identifying the right target consumer, the right tone, message and form of message based on test and learn methodologies from data; using the best channel based on consumer behaviour in those channels; finding the proper mix of different kinds of content to help create a mosaic understanding of a brand's story, ie the right mix of product posts, brand equity messages and customer support; and wrangling the stories customers themselves put out. Traditional marketing mix modelling has been completely transformed by the use of technology and data through closed systems that can help track attribution and can use new proxies of conversion and success to help calculate ROI in a more holistic manner. Consumer insight generation is no longer limited to (and subject to the challenges of) primary research. Marketers can now observe directly the intent, behaviour and outcome of consumer interactions with our products and each other, and the impact our products have on culture, and create products, programmes and platforms for their consumers to engage not only with their products but with the brand itself.

Data allows us to see new, different, and better. Data can be used to increase our domain of expertise and it can help us reveal otherwise unseen patterns to feed our ability to think imaginatively. Data can fill in those gaps in human expertise in a way that humans never can. Creativity's role, then, in marketing and in the human experience, is to remain the motivating force to use these inputs in a way that reflects our values, but also to support this new input into the creative process through data.

Market research is a key aspect of the exploration and decision-making process of good promotion and product development. Now, new and more detailed data sets can improve the insight generation and optimization

Figure 1.3 Data vs Creativity

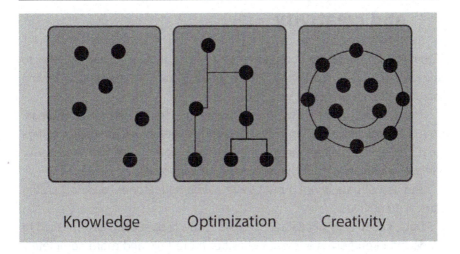

Knowledge   Optimization   Creativity

in the creative development process. What data (and in particular 'big data') offers us is a way to observe the nuances of human behaviour that samples of 300 just won't do. It allows us to slice customers into cohorts where we can observe the subtle impact of attributes, decisions, and influence on consumer choices.

Data is also becoming a shared language amongst different stakeholders within corporate organizations beyond marketing. The developments in technology and data raise a key issue, namely who decides on the allocation of marketing budgets? Marketing budgets are no longer distinguished from digital marketing budgets. Instead, the chief marketing officer and the chief information officer will often have to meet in the middle to create a new, integrated marketing approach that balances consumer needs with brand needs as they relate to data usage. These teams will need to navigate creative agencies, software vendors, media agencies, IT solutions, and publishers to not only sort roles, responsibilities and budgets, but also data federation, integration, ownership and stewardship in the ever-evolving campaigns and products driven forward by creativity.

Some would argue that since creativity in marketing existed first, data needs to fit in the context of its rules. Others would state that since data is more structured and rigorous, then creativity needs to be applied within the context of the rules. Marketing needs to be more than evolved; it needs to be transformed. And data is just the candidate to do it.

1.7 Marketing's embrace of data and creativity

Creativity and data are complementary forces that need one another to evolve the field of marketing and continue to make marketing a thriving practice of culture.

The practice of creativity within marketing isn't a wild romp of ideas. In marketing, there are objectives, guardrails, personalities – many things that shape the 'sandstone' of the idea into something that inspires or reflects a universal truth that resonates with people.

The use of data is not meant to be a limiting factor or roadblock in the use of creativity.

Data, specifically big data as it exists today, is best used as a method to understand ourselves and our behaviour more fully and more completely by allowing us to observe actions we may not otherwise be able to see. If used incorrectly, though, it can also be a way to deeply misunderstand ourselves, much like trying to see the forest for the trees without perspective, a helicopter, or binoculars. It's important to apply the use of data with the right focus, purpose, and perspective to make it meaningful, just as a marketer applies creativity.

Marketers use research and analytics to shed light on who buys what and why; who influences buyers; and when, in the consumer decision journey, marketing efforts are likely to yield the greatest return. This type of insight generation helps shed light on not only the 'what' but in some cases, we can also see the 'why'. Marketers can better understand the types of experiences that customers want and what they value, by measuring these experiences (social media, mobile-enabled questionnaires, facial sentiment). They can better identify innovations they value by measuring the incremental differences in innovations and the types of improvement in people's lives through self-tracking, changes in purchase behaviour, and a whole host of other ways. And most importantly, marketers have the ability to tell shorter stories through social media and highlighted user-generated content, or tell big stories to the right customers targeted through channels enabled by large partners such as Google, Apple, and Facebook, who are creating moments within their consumer experience that qualify as right place, right time, right messages.

The chapters that follow are meant to elevate the possibilities of data into something more than 'just another tool' to help marketers. It is not just a new category of 'science' in the traditional equational understanding of marketing as an 'art' and 'science'. Data, like creativity, can help guide marketers through uncertainty and can bring into focus a range of possibilities beyond what is plainly in front of us. Data, like creativity, is a way of thinking and working through business problems and can elevate solutions into ideas that impact culture.

Notes

1   Miller, Geoffrey (2009), *Spent: Sex, evolution and the secrets of consumerism*, Random House, London, UK, p. 15

2   Beau Lotto website, *Lab of Misfits* [online] http://www.labofmisfits.com [accessed 1 May 2016]

3   Ibid.

4   IBM Institute for Business Value, 'Capitalizing on complexity: Insights from the Global Chief Executive Office Study', *IBM*, May 2010 [online] http://www-935.ibm.com/services/us/ceo/ceostudy2010/ [accessed 1 May 2016]

5   Rothman, Joshua, 'Creativity Creep', *The New Yorker*, 2 September 2014 [online]. http://www.newyorker.com/books/joshua-rothman/creativity-creep [accessed 1 May 2016]

6   Bogart, Leo (1967) *Strategy in Advertising,* Harcourt, Brace & World, Inc, USA

7   Van Rijmenam, Mark, 'A short history of big data', *Datafloq* [online] https://datafloq.com/read/big-data-history/239 [accessed 1 May 2016]

8   Cukier, Kenneth 'Big data is better data', TEDTalks, June 2014 [online] https://www.ted.com/talks/kenneth_cukier_big_data_is_better_data?language=en

9   Koller, Daphne, 'Stanford team trains computer to evaluate breast cancer', 9 November 2011 [online] https://med.stanford.edu/news/all-news/2011/11/stanford-team-trains-computer-to-evaluate-breast-cancer.html [accessed 1 May 2016]

10 Harrop, Peter and Das, Raghu, 'Printed and chipless RFID forecasts, technologies & players 2011–2021', *IDTechex*, October 2010 [online] http://www.idtechex.com/research/reports/printed-and-chipless-rfid-forecasts-technologies-and-players-2011-2021-000254.asp [accessed 1 May 2016]

11 Grubb, Jeff, 'The Earth will spend $91.5B on video games this year', *Venturebeat*, 22 April 2015 [online] http://venturebeat.com/2015/04/22/video-games-will-make-91-5b-this-year/ [accessed 1 May 2016]

12 Bradbury, Ray (1950), *The Martian Chronicles*, Doubleday, USA

13 Hamilton, Peter F (2002-2012), *Commonwealth Saga,* Pan Macmillan, UK

14 Asimov, Issac (1942–1993), *Foundation Series*, Doubleday, USA

15 Dick, Philip K (1956), 'The Minority Report', Fantastic Universe, USA

16 Smolan, Rick (2012) *The Human Face of Data*, Against All Odds Productions, New York

17 IBM CMO Study 2011, 'CMO's Digital Challenge', 11 October 2011 [online] http://www-03.ibm.com/press/us/en/pressrelease/35633.wss [accessed 1 May 2016]

18 Patel, Karan (2013) 'Incremental journey for World Wide Web: Introduced with Web 1.0 to recent Web 5.0 – a survey paper', *International Journal of Advanced Research in Computer Science and Software Engineering*, **3** (10), October 2013

19 Klaus Schwab (2016) *The Fourth Industrial Revolution*, World Economic Forum, UK

20 BBC special sponsored by Huawei, 'A better connected world' [online] http://www.bbc.com/future/bespoke/specials/connected-world/dataconnectivity.html [accessed 1 May 2016]

21 Tadena, Nathalie, 'Marketers say they would spend even more on digital ads if measurement improved', *Wall Street Journal*, 6 July 2015 [online] http://blogs.wsj.com/cmo/2015/07/06/marketers-say-they-would-spend-even-more-on-digital-ads-if-measurement-improved/ [accessed 1 May 2016]

22 Wegener, Rasmus and Sinha, Velu. 'The value of big data: how analytics differentiates a winner', *Bain & Company* [online] http://www.bain.com/Images/BAIN%20_BRIEF_The_value_of_Big_Data.pdf [accessed 1 May 2016]

23 Madrigal, Alexis C, 'I'm being followed: how Google – and 104 other companies – are tracking me on the Web', *The Atlantic,* 29 Feb 2012 [online] http://www.theatlantic.com/technology/archive/2012/02/im-being-followed-how-google-151-and-104-other-companies-151-are-tracking-me-on-the-web/253758/ [accessed 1 May 2016]

24 Luma Partners, 'Marketing Technology Lumascape' [online] http://www.lumapartners.com/lumascapes/marketing-technology-lumascape/ [accessed 1 May 2016]

25 Scott Brinker blog, *Chief Marketing Technologist*, http://chiefmartec.com/ [accessed 30 September 2016]

26 Interview with Brandwatch CMO Will McInnes. Personal interview, 18 December 2015

Transformation within the (marketing) organization 02

2.1 An example of how a creative company uses data

Cirque du Soleil is a creative company. It's a billion-dollar company whose main product, live experience, is largely difficult to replicate and scale. Their secret: 'If you have a very good artistic product it's very well, but you have to have good business management', says Gilles Ste-Croix, one of the company's co-founders and current artistic director.[1] It's a company whose alchemy of balancing a creative ethos with the rigors of data has been well documented in case studies, research, and the news. In 2016, the company has evolved into an organization that combines their customer experience vision and data-driven decision making to strike a successful business balance.

However, the company wasn't always that way. Launched in 1984 in Montreal and in the United States in 1987, Cirque Du Soleil began as a travelling show focused on the feel of circus performance with the grace of acrobatics and without the logistical challenges of maintaining animals. Driven by the group's founder, Guy Laliberte, a small core team of creatives revived the circus experience by creating a collection of permanent shows to tour North America. Each show had its own story and, crucial for the creative process, also had the time and room to grow and evolve to become polished into a diamond. This creatively driven, iterative process created a winning streak of successful shows for nearly two and a half decades. Then, in 2008, at the height of its popularity (and profitability at that time) Cirque du Soleil did what any company on top of the world does; they expanded again – to China, to more shows in Las Vegas, to South America.[2] Moving from one new show a year to three, Cirque du Soleil entered new markets with new shows lead by an ethic of growth at all costs. By 2012, unchecked expansion and failed experiments, such as its 2009 vaudeville foray Banana Shpeel, resulted in poor reviews, early closures and falling profits.[3] The death of one of its aerialists on stage in June 2013 marked a low for a company whose brand was based on the principle of celebrating the performers and performance first. The reasons for the failures differed. In retrospect, the show Iris, in Los Angeles, played in a seedy neighbourhood of Hollywood which, despite heavy tourist traffic, was commercially unviable. Zaia, in Macau, simply didn't appeal to local audiences. Another show, Zarkana, couldn't make enough money to cover its production costs for playing in New York City's 6,000-seat Radio City Music Hall. At an all-time low, 2013 was the first year Cirque du Soleil did not turn a profit.[4] The leadership team could not figure out why there was not market fit. In fact, much of the realization that there was a problem at all came as anecdotal understanding after millions of dollars were invested in production and marketing. In 2013, the organization needed to rewire itself with the same precision it executed in performance.

Laliberte, through a process of investment, restructuring and internal re-organization, led Cirque du Soleil back to theatrical and financial success. What drove this quick turnaround? One crucial factor that has helped it succeed was adhering to its brand on creativity in its show vision. Their mission, from the start, was to create experiences that their consumer could never expect. Creativity remained paramount, but the leadership team knew that they needed a sharper ingredient to add to their creative prowess. Data and customer input, according to Mario D'Amico, the VP of marketing, became that factor in creative excellence: 'We use data to brief the members of our creative team, to help them understand who's applauding when the curtain goes down. We don't tell them to use a red dress or a blue dress, or what to do in a certain scene, but we do educate them. Then we get out of their way so that they can create.'[5] In other words, it's about providing enough input (not restriction) to help ground creative exploration and development without adhering to the exact outputs of the data. Data does not equal insight.

Another crucial decision was its dedication to building an internal infrastructure to power the organization, a change led primarily by the marketing department. A critical analysis of the successes and failures during that time had to do with the relative shallowness of assessing new markets and local market reaction. Live experience shows, in their first three years, see 60–90 per cent of their traffic from the local area. Cirque du Soleil competes not only with similar live events, but also with nearly any entertainment option for consumer dollars. This type of insight did not come from ticket sales data (that often only shows the ticket purchaser's information when the average size of tickets purchased is three); it came from the web analytics that demonstrated site traffic changes as shows came closer.[6]

The third innovation was the company's focus on consumer experience beyond the show itself. Rather than focusing only on entry and exit analytics related to the show, they began collecting metrics on how people talked about the show before purchase, their experience of the content about the show (including the website, e-mail, review sites, and third-party ticket resellers).[7] By examining the consumer experience from pre-purchase to show experience to follow-up on new shows, Cirque du Soleil was able to create and extend its award-winning 'brand' beyond the shows themselves. This last innovation was a multi-year initiative with executive support. 'We're looking at the customer experience more holistically,' said Axel Bedikyan, the director of strategy and market intelligence.[8] Specifically, the company completed a business intelligence project earlier that year to expand data access to all in the company.

'The primary goal of the project was to render every person who wants information autonomous, and allow access and analysis company-wide', he says. Cirque du Soleil had two main business units – its resident division and touring show division. Information relating to each department was collected and housed separately, sometimes on individual computers. 'We had multiple versions of the truth,' Bedikyan says. 'It was difficult to aggregate and consolidate the information from the two units to get a full understanding of the big picture.'[9]

Bedikyan and his team integrated siloed information and added more detail to its database of information about customer relationships.[10] Now, anyone in the company can analyse information related to the pre- and post-show experience via dashboards, as well as overall customer and market information. The 'customer experience' moves beyond just the show to advertising, website activity, purchase information, customer interactions between purchase and the show, the actual show experience, exit surveys, and CRM (Customer Relationship Management) marketing. In fact, a survey conducted by a group called Data IQ in the UK has revealed that 53 per cent of the 144 UK-based organizations polled planned to increase their level of investment in data and marketing in the coming year.[11] Cirque du Soleil used their CRM infrastructure to not only add Customer Lifetime Value (CLTV), but to better target their customer communications and loyalty programmes.

The company is ultimately creatively driven, but their process has evolved. A small creative team meets bi-monthly. David Lamarre, CEO and President of Cirque du Soleil, cites four criteria they discuss for accepting a new project: 'a significant creative challenge; an affinity for the people we might do business with; a strong fit with our business model and financial viability; and, finally, socially committed partners.'[12]

2.2 The process of creativity and data in marketing

It's important to acknowledge that the analytic and creative process is unique across the many different brands, agencies, partners and vendors that exist in the marketplace. What stands out that is that marketers are all moving toward a more customer-centric view of their roles. Outlined below is a framework to leverage both creativity and data in a way that embraces a curiosity about the lives of consumers where a brand can participate (rather than on the brand relationship itself). This process is based on the scientific method (which puts observation before goals), as discovery is key in the creative process. Here are the seven steps:

1 Observe the world.

2 Define the challenge.

3 Gather (in one place) information (and data) about the consumer.

4 Generate insights.

Figure 2.1   Process for creativity and data

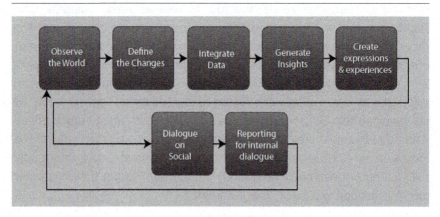

5 Create targeted messages and/or experiences.

6 Dialogue with audiences.

7 Report and learn.

2.2.1 Step 1: Observe the world

One way to observe the world is to look through beautiful statistical views, charts, and graphs. The most well-known (and free) among them is Google Trends. However, there are other trend insight tools such as GetChute, CrowdTangle, and Banjo.

GetChute is a visual content engine that helps marketers create, store, and optimize their user-generated content and campaigns. Their insights engine helps spot trends amongst the visual revolution.

CrowdTangle helps publishers to find content and stories on the internet before they 'go big', by creating a detection model of viral stories on Facebook, Instagram, Vine, and other social media channels.

Banjo has flipped the question from 'what's on social media?' to 'what is going on in the world?' By triangulating on one of 35 billion 'squares' that make up a map of the world, Banjo searches for social and other means of public data happening in that region. This observation of the world can create baselines of information coming from those regions; when an event occurs in that area that increases the number of images, an alert sets in motion analysts to find out more.[14]

The important element in these companies is not the thread of visual social media, but rather a process to gather information without a particular agenda.

2.2.2 Step 2: Define the challenge

The next step is to define the challenge (as a scientist would define an objective). It must be measurable and framed against benchmark or historical data. This can include competitive analysis data, equity research that offers sector benchmarks, or third-party syndicated research from firms like Kantar, MRI, or Comscore.

Defining the challenge is more than meeting a benchmark.

1 To create truly innovative work, it's important to frame the challenge in a single strong sentence. Instead of 'increasing sales', a more specific goal is to 'attract new customers' or 'develop the best super customer'.

2 It is also helpful to define a challenge that plays against an assumption about the market, particularly the customer. This can facilitate out-of-the-box thinking.

3 And of course, be clear on who the customer is in relation to the challenge. Is the challenge in communications or in distribution? This helps with turning the marketing problem into a set of steps for both analytic and creative teams.

4 It's also important to be clear on the type of communication challenge you are tackling. Awareness programmes are different than conversion programmes in length, depth, strategy and creativity.

5 During this phase, it's also important to plan the measurement strategy.

2.2.3 Step 3: Integrate data sources to create one customer profile across all channels

The process of collecting, normalizing, formatting and producing integrated marketing data requires a high level of data management expertise that senior marketers need to get from their IT departments or external vendors. Partners such as Adobe, IBM, HP and Oracle are leading the charge on a product offering called a 'marketing cloud', an integrated technology, content, and data solution that helps measure, personalize and optimize marketing campaigns and digital experiences for optimal marketing performance.

2.2.4 Step 4: Generate insights

Insight generation is the place where marketers often start, so this is second nature. This is the place where our natural assumptions about the challenge should surface, be challenged or reinforced, and validated. We often do this step first without allowing for discovery. Generating insights is a push and pull practice to work through our assumptions and to be surprised with what surfaces beyond in-depth interviews, syndicated research, collation, analysis and visualization of data.

Insight generation often feeds into the internal product and marketing functions as well as the organizational understanding of the consumer. The product and marketing functions yield influence on the processes and operations of each. The product, when in market, is impacted by category dynamics, and the marketing, when in market, is shaped by cultural dynamics. The consumer sits in the middle between culture and marketing and is influenced by the interaction of the two through media.

Data can transform the insight generation process from an understanding of a sample size of a population to understanding diverse samples within the entire population. 'Samples' become 'sub-samples' that can help us understand the dynamics at play when making decisions about purchase of, or participation with, a brand. Data becomes a proxy of the consumer, a language through which companies can listen to the consumer. This does not refer solely to social media data. Data that tells us about the consumer can be web data, search data, location data, product usage data – any data that tells us their opinion of the product through their words, their intention or their behaviour. Also described as an information market, we come to understand the context around the purchase of the product through these other means of data. Data's role has traditionally been to serve as the intelligence centre for the marketing function. Now there is a much greater role for data to play in marketing.

There are several groups that help fuse data to help better understand the consumer. Brandwatch is a technology and analytics firm that tracks social conversations.[15] Their CMO, Will McInnes, provides this perspective on the evolution of creative data and data-informed creativity. For him, the word 'creative' doesn't refer to the 'Big Idea', but to an application and process both novel and practical. Brandwatch is most interested in the power of mixing and fusing different types of data together. What they are finding are novel results that deliver business value. For example, a well-known American beer company leveraged Brandwatch's technology to extract from social data information about the hottest bars in the top 20 cities for their distributors to approach. Then, they fused it with liquor licensing data as well as their own CRM data to draw up a hit list of sales targets.[16]

Another example is from the ice cream brand Ben and Jerry's. Already leaders in social media with millions of followers, they were interested in leveraging social media as something more than social analytics for its channel. The client's observation: Ben and Jerry's is premium-priced. The question was, were they too expensive or too cheap? Brandwatch then broke down the business question into a data-mining exploration. Using Brandwatch, Ben and Jerry's mined social sentiment data to correlate to price change to see if the consumer was sensitive to price.[17] There was no correlation to price or taste. What they did notice, however, was a large number of conversations about when to buy the product, eg now, later, after work, after school. The brand then looked more closely at sales data and found a pattern in sales. Saturdays were peak days. Looking for a relationship, they found that greater volumes of conversations were happening on Thursdays and Fridays. Some of those Thursday–Friday conversation peaks were much greater than others. In those periods, they saw conversations such as 'it's raining, I'm going to go buy some ice cream and watch a movie' surface in the word cluster analysis. They decided to overlay weather data in specific regions and found that there was a correlation between weather data and the volumes of conversation. Through analysis of Twitter data, they discovered ice cream was a premeditated purchase rather than the impulse purchase much of ice cream advertising sits on. They also decided to advertise on a Thursday rather than a Saturday to deliver their messaging during their consumer's time of consideration.[18]

The data process helped focus the conversation in the right ways. There were other avenues that the team pursued. Was it location, was it audience, was it the air time of commercials? Each of those questions represented a hypothesis. Asking those questions is not simply in the realm of 'creative'. What we think of as creative today is not simply someone with the ability to draw, write or paint, with a love of art. To achieve these results, McInnes shares these thoughts.

> I would start with the platforms or the access. You need a tool kit. There are some great tools that people use which are free and they kind of mash them together, or there are platforms like Brandwatch, but most of our clients are operating in their own kind of tailored marketing stacks. Brandwatch isn't the only thing that they're operating. I think you need to have the human skills, which is really important. Our happiest clients who are doing the smartest work have got really smart analysts. The people who are trying to do this just as a small part of that job are the ones that struggle to get the most value. People, platforms, access, and senior support. Where technology can begin to help the process is to help with 'productizing' workflow.[19]

Figure 2.2 Process for social media insights

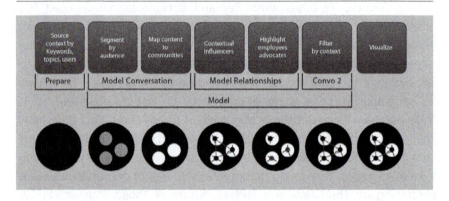

2.2.5 Step 5: Create targeted message and/or experiences

In this phase, marketers can create messages or a sequence of messages to deliver to consumer audiences. Marketers may also work with creative or specialist agencies to create campaigns around a central idea delivered across omnichannels, product extensions, or digital products to address customer needs and mindsets.

Content marketing

Frank Speiser is the founder and chief product officer for SocialFlow, which is a social media optimization platform used by brands and publishers. SocialFlow's core product optimizes delivery of publisher and brand content on social platforms to their friends and followers. Posts are automated by way of SocialFlow's platform and their algorithm posts content at a time that will maximize clicks, views or engagement. Speiser's platform is powered by a machine learning platform, affectionately dubbed 'Sanders' (he tells a story about naming the artificial intelligence platform after both the mathematician Charles Sanders Pierce and Colonel Sanders, the brand mascot for Kentucky Fried Chicken.[20] This artificial intelligence platform helps advertisers to engage their consumers by delivering relevant content that earns their attention, rather than interrupting their focus on publisher content with a commercial message.

His newest product, Attention Stream, provides advertisers with a way to sponsor content in the category of interest posted on publisher feeds rather than interrupting a target audience's stream. This product allows publishers to monetize and advertisers to offer a relevant message. As a result, the 'customer' of the publication is actually the brand and audiences can go back to being 'consumers' of the editorial content. This allows customers a better opportunity to reach the publications' consumers.

Speiser has seen his customer advertisers reinforce that shared moment of relevance with a campaign of more brand-centered marketing with resounding success. A beauty brand, working with a fashion magazine and AttentionStream, saw a 76 per cent increase in social impressions over their typical ad buy, with 4.4 times more clicks.[21]

This is far removed from the services provided by 'big idea' ad agencies yet can be equally, if not more, effective. By earning trust through delivering relevant content, marketers can see results that are meaningful and that are relevant to the brand instead of simply entertaining (which sometimes results in poor attribution back to the brand). Speiser helps data-driven marketers to ask questions beyond 'who is our target?' and 'on what media do they spend their time?' to 'how do I share time with them that's meaningful?'[22]

Targeted/sequenced website content

Companies such as Adobe have created products like Adobe Experience Manager (AEM) and Target to help sequence and target messages based on an incoming users' social information. Products like Gigya, Janrain or LoginRadius provide toolkits to enable social credential sign-in, which bypasses the need to create distinct usernames/passwords for any website we visit. By using social sign-on, companies can leverage those credentials to request access to a user's social content to analyse for content preferences and sequencing.

2.2.6 *Step 6: Dialogue with customers through social conversation*

Have one-to-one conversations throughout the customer journey. This is the content strategy and communications element of the marketing strategy that feeds back into product, brand building, and customer service.

Digital media (be it social media, online reviews on e-commerce sites, or help forums provided by brands to aid in self-service customer support) has opened the door for iteration, the next chapter of the story, and more. The creative process for either product or campaign does not end once in market. The ability to enter into a dialogue with customers on the effectiveness of the message or product is critical. If a marketer communicates with the customer to deliver a message about the superiority of the product's performance, it's important the product delivers on that.

2.2.7 *Step 7: Reporting*

The role of reporting, which we discuss in Chapter 5, is to facilitate dialogue amongst stakeholders. This is a critical step in the analytic and creative process, particularly for marketers. This is often the step that launches the broader conversation of accountability in decision making and action taking. Reporting, though, isn't about measurement alone. Good reporting on progress and status is meant to convey a beginning, middle and end to remain in the audience's mind. Business intelligence tools like Excel, GoodData and Tableau now provide analysts with an ability to work more deeply with data to summarize, aggregate and visualize for faster comprehension. Of course, good data visualization and reporting do not amount to storytelling. Void of language, reporting is unable to independently transmit ideas, clear purpose and emotional impact. However, storytelling applied in the service of data actionability, ie using the human language to provoke a measurable reaction on the part of internal stakeholders in the face of a specific set of metrics, can help drive business decisions. A combination of data visualization, language and images can help.

2.3 Data and creativity in storytelling

The cycle between analytical and creative thinking isn't simply the domain of the creative process – the process of thinking and feeling is reflected in the learning process too. In Daniel Coyle's book, *The Talent Code: Unlocking the secret of skill in sports, art, music, math, and just about everything else*, he describes the process in which human beings master skills.[23] He outlines the steps of deep practice where a person begins learning by absorbing the whole thing s/he practises and begins to break the task down into chunks. This analytical process is about reviewing the smaller chunks over and over again until all errors are unknotted through practice. Only through repetition, intensity, and then flow, does the practice turn into mastery. Like learning, the elements of analytics and creativity feed into one another and often result in an unexpected journey to achieving the goal in marketing.

Creativity, in the traditional marketing sense, has often referred to branding that then evolved into narrative storytelling. The colours, fonts, and words used in product packaging to describe the promise of quality and personality in the product, gave way to radio and TV ads. The space that existed between the promise and the product built (and sometimes destroyed) was the brand equity. Today, the promise has been replaced by experiences the customer has with the many different touch points surrounding purchase including review sites, social media, rating systems, word of mouth, e-mail marketing and many other forms of information available about the product – a plethora of data for the marketer to sift through. This overwhelming amount of content and media doesn't simply come from the brand anymore. It comes from other customers, competitors, reviewers, friends, co-workers and more. Each of these experiences with the brand is underscored by a data point for the customer and the data creates their own message they put out in the world that gets counted as another like, share, click, purchase, rating. In this way, data became a language by which marketers could listen to and hear their consumers, and creativity a way to respond to them.

If marketers and creatives listen closely to the insights, the stirrings of a story can emerge. Laura Ziskin Productions, a film production company known for producing films like Sam Raimi's *Spiderman* trilogy and Lee Daniel's *The Butler*, launched a pro bono campaign and fundraising platform called Stand Up 2 Cancer (in the name of full transparency, I worked on this campaign and for Laura Ziskin). It was the first roadblock show across all four networks (CBS, ABC, NBC and FOX) during prime time to raise money and awareness for cancer. Laura herself had fought cancer and was passionate about turning her experience into a lesson for others. During one of our planning sessions, she shared her experience of when she first found out. In her journey to understand the disease and to make sense of something that had turned her life upside down, she clung to the statistics. She rattled off statistics about mortality, morbidity, recurrence rates, funding needs and budgets for research vs. advocacy. After 10 minutes of straight statistics, she slowly rose up between her daughter and her business partner (also a woman), and said, 'one in three women will be diagnosed with cancer in their lifetime. May it only be me.'

The production company recorded a public service announcement (PSA) to Pearl Jam's 'Rise' to demonstrate through storytelling the power of standing up to cancer. The single statistic inspired an action that has come to represent a movement. In their first year, they raised $245 million.

In fact, the Cannes Lions festival, an annual festival of creativity in the creative communications and advertising fields, has recognized Creative Data as an Innovation category. The categories are broad and recognize that the transformative power of data in the creative process isn't limited to one expression. The categories represent the impact of data on the creative process, including personalization and interactivity, as well as the role of data in the insight generation process. They also represent how an organization can use data and data technology as an inspiration and driver in product development, or in some cases, as the product itself. In 2015, the jury announced 11 small prize winners in the Creative Data category, yet none of them took home the main prize, the Grand Prix. Year one for any new prize category is often about defining what the category is about; creative data is quite new. 'We felt this was year one, and that in a category with 11 subcategories that were quite different – from the notion of data integration to enhancing a story – we just didn't feel adequate' to identify a Grand Prix winner, said Jury Chair David Sable, Y&R Global CEO.[24]

A third area is the use of data in innovative ways – including real-time data, social data and aggregated consumer or product data to share an inspired POV in storytelling – such as Nike Fuelband, Wearefine, and other gorgeous visualizations popularized for the general public by creative data artists and journalists like Aaron Keblin and Jer Thorpe. Here, data is used to tell a rich consumer narrative, not only through data visualization but as the driving force in the story itself. We will explore each of these in Chapter 8.

2.4 How marketing practice is transformed by data

Different kinds of data sets are changing the principles of marketing. Marketing has traditionally been made up of the 4 Ps: product, price, placement and promotion. Technology and data allowed us to deepen the exploration in each of these four processes and has even extended marketing to 10–12 processes. For now, however, only the 4 Ps are explored.

2.4.1 Price

Here are four ways to calculate pricing. The first, cost-plus pricing, calculates the price based on production costs plus the company's margin. The second, target pricing, sets the price to achieve a target return-on-investment (ROI). These two methods are centred on the business and its needs. Data, as a proxy for the customer voice, impacts the second two methods: value-based pricing and psychological pricing. Value-based pricing is based on the value it creates for the customer. Psychological pricing is based on factors like positioning, perception of fairness in pricing, and what are popular pricing points for the product. The rise of social media and digital tools, as well as mobile device usage for in-store price comparisons, has now magnified price transparency across all channels. As a result, this type of open data allows consumers to develop new consumer journeys and purchase patterns that may eat away at marketer margins on subsequent purchases. Marketers must now create strategies for every step of the customer's journey to purchase and loyalty. One strategy includes 'price matching,' employed by Target, Toys R Us and Walmart, particularly during the holiday season. Price matching includes the practice of empowering in-store employees to match pricing from competitive stores and sites.

The bottom-line results of price matching are mixed, but of retailers that have taken part in the 2014 Omnichannel Survey, approximately one-third (32 per cent) of respondents said they would allow price matching in some instances.[25]

Nordstrom incorporates price matching as part of its overall service-oriented approach. Walmart takes another approach by using price matching as a 'backdoor loyalty driver'.

2.4.2 Promotion and placement

Marketing promotion has also been transformed by data – specifically on two levels. Consumer actions and transactions on the internet are measurable through ad-tech and direct marketing companies. In a well-researched, often-referenced article by the *Atlantic*, more than 105 companies receive data about each click we make on the internet. Tools like Collusion (collusion.toolness.org) compiled a graph of the companies that are capturing data about people's digital journeys.[26] These companies are collecting data to help sites, advertisers and their partners to gather the data necessary to target consumers better. As a result, marketers can now better understand the lower funnel experience – what was the last point of engagement before purchase, does a person come back, and what do they say about the product to others? But we now also have the ability to better understand the impact of the brand on culture through things like search intention, social media conversations, or number of Meetup groups created to facilitate connection around a topic, purpose, or shared experience. These actions and expressions are all captured in ways that data-transforming technologies can federate and integrate into actionable insights.

In the most tangible example, the internet allows us to distribute our products and services in a wholly new way that allows for greater product choice, price transparency and better product fit for our needs. Companies like Amazon and Yelp have evolved the traditionally word-of-mouth communication that ended with a 'goodbye' to useable data sets of ratings, reviews, and transactable products and services.

Understanding where big data can drive competitive advantage is essential to realizing its value. For many companies, the insights drawn from big data have already resulted in profitable, sustainable growth in three areas: customer relationships, product innovation and distribution. Data puts the customer at the heart of any business or marketing strategy. Organizations can bring together social media feeds with disparate sources, including weather data, cultural events and internal data such as customer contact information. Further, advanced analytical tools allow for faster, more effective and less costly processing and create the potential to rapidly develop new insights.

A US-based retail bank might look at social media activities to identify at-risk customers, while an Asian bank analyses customer-call audio logs to compile sentiment of the customer experience. This kind of opinion gathering not only captures first-hand feedback and avoids the inherent bias of customer surveys, but also quickly develops customer and performance targets. Reporting is standardized to a weekly, daily, even real-time cadence. Macy's (a US chain of department stores) uses big data to create customer-centric assortments.[27] In the past, Macy's analysed data points around merchandising such as sell-through rates, out-of-stocks, or price promotions. Now, with big data tools, the company can analyse these data points beyond product or SKUs (stock keeping unit number) to factors such as size, packaging and weight as well as time and location of the products at any given time from manufacturing to ordering. From there, data can help generate thousands of scenarios to gauge the probability of selling a particular product at a certain time and place in order to optimize merchandise assortments by location, time and profitability.

Today's technology goes beyond pattern matching: Twitter's Bluefin Labs uses advanced technology to 'watch' videos and 'listen' to audio to learn which customer segment prefers which ads in which TV show genres. By targeting on the micro-segment level, we achieve higher returns on advertising investment.

2.4.3 Product

From a product perspective, big data can improve product itself. When ZestCash, a money lender to lower-income borrowers, began using cell phone records as a proxy to ascertain credit risk, the company improved its margins by 20 per cent.[28]

In the creative development process that makes up so much of the promotional and product development process, we look to the converging forces in culture, in the category, in consumer behaviour, and in the company itself to help us orient ourselves. Here is the relationship between brand, consumer, category and culture, and the question of how data can help us better understand the relationship between these as it relates to the product and marketing.

There are five broad categories of impact that a combined data and creative process can have:

1 **Measurement and optimization**. Most data practices begin with measurement. The first step of most analytic and data programs is to

focus on the things we know how to measure – sales, media. The next step is to package those measurements into a reporting structure to begin a dialogue of what's important and what's not. By creating internal benchmarks of what's normal and what's not, we have an opportunity to see what's really going on in an organization. It's also important to understand that what's normal internally may not be normal for the industry. The next step is to monitor progress based on those measurements. Partners who can help this process will be covered in Chapters 3, 6 and 8. The principles of measurement, however, will be covered in Chapter 3.

2 **Generate insight**. Data can help generate consumer insights as well as improve customer analytics (including segmentation, cluster analysis of data, etc; many things fall into this category). However, there is much more exploration, as data from our manufacturing process is changed by the Internet of Things. This might also include new distribution methods or partnerships that may improve placements of products, or distribution. In the promotional realm, data can also help identify the context for creating relevant creative work; for example, do blondes drive better lingerie sales than brunettes? (See Chapter 9.) Data can now become the language of the consumer – a way to initiate a two-way dialogue.

3 **The role in media**. Data is already playing a huge role in guiding the media planning and buying process. This includes understanding all the components of data a media partner may bring to the table – the DMP (Data Management Platform) that handles your first-party data, the limitations of third-party data, better strategies in retargeting – but should also include the combinatory effect that data and creativity can have in proactive personalization within marketing, irrespective of channel. This might include better service support, e-mail correspondences and recommendations. This is also the domain of better customer acquisition through both targeting and identification. We will cover this more extensively in Chapter 6.

4 **Creative and content strategy**. Data can help make better creative work as well as establish the foundation of meaningful communication with our consumers, for example the ability to 'humanize' the quantified facts about a product or service. This also includes the evolving field of content strategy, which includes the creation of content offering value to the customer without any regard for the brand or brand metrics marketers are trying to move. We will cover this in Chapter 7.

5 **Data (and creative) as product**. Companies can create new products and services for consumers with 'data as a product', ie information on factors that can impact us as well as information about our own behaviour as people. For example, the Weather Channel provides value to its customers by providing information on the weather. The way they distribute it, however, is by offering it in a context that benefits customer lives such as gaming, retail like Home Depot, and smart phones. Data as a 'product' is what powers apps, websites and 'things' connected to the 'Internet of Things' movement. For example, Nike launched Nike Fuelband, a now-defunct product that made fashionable an entire category of 'quantified self' tools (a movement to incorporate technology to track data and information on ourselves including heart rate, EEG, EKG, mood and other inputs). For a marketer, these types of devices can extend the data collecting ability to better understand their brands in the context of a consumer's life.

2.4.4 What is creative data?

Each year, Gartner releases a study about the most hyped terms in emerging technology.[29] The hype cycle follows an established trend – from hype to reality to institution. Several of the hype cycles popular with clients are data related, including those for data science, business intelligence and analytics, identity and access management, Internet of Things, and more. Data has certainly become prolific as a concept spawning related concepts, and has established itself as a corporate transformation practice. In the specific realm of marketing, new vendors, technologies and techniques are now helping brands work with consumer and internal data in a number of different ways to better understand consumer behaviour as well as empower marketers and analysts without technical backgrounds to access business intelligence. Some of these emerging technologies apply specifically to marketing. Today, marketing is seeing a convergence of its channels (mobile, social, cloud and information). Companies must focus on new and more sophisticated ways to reach consumers who are more willing to participate in marketing efforts to gain greater social connection or product and service value. New terms like Hybrid Cloud Computing, Internet of Things (IoT), Machine Learning, People-Literate Technology and Speech-to-Speech Translation are now part of business lexicon and pop culture. We will cover these in more detail in Chapter 10. The main point to note is that this model outlines the speed and trajectory of how concepts and technology around data evolve quickly.

Figure 2.3   Gartner Hype Cycle

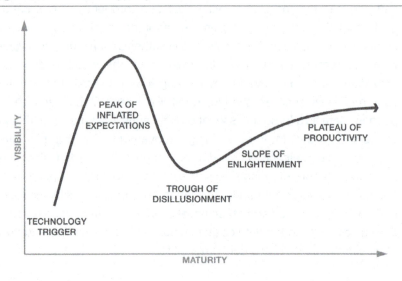

Understanding the Internet of Things from a data point of view can provide a model for marketers to both understand consumer behaviour and to communicate with the consumer. In 2008, Nike revolutionized the experience of running by combining a relatively standard system of tracking personal progress through fitness monitors and added in layers of utility and social interaction. By creating an online place, Nike not only connected runners to other runners, but were able to help runners better understand themselves by providing benchmarks of running times and distances of similar runners. Nike found that if there were less than five uses of the Fuelband within the first month, runners abandoned the community. Nike also found that if a runner was active at least once a month for six months, he/she often became a leader in the community and was more likely to organize group runs. Those who took images of their run and shared them with friends were more likely to bring new sign-ups than those who didn't.[30]

The process of getting to these insights and innovations, however, required a lot of re-work. The first thing that needed to happen was to create data collection systems that brought together all the data. The collected user data itself was stored in an external database while the web analytics lived within Google. The social data, not linked and not aggregated, lived as a process of a marketing analyst adding in new user names each day to see what consumers were doing on open social networks.

The second challenge was to ensure that historical records were kept to see changes in behaviour over time. Called transaction records, they were a log of each stage of the consumer experience captured in data. The next step was to validate that the way the data was interpreted was correct. Did a sudden drop in activity mean that the customer stopped using the Fuelband, or stopped sharing data? All these questions were vital in the process of interrogating the data to turn it into insight.

Why does all this data fusing matter? By thinking through the plumbing of data, it forces everyone in the room to begin to see the person in a holistic way, and we start to see their journey not simply as a consumer but as a whole person engaged in their lives. Running is not an inherently social sport, but through data and with sharing data, we begin to see just how much community there really is. By considering the technology needed to support this influx of data, we are forced to prioritize what we feel is important to view; this then allows us to see the white spaces in the experience that another product or communication can help solve.

2.5 Good rules to live by when using data creatively

How can we turn this continuous trail of interaction into something valuable in the marketing process? To turn data into valuable knowledge and insight for the marketing process is a matter of asking the right questions and applying focus, purpose and perspective to how including data and analytics might transform the creative process.

2.5.1 Measure everything meaningful

These days, it does feel like everything is measurable. We can personally track our mood, our weight, our opinions or the evolution of our friendships. Yet, the utility of such measurement can fall short if we aren't clear about the purpose of the measurement to begin with. Freud once wrote: 'It is impossible to escape the impression that people commonly use false standards of measurement – that they seek power, success and wealth for themselves and admire them in others, and that they underestimate what is of true value in life.'[31] Value is often overlooked as a key performance indicator (KPI) for a number of reasons. When thinking about data from a measurement standpoint, it's important to ask the right questions. Here is a list of questions to help guide the process as it relates to marketing:

1 What is/are the goal(s)? In business planning, it's common to refer to a goal as an observable or measurable result to be achieved in a fixed timeframe. Oftentimes, marketers set goals that require them to understand the complex dynamic involved in achieving them. 'Increasing sales by 20 per cent' is indeed measurable, but doesn't necessarily help in the business (and marketing) planning process. Data and measurement is a way to scaffold the efforts by setting up measurable goals for actions and programmes that help achieve the greater goal.

2 How can data be collected? The answer to this question should always come with a confidence level. Today, we have many metrics made available to us by the technology vendors and media partners that help us deploy our campaigns. Likes, posts, views and click-through rates have, on one hand, helped standardize how we can compare marketing across industries, competitors and campaigns. However, these methods of measurement often have wide gaps between them to help us paint a fuller picture of the questions we are trying to answer. A classic example is the run on Facebook 'likes' we saw when Facebook introduced Brand Pages. Over time, brands discovered that the best way to encourage 'likes' was to offer coupons and discounts. In many cases, however, that wasn't necessarily the best thing for awareness, brand building, or even preference. It's important to understand the 'like' as a function of your marketing programme, but it does not help measure the effectiveness of the programme in building brand (if that is your goal). In these cases, we are measuring a behaviour that requires us to ask how it is related to our goal. In the case of driving sales, it may indeed by effective. But if the consideration is building brand equity, the action of coupon promotion may not seem like the best choice.

3 Are there limitations in reporting standardization? Oftentimes, for continuity purposes, we may choose to focus on measurement of KPIs that are shared amongst campaigns. We may measure things like click-through rate (CTR) in digital marketing or impressions because it makes comparison easier. But it doesn't necessarily have the diagnostic ability that good metrics can provide us. In these cases, we must allow data to be what it is and create new sets of measures that truly reflect what we are looking to accomplish.

4 Is it possible to measure the relative strength and weakness of individual channels and programmes, the relationships between them, and the overall effect of the programme? Measurement can be a powerful tool in understanding not only the effectiveness and efficiency of particularly programmes and tasks we set for ourselves, but can also be a way to show the relationship between these programmes. For example, we have the ability to target digital campaigns to one set of audience members and then target similar audience members with a combination of digital and addressable TV campaigns. This helps us see the impact that a robust media mix can have.

2.5.2 Data is biased

Selection bias – when something is more likely to be selected than others (also known as preference) – is something we as people do all the time. This is the effect of suddenly noticing things we didn't notice that much before, wrongly assuming that the frequency has increased. A similar thing happens to pregnant women who suddenly notice a lot of other pregnant women around them. It's not that these things are appearing more frequently, it's that we've (for whatever reason) selected the item in our mind, and in turn, are noticing it more often. Creativity is biased as well, but it's not the fact that it's biased that's a problem; it's the false belief that it's an absolute truth that can lead us down a difficult path. This is important to remember when collecting information on customer behaviour. If the data reveals something unexpected, it is okay to review the methodology to ensure that moderators weren't biased, or that the correct statistical principles were applied in the analysis.

2.5.3 Garbage in, garbage out

'Garbage in, garbage out' refers to the fact that models, computers and algorithms, since they operate by logical processes, will unquestioningly process unintended, even nonsensical, input data ('garbage in') and produce undesired, often nonsensical, output ('garbage out'). A term first adopted from computer science, it refers to the fact that because a computer software program manipulates data, the 'formula' that defines how that data is manipulated is only as good as the data used. Marketers experience the same thing; they may have sophisticated spreadsheets to help manage the marketing mix, but if there's incorrect data, they aren't useful.

2.5.4 *Data is irrelevant without context*

More formally known as Gödel's Incompleteness Theorem, the general premise is that a system cannot define itself completely based on its own description. According to Gödel, 'Any effectively generated theory capable of expressing elementary arithmetic cannot be both consistent and complete.'[32] In other words, marketers always need other data sets to contextualize the data within the data set. Marketers receive all types of data, particularly from digital marketing. For example, a stock image company spent the majority of its marketing budget on PPC (pay per click) techniques in search, display and social to drive consumers to purchase images. Their metrics showed that the US market share was slipping so they recommended increasing spend there. What they didn't compare was the cost per acquisition year over year. When they did so, they found that the increased spending was decreasing their effectiveness in the channel, and so they re-diverted their spending to another channel.

2.5.5 *Interrogate (and straighten out) your data*

The raw data – the millions of lines of numbers, words, images – is the basis by which data and analytical people work. If there is ever error in the collection or storage of the data, the conclusions will be invalidated. That's why it's important for marketers to ensure data fidelity and perishability (is the data in your models or about your customers out of date?).

2.5.6 *Data is a shared language*

Beyond an intelligence centre, data can also help the collaborative process within an organization to unlock creative possibilities. Data helps organizations:

1 get everyone on the same page;
2 create a shared language amongst stakeholders in the marketing, technology, business and information groups;
3 develop new skills to foster dialogue (and new ways of seeing).

Getting everyone on the same page

Discovery networks is a prime example. Discovery wanted to create an education programme and decided to launch a full-scale consumer survey in partnership with schools. They found that nearly 80 per cent of those

Figure 2.4 Analytic and data workforce Sourced from Spencer Stuart Cmo Survey, 2014

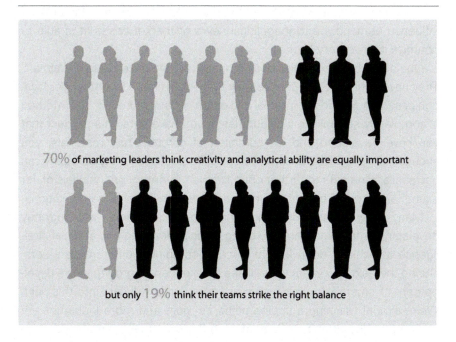

70% of marketing leaders think creativity and analytical ability are equally important

but only 19% think their teams strike the right balance

surveyed said they watched Discovery, yet subscription levels showed well below 50 per cent market penetration.[33] What they realized was that consumers were saying they watched Discovery networks because they felt like they should – not because they did. After all, who doesn't want to model for their kids a life-long habit of learning? In truth, this happens often. Consumers prioritize features they think they want when giving consumer feedback, but when we analyse the data for true drivers, we find something else to be the case.

Create a shared language amongst stakeholders in the marketing, technology, business and information groups

Data can also serve as a way to bring the marketing teams together. Most marketing organizations use some data, whether it's web analytics or traditional consumer research. Companies, particularly marketing groups, can get the most out of data by combining different data sets, not only from their own processes, but also from external and public sources.

In addition to employing and mixing their own data resources, companies should go one step further and look for useful data beyond company borders to help contextualize performance and understanding. Combining data sources is becoming more common as many companies are beginning to combine their internal and external data sources. If a company has detailed information on its customers and external macro-factors that influence demand, be it geopolitical news or market crises, it is able to optimize its inventory further.

One of the best examples of a company utilizing mixed data is Walmart. They have been able to optimize their up-to-the-minute inventory per location based on all kinds of internal and external data sources.[34] This method is completely scalable to all industries: if you have data on a product that you have developed and it's compiled of different raw materials, you already have a few useful data sources at your disposal. Any company can use similar data sets to further optimize their inventory on the basis of, for example, the price level of raw materials, demand or weather conditions.

Many different start-ups and long-running companies are currently developing smart algorithms by using machine learning and artificial intelligence to achieve deep insight through combining different data sets. During the next few years we will see an exponential growth in the development of smart algorithms, as more companies will dive into this field. We're almost reaching a tipping point, as more and more industries are realizing the importance of big data and the industrial internet, and starting to raise the demand for the right technology.

In order to work with big data, an organization, including the board, has to have a shared understanding of what big data is, and what it can be used for. Each department relies on the data that is being analysed and uses that insight as the basis for decision making. It should also be ensured that the data and the algorithms created are reliable and correct. The result of this should be a data-informed culture.

For example, in process industries involving material handling, big data helps companies to monitor their products and equipment better. Sensors allow them to know exactly where everything is. By combining this insight with data on how employees work or how the products are used, companies can optimize safety and improve efficiency in their inventory.

Instead of starting off with applying a data approach to the whole business process all at once, a company should begin with a process that is easier to grasp and can be tested by using a proof of concept. Formulating a proof of concept is a very important aspect of getting started with big data, because developing a data-driven strategy and implementing it is not an easy job. Typical big data projects last approximately 18 months, so you should start small by learning and experimenting around what it can do for your organization. When you have done that, then you can expand.

Develop new skills to foster dialogue

Data thinkers can help increase diversity and difference; including data in the conversation requires team members to spend time in different places in their mind and work with people with different worldviews and skillsets. The simplest way to get to different ideas is to work with different people in different ways. It's very easy to work in a marketing group, particularly a successful one which does one type of thing well. That expertise tends to lead to over-developed muscle memory and a habit of seeing the world as full of similar-shaped problems. Using different methods to solve problems –through creativity or through data and analytics – keeps the team interesting and interested in each other, which provides greater value of perspective and new learning for customers.

2.6 When data is and is not useful

Data, for all its usefulness in understanding more and more deeply about a customer or our marketing performance, has its limits. Data does a good job of reflecting historical performance. However, at best, data is only a proxy. As a result, the practice of predictive analytics is an estimate of future behaviour. Quantum mechanics, a field of science pioneered by Albert Einstein and Max Planck, tells us that scientists can't precisely know both the position and velocity of an electron at the same time.[35] Specifically, the Heisenberg uncertainty principle describes to us that the more scientists know about something's velocity, the less they know about its position; and the more they know about its position, the less they know about its velocity. The measurement and collection of marketing data is much like this. At best, the data we collect is like the Heisenberg uncertainty principle; it's a collection of data points that represent the movement or preferences of customers, but those preferences can change or be in between those measured points. So it's hard to use data prediction as anything more than a guiding tool. It rarely gives marketers the answers.

Data is not useful if it's not applied correctly. If the aim of the conversation is to reduce uncertainty and risk, data can be used to select areas of reduction. However, only using data for that purpose can improperly cast data as a tool that is anti-creative.

Data also requires the right questions to shape it. The challenge with a lot of data models today is that the constructs of the questions used to interrogate it, ie the algorithm or model, are hierarchical.

Data is, however, useful in solving business and communication problems, but the technical skills are no longer enough.

There is a set of common tasks in data which, unlike business and communication problems, occur for each task. These include gathering, wrangling (which includes standardization and cleansing of data sets), working with the data and visualizing data. This process is more clearly described in the next chapter.

Analysts and data scientists must work in collaboration with creative strategists, and these tasks can be broken down into subtasks. The subtasks are unique to each category of problem, but usually at least one of the subtasks can be answered by data – either through addition of knowledge and expertise or in the uncovering of relationships between observations, musings and attributes. The link between business understanding and data understanding is an iterative process that requires creativity on both the business side and the data side. Specifically, when we talk about the creative side of business, we're talking about strategists and analysts at agencies, product managers, and heads of marketing focused on branding. When we talk about the data side of the business, we are speaking of the data wrangler, data scientist or data interpreter. The key to success is the ability of the creative team (be it design, strategy or marketing) to see novel formulations (what would the behaviour of the consumer be related to – the weather, the traffic patterns, the release of the new Beyoncé album?). These formulations do not need to be accurate, but if they can be used as proxies then it's possible for the data side of the business to source and apply the right data sets to the process.

Tye Rattenbury, formerly a data scientist for Facebook and before that for creative agency R/GA, reckons that often, data can do two things well: optimize the details of the ideas and understandings we have (which can shift an idea from good to great by adding specificity) and very rarely it will come up with an insight that a human being couldn't gain through the collaborative strategic-creative process currently employed by agencies.[36]

There are more things data can do. There are things within the range of human experience that we can observe and describe about ourselves and data provides us with a method of paying better attention and observing things undetectable to the human eye. There is an entire world of observation and description that lives beyond our human capabilities. For example, the realm of sports is in the midst of revolution through the use of machine learning on data sets captured through video and biomechanics.

Through these trained algorithms of machine learning, we are able to identify potentially complex yet meaningful patterns in the data.

For example, during any match played in the NFL, video and machine learning can provide real-time information and analysis on player movement and performance. Despite access to this information, the ability of coaches to observe, process and evaluate the actions of 18 players is limited. Don Norman summarizes this predicament in his book *Things That Make Us Smart: Defending human attributes in the age of the machine.* 'Human memory is well tuned to remember the substance and meaning of events, not the details. Humans can essentially attend to only one conscious task at a time.'[37]

There are realms of human behaviour that are relevant to marketing beyond attitudes and usage. As marketing evolves into an interactive, near-real-time dance between consumer and brands, we must understand where data is best applied and when we can (and should) rely on human judgement.

Notes

1 Gittleson, Kim, 'How Cirque du Soleil became a billion dollar business', *BBC*, 12 December 2013 [online] http://www.bbc.com/news/business-25311503 [accessed 1 May 2016]

2 Ibid.

3 Quigly, James and Baghi, Mehrdad, 'Case Study: Cirque du Soleil', *Financial Times,* 16 March 2011 [online] https://www.ft.com/content/4191c332-500a-11e0-9ad1-00144feab49a [accessed 3 October 2016]

4 Ibid.

5 Ibid.

6 Glagowski, Elizabeth, 'Cirque du Soleil balances the art and science of creativity', *Teletech*, June 2014 [online] http://www.teletech.com/thought-leadership/articles/cirque-du-soleil-balances-art-and-science-creativity#.VmyJvRorLdR [accessed 1 May 2016]

7 The Level Summit, 'From the archive: marketing Cirque Du Soleil to the world', May 2014, http://www.levelsummitamericas.com/archive-marketing-cirque-du-soleil-world/

8 Glagowski, Elizabeth, 'Cirque du Soleil balances the art and science of creativity', *Teletech*, June 2014 [online] http://www.teletech.com/thought-leadership/articles/cirque-du-soleil-balances-art-and-science-creativity#.VmyJvRorLdR [accessed 1 May 2016]

9 Ibid.

10 Ibid.

11 Duval, James, 'What is database marketing and when can it be used?' *Customer Think*, August 2013 [online] http://customerthink.com/what_is_ database_marketing_and_when_can_it_be_used/ [accessed 1 May 2016]

12 Barmak, Sarah, 'The astonishing second act of Cirque du Soleil', *Canadian Business,* 13 Oct 2015 [online] http://www.canadianbusiness.com/innovation/ cirque-du-soleil-second-act/ [accessed 1 May 2016]

14 Macmillan, Douglas, 'Banjo Raises $100 million to detect world events in real time', *Wall Street Journal*, 6 May 2015 [Online] http://blogs.wsj.com/ digits/2015/05/06/banjo-raises-100-million-to-detect-world-events-in-real-time/ [accessed 1 May 2016]

15 Interview with Brandwatch CMO Will McInnes. Personal interview, 18 December 2015

16 Ibid.

17 Cairns, Ian, 'How Unilever became a pioneer in social analytics', 10 Nov 2015 [online] https://blog.twitter.com/2015/how-unilever-became-a-pioneer-in- social-analytics [accessed 1 May 2016]

18 Ibid.

19 Interview with Brandwatch CMO Will McInnes. Personal interview, 18 December 2015

20 Interview with SocialFlow founder and chief product officer Frank Speiser. Personal interview, 10 December 2015

21 Ibid.

22 Ibid.

23 Coyle, Daniel (2009) *The Talent Code: Unlocking the secret of skill in sports, art, music, math, and just about everything else.* Bantam Books, New York

24 Neff, Jack. 'No Grand Prix in first year for Creative Data Lions', *AdAge*, 26 June 2015 [online] http://adage.com/article/adtile/grand-prix-year-creative- data-lions/299243/ [accessed 3 October 2016]

25 Retail Touchpoints, 'Data-driven personalization drives advanced pricing strat- egies' [online] http://www.retailtouchpoints.com/features/special-reports/ data-driven-personalization-drives-advanced-pricing-strategies [accessed 1 May 2016]

26 Madrigal, Alexis C, 'I'm being followed: how Google – and 104 other companies – are tracking me on the Web', *The Atlantic*, 29 Feb 2012 [online] http://www.theatlantic.com/technology/archive/2012/02/ im-being-followed-how-google-151-and-104-other-companies-151-are-tracking- me-on-the-web/253758/ [accessed 1 May 2016]

27 A T Kearney, 'Big data and the creative destruction of today's business model', January 2013 [online] https://www.atkearney.com/strategic-it/ideas-insights/article/-/asset_publisher/LCcgOeS4t85g/content/big-data-and-the-creative-destruction-of-today-s-business-models/10192 [accessed 1 May 2016]

28 Ibid.

29 Gartner, Inc. (2015) Hype cycle [online] http://www.gartner.com/technology/research/methodologies/hype-cycle.jsp [accessed 1 May 2016]

30 Interview with Nike VP of global brand marketing Jeff Cha. Personal interview, 5 April 2012

31 Freud, Sigmund (1962) *Civilization and Its Discontents,* ed. and trans. James Strachey, Norton, New York, USA

32 Priestley, W M, 'Gödel's Incompleteness Theorem', *Encyclopedia of Science and Religion,* 2003 [online] http://www.encyclopedia.com

33 Interview with Angela Wei of Discovery Communications. Personal interview, 5 April 2014

34 Industrial Internet Now, 'A fresh mix of data creates new insights', 19 March 2015 [online] http://industrialinternetnow.com/a-fresh-mix-of-data-creates-new-insights/ [accessed 9 May 2016]

35 Jha, Alok, 'What is Heisenberg's Uncertainty Principle?' *Guardian,* 10 November 2013 [online] https://www.theguardian.com/science/2013/nov/10/what-is-heisenbergs-uncertainty-principle [accessed 9 May. 2016]

36 Interview with Salesforce director of data science and learning Tye Rattenbury. Personal interview, 10 November 2015

37 Norman, Don (1993) *Things that make us smart: Defending human attributes in the age of the machine,* Addison-Wesley Longman Publishing, Boston, USA

Understanding the data and analytic processes that enhance marketing

3.1 Data literate vs data fluent

To be a successful marketing executive today now requires literacy in data. This is not the same as being fluent. A data-literate marketing executive can ask the right questions and seek the right assistance to accomplish their goals. For example, a common requirement in measuring marketing success is to understand how sales numbers are related to promotional activity. Someone who understands data would understand that a simple linear regression is an appropriate technique to accomplish the task; someone fluent would consider the specific methodologies to use. A marketer's job in this context is to create the environment where data and creativity work together.

In 1980, John W. Tukey of Bell Telephone Laboratories and Princeton University wrote a seminal paper published in the *American Statistician* entitled 'We Need Both Exploratory and Confirmatory'.[1] In it, he described the need for what he calls 'exploratory data analysis (EDA)' as a way to analyse data for generating ideas that could be confirmed later. He believes that:

> Exploratory data analysis is an attitude, a flexibility, a reliance on display, not a bundle of techniques, and should be so taught.

Rather than looking to data to confirm suppositions and gut instinct or looking for data to illuminate the full answer, data analysis can be a way to jump-start the creative process.

Here is a list of 25 questions compiled through interviews with creative senior marketers and product development leads that can help guide the interrogation of data analysis generated to spark the creative development process.[2,3] A data-literate marketing lead will be able to ask any of the following questions, understand the context provided by the data and make decisions based on the responses. If there are any terms introduced that are unclear, they will be clarified by the end of the chapter.

25 data questions to spark the creative development process

1 What is our business goal?

2 Which analytic approach did you select?

3 How was this data collected?

4 Is this the right data or did you use other sets of data as a 'proxy' to answer the question?

5 How recent is the data?

6 Did you fuse this with other data sets?

7 Did you omit, prune or parse (parting based on a set of instructions) data before analysis?

8 How did you treat missing data?

9 What were your assumptions about the behaviour, the data, the vector?

10 How are outliers treated?

11 If necessary, did you A/B test this result?

12 What model/algorithms did you try?

13 What methods did you use to transform the data?

14 Is this the appropriate model for this type of data?

15 What is the model's accuracy?

16 Why did you choose those models?

17 Was the learning supervised or unsupervised? (If you don't know!)

18 How did you measure data science quality? What is the r-squared value?

19 How can this best be visualized?

20 Is the visualization truncated for better storytelling?

21 Does this model help eliminate existing hypotheses or help form a new one?

22 Is the visualization honest?

23 Can this point be illustrated with a relevant example?

24 What are the key points we're trying to communicate?

25 Is this normal for the brand? Is this normal for brand competitors? Is this normal for customers? If not, what's the context of this behaviour? Seasonality? Cultural events? Political events? Category shifts? New competitors? Other product lines?

3.2 Three uses for data in relation to creativity

This chapter aims to address the terminology, techniques and tools that can be used to accomplish specific marketing objectives that involve data in the creative process. These marketing objectives can be broken out into three main areas:

- marketing measurement of creativity's impact;
- marketing's role in growth (known more colloquially as Growth Hacking);
- insight generation: understanding the customer and market.

3.2.1 Better measurement for success

Measurement has always been a critical part of the marketing process. With the introduction of new data sets and technologies, there is more measurement available to a marketer, especially as it relates to the creative development process. The influx of data and observations of customer behaviour through data has improved our ability to measure more often, and usually, more accurately. This section is not meant to discuss all types of marketing measurement, but rather marketing measurement as it relates to creative process in marketing.

In an ideal world, the impact of creativity in marketing will contribute to shareholder value of the business. The financial returns of the company as a function of the impact of all forms of communication to influence consumers will result in a very clear marketing mix model (the econometric formula used to assess sales lift of different marketing tools and to identify the most effective). In each of the following sections are sample metrics that can be included in the model. As with any solution, the metrics (and the model itself) are imperfect but can point us in the right direction. The model must include media impressions and other standard metrics: economic data; industry data (like market projections for growth); product data like pricing, feature success and performance; advertising data (including copy testing), promotional data and competitive data; and performance data like sales, revenue and profits. The model can also include data that represents the impact of creativity.

A number of studies have proven that creativity is an important factor in effectiveness – as much as deep understanding of the consumer and precise targeting of the message to specific groups. According to a 2015 Millward Brown study, creatively awarded campaigns are 11 times more efficient than non-awarded ones in terms of the level of market share growth they drive per Excess Share of Voice (ESOV is defined as share of voice minus share of market).[4] A 2013 *Harvard Business Review* study, drawing on research of nearly 437 campaigns for 90 FMCG (fast-moving consumer goods) brands, found that 'A euro invested in a highly creative ad campaign had nearly double the sales impact of a euro spent on a non-creative campaign.'[5] This same study stated that certain TYPES of creativity are more impactful in advertising, such as elaboration, the addition of unexpected details or extending simple ideas so that they become more intricate and complicated (30 per cent more impact on sales), and originality, which includes elements that are rare or surprising or that move away from the obvious and commonplace (when combined with elaboration, 96 per cent per cent more impact on sales).

Many of these studies are meta-studies (studies of studies) that look over hundreds of campaigns to measure effectiveness. For measurement to be useful for marketers beyond a statistic, it is important to consider the types of metrics that can help before, during, and after marketing planning. How does one go about measuring creativity's impact on marketing?

More is not always better unless we use the data correctly by measuring the right goals. According to *Marketing Accountability* by Malcolm McDonald and Peter Mouncey, there are three levels by which marketing investments should be measured.[6] The first is shareholder value add based on the marketing programme. We measure value as programmes that contribute to sustained competitive advantage for the company. According to McDonald and Mouncey, nearly 85 per cent of global company value is based on intangible assets. For example, in 2006, P&G paid nearly £31 billion for Gillette, of which only £4 billion was accounted for as tangible assets.[7] 'Intangible' value is a result of many factors beyond marketing, of course, but marketers want to be able to capture that which is related to marketing. This level of measurement involves an understanding of the relationships between sales, customers and operations. The second level they describe is linking marketing activities to consumer and expected and actual outcomes. This is where marketers will look at specific programmes, of which many have tentacles into and out of marketing promotion, that cut across the entire organization. For each of these programmes, we need to be able to assemble metrics both impacting and emanating from marketing. An example might include a global, consistent consumer segmentation by which marketing, operations and finance can orient their decisions around or the use of an assets delivery programme through technology or a global loyalty programme. The third level is what McDonald and Mouncey describe as micro measurement, a term that describes the measurement of the promotional elements like advertising effectiveness.[8]

I propose extending this framework and focusing on the metrics that creativity can have an impact on, such as ease of use and usage relevance by the customer. 'Ease of use' and 'usage relevance' are new, important metrics to the traditional list of marketing metrics to help measure the impact of technology in the consumer journey. One of the interviewees for this book, Patrick Martin, the principal of business strategy for Zappos, stated that there is strong recall and much brand love for Zappos, but that doesn't often convert to usage unless they also score high in ease of use and usage relevance.[9] We will cover this in detail in Chapter 7.

3.2.1.1 Shareholder value[10]

Marketing metrics linked to measurement of corporate value are often related to sales and margins and market share growth. But, in context of the fact that corporate value is 85 per cent intangible assets, we need to consider metrics that can help us understand how we grow this over time. Creativity helps grow brand value (which translates to shareholder value) by differentiating the product.

Therefore, metrics like brand equity and imagery, percentage of positive reviews and position in Google search results can all be used to represent the progress of marketing's work. Other intangible assets like overall customer satisfaction with a company's product or service can be quantified using metrics like Net Promoter Score (an index ranging from -100 to 100 that measures the willingness of customers to recommend a company's products or services to others).

With the introduction of new and different data sets like social media, we can more accurately measure these and measure them more often. Imagery can now be measured using social media data. Other ratios related to placement of the product including merchandising metrics like accessibility and availability are also useful for measurement to help marketers to maintain high levels of customer satisfaction.

The important thing to note is that each of these metrics must be measured against the targeted segments that the company understands to be either their 'best customer', 'target customer for growth', or 'target customer base'.

3.2.1.2 Linking activities to outcomes[11]

The next layer of marketing metrics is concerned with the marketing programmes themselves. One of the more significant factors that affects business success is the profitability of products. A major factor to consider in profitability is that the price premium businesses can charge as a result of the meaningful differentiation from their competition. Sometimes even product differentiation is not enough. In these cases, creative marketing programmes can have a great impact on the business goals. These are the types of programmes that might include modifications to the physical product, packaging, labelling, positioning and promotion. In the case of marketing programmes, there are a number of different metrics based on the goal of the programme. The important thing is to use the right metrics to assess the impact of the creative rather than effectiveness and efficiency. Metrics may include shifts in brand tracking studies as well as longitudinal surveys that help marketers to monitor a brand's health and adjust marketing programmes.

Consider a programme like 'Small Business Saturday' for American Express (AMEX). Created six years ago, it is now a US holiday held every Saturday after Thanksgiving to encourage holiday shoppers to patronize small and local stores. American Express has a long history in advertising and event sponsorships, and could have used these tactics to promote small business. Rather than focusing on the message of promotion, the programme emphasized the action of spending with small businesses. A good portion of American Express's income is from small businesses, but rather than focusing on opening more accounts, American Express focused on driving more revenue by helping grow business for these small companies. The metrics of the programme were related to more than simply return on investment (ROI). AMEX ran advertising, built kits for retailers and created a lot of videos highlighting small businesses. The initial metrics for success were revenue generated for small businesses, engagement of small businesses and loyalty. As a result, AMEX saw the number of new accounts increase dramatically. Since 2012, American Express, in partnership with the National Federation of Independent Business (NFIB), has released its success metrics. From 2014 to 2015, there was a 14 per cent increase in small business spending.[12] User search volumes for 'Small Business Saturday' have been growing at a steady pace, with the data especially popular in New York, Phoenix and Boston. Of those aware of Small Business Saturday, nearly half (47 per cent) shopped on the day.[13]

3.2.1.3 Promotional metrics[14]

In the absence of a single way of measuring ROI for different channels, marketers can move toward an apples-to-apples way of comparing returns across a range of media. By measuring the impact of advertising on consumer recall, on the public's perceptions of the business, and on sales leads and revenue, marketers can see the impact of each channel individually and in orchestra with one another. This is the work of attribution modelling.

Attribution is simply the ability to evaluate the performance of each touch point in the buying process. A key premise of attribution is that all touches play a role in impacting the buying process. To create any type of attribution model you need data related to both converting and non-converting opportunities. Therefore, attribution requires the capturing of consumer touchpoint data over a historical period to determine which touchpoints are the most effective at which stages in the buying process to support investment allocations and produce higher aggregate results. The most useful attribution model for creative impact is fractional attribution. Fractional attribution assigns a calculated 'weight' to each marketing touchpoint (or creative element) throughout the buyer's purchase journey. Typically, this weight is determined by the corresponding relative impact that particular touch will have on producing the desired business outcome, such as purchase. Determining the weights requires an understanding of which touches perform best through iterative testing. In other words, marketers need to collect the data over several campaigns to calculate the weight through statistical significance of the various touchpoints. Companies like Media Math, Adometry and C3 Metrics specialize in attribution software to manage a closed-loop system to measure the impact of creative, channel, and campaign.

According to the same *Harvard Business Review* article, 'Creativity in Advertising', levels of creativity vary across product category.[15] In categories such as cola and coffee, advertisers and customers often favour creativity, whereas other functional categories like shampoo and body care focus on product demonstration. Overall benchmarks scores ranging from 2.62 for shampoo to 3.60 for cola can have meaningful impact on marketing mix model results.

3.2.2 Marketing for growth

Companies like Airbnb, Uber, Twitter and Dropbox are well known for their exponential growth and 'disruptive innovation'. A term coined by US-based venture capitalist Bill Gurley, it is an 'an innovation that helps create a new market and value network, and eventually goes on to disrupt an existing market and value network (over a few years or decades), displacing an earlier technology.'[16] Their method of growth was not traditional marketing and advertising, but tapping into new and unconventional acquisition channels, iterating product features and developing a close relationship with customers through social media using a rigorous analytical and creative approach. This method, known as 'growth hacking', connects the product directly to distribution and has become a new type of marketing that brands large and small are adopting. One example is Dropbox's early incentive to gift free storage space to those who shared the service with their friends. Mailbox created demand by producing a very elegant interface and creating a sense of anticipation and exclusivity by showing the number of people waitlisted before new prospects could join the list.

Growth marketing is constantly evolving. In the early days of social media, people drove traffic to sites using SEM (Search Engine Marketing) and Social Media Marketing. Since then, Facebook and other channels have opened up their media buying tools to large brands who have now flooded the platforms with money and keep small start-ups from bidding on common keywords or interests graphs of consumers.

Now, growth marketing has extended to partnership marketing by leveraging the resources (and e-mail lists) of larger brands. This process is described more deeply in Chapter 9 as an in-depth case study at Adore Me.

3.2.3 Understanding the data-mining process in insight generation

Data used for reporting measurement results is sometimes confused with insights. The insight is not the technical understanding of the connection of one data point to another, but the understanding as to why those two data points are related (if at all) and the contributing factors of the relationship. Is an increase in social media spending responsible for the increase in sales or is the strong creative campaign coupled with smart social media targeting responsible for broader engagement with a younger, more digitally focused consumer who increased visits to the website, which increased the number of e-mail subscribers, which drove better targeting of offers and promotions? Insights here are defined as actionable, data-driven findings that create business value. Below are a few ways to think about how data can be used to generate an understanding of the customer and the market to help with the creative development of marketing programmes.

The process of turning a marketing task into an analysis or data-mining task is a fairly well-delineated series of steps. The steps involve a combination of a marketer and analyst team's creativity, business knowledge, IT skills, a robust understanding of statistics, and what many refer to as common sense, or as I like to call it, sense.

3.2.4 Types of analysis to generate insights on customers, product, and communications

Customer analysis includes the following formulae:

Affinity Analysis

This analysis helps marketers see what activities customers often perform together. This might leverage co-occurrence analysis or other methodologies like association rule learning or similarity matching (which is covered later in this chapter).

Calculating Customer Lifetime Value (CLTV)

This is a prediction model used in marketing that can estimate what the lifetime relationship of an individual customer will be worth to a business. This marketing function might utilize classification modelling.

Recency, Frequency, Monetary Analysis (RFM)

A marketing technique that is used to calculate the best customers of a business based on a triumvirate of factors: how recently a customer made a purchase, how frequently they purchase and how much they spend. The theory that drives the technique's use is the marketing paradigm that 80 per cent of your business comes from 20 per cent of your customers. This allows the efforts of the direct marketers to be specifically targeted to the best 20 per cent of customers. This type of analysis might include the clustering technique.

Churn
The primary goal of churn analysis is to identify those customers that are most likely to discontinue using your service or product. The marketing analysis might be regression analysis.

Influencer Network Analysis
This type of analysis helps us understand the relationships between customers. This analysis is common in social network systems and is used for influencer marketing. It uses methods like link prediction.

Product Analysis includes the following formulae.

Merchandise Planning
This includes Affinity Analysis but also includes the ability to help keep inventory from getting old or to help the consumer to select products you believe they want. Inventory now arrives before customers order it to reduce wait times. This marketing function might leverage regression analysis.

Pricing
Database mining can also help marketers determine the best price for products around customer sensitivity. This marketing analysis might include regression analysis or, if a complex issue, predictive analytics like simulation.

Product Recommendation
This type of analysis includes a process called collaborative filtering that makes automatic predictions (a type of filtering) about the interests of a user by collecting preferences or taste profiles from many users (the collaboration part).

Communications Analysis includes the following formulae.

Targeted Communications
This type of database marketing improves customer communications and includes using information to personalize correspondence, making it easier to build up a rapport and therefore increase loyalty, customer retention and sales. The calculation of how likely it is a customer will respond is an important component of effective targeted communications. This

analysis requires several different models, including regression, causal modelling as well as clustering and segmentation algorithms.

Lift

Lift analysis is often used to answer the question of how much more prevalent a pattern is than what would be expected if things were left to chance. Lift helps determine whether the co-occurrence in data is significant rather than as a result of popularity. Lift leverages other algorithmic techniques for causal modelling.

These concepts are explored more deeply in Chapter 7 as an in-depth look at Zappos.

3.2.5 A deeper look at segmentation

3.2.5.1 Segmentation, cohorts, and personas

Market segmentation is a basic tenet of marketing. Segmentation is a grouping of customers built upon any number of attributes such as income, location, education level or age. They can also be built upon psychographic attributes. Popular actionable segments that are used every day are geographic, behavioural, seasonal, and benefit segments.

Nielsen PRIZM is a popular market segmentation system that is based on zip codes, where people are chunked into subsets regarding their location, income and behaviour.[17]

The company GfK MRI surveys the United States twice a year to create their segmentation. These surveys are all built on top of US Census data and supplemented by sending out surveys to a large sample of people to create segments throughout the United States.[18] Experian Simmons is similar and also extends to the UK and European markets as well as the data and research providers Comscore and Hitwise, which focus exclusively on digital behaviours.[19]

When a segmentation is defined based on experience and life stage, this is called a cohort. Cohort analysis is very common in the United States; we often talk about 'Millennial' traits as well as 'Generation Z' attitudes (the cohort that succeeds the Millennial generation). When a segmentation is quantitatively validated, marketers talk about each group of customers as a generational cohort.

Developing personas is a method of market segmentation wherein marketers collect a combination of qualitative and quantitative data to build archetypes of the members of our target audience. In other words, marketers can take data to tell a predictive story about customers based on past behaviours and attributes to understand habits as well as data such as search intent.

There are a number of important formulae related to segmentation. Clustering techniques are often used when quantifying a segment. Data science methodologies such as EM (expectation-maximization) are good for this type of analysis and when used in conjunction with a marketer's domain expertise can help define customer segments that can be used throughout the organization. The techniques will be covered later in the chapter.

3.2.6 Terminology: a word on data science, big data, analytics and more

There are many terms bandied about when speaking of data, analytics, and data mining. Let's take the time to clarify the relationship between data, analytics and the process of data mining. In Chapter 1, we defined what data is and the different types of data that are useful to marketers. Analytics is the application of an algorithmic process (usually statistics as a descriptive or predictive tool) to data in search of meaningful information.

Big data is not the same as analytics. It is true that both seek to glean intelligence from data and to translate the findings into business advantage, but big data refers to the complexities and considerations that come from analysing large sets of data. The challenges are more than technical (IBM describes them as the 4 Vs of 'big data' – volume, variety, velocity, veracity);[20] they also come with a lot of challenges, as many good data scientists forget some of the basic principles of statistics including sampling populations and biases (the premise of which is our next chapter).

Classical statistics (both frequentist and Bayesian) fall into the category of mathematics. Statistics sit largely at the intersection of probability and optimization. In contrast to data mining (described below), they are mostly employed towards better understanding some particular process we observe through the collection of data. Once collected, a formally specified model (again, from the area of study of statistics) is applied to the data to extract that model from the full, noisy data set (ie estimation), and this is distinguishable from other possibilities (ie inferences based on known properties of the sampling distributions). In laymen's terms, this means that we understand certain things about how groups of numbers work if they follow certain rules, so we estimate the likelihood that they follow those rules rather than other possible rules. The most common model is called regression analysis. It assumes one dependent and one independent variable (meaning one set of numbers is dependent on another set of numbers) and the analysis looks to estimate the relationship between the two.

Data mining is the process of analysing data from different perspectives and summarizing it into useful information, which includes statistics, but can also include pattern recognition techniques from Machine Learning. Usually, the data sets are larger than most of the typical statistical tools used, and are often messier. The goal is either to generate some preliminary insights where little insight exists, or to help predict future observations more accurately. Moreover, data mining procedures could be either 'unsupervised' (we don't know the answer – discovery) or 'supervised'' (we know the answer – prediction). Note that the goal is generally not to develop a more sophisticated understanding of the underlying data generating process – it's much more exploratory and is meant to summarize what's going on. Common data mining techniques would include Cluster Analysis, Classification and Regression Trees, and Neural Networks (described in the next section).[21]

Machine learning involves the study of algorithms that can extract information automatically (ie without human guidance, but sometimes with supervision through the model and parameters). Machine learning is a broad field; so long as there is some inductive component to it that's achieved through an algorithm, it qualifies as machine learning. Neural Networks is a sub-topic of machine learning, as is Anomaly Detection. Natural Language Processing is a phrase used to describe a specific problem that ML tackles, as well as the evolving techniques in AI beyond ML being used to tackle the problem.[22]

Machine learning can be one or several algorithms packaged together to achieve specific goals within Artificial Intelligence (AI). A popular machine learning tool for classification purposes that has been made available to the public is IBM's Watson, as is Google's recently released deep learning API, TensorFlow. Machine learning (in common with most data models) does have a bias to it. Even when we have no specific purpose or target for a grouping (which we call unsupervised), a person still has to define which data elements to include in the model.[23]

Artificial Intelligence is the broader study of how to create intelligent agents beyond machine learning. AI, in general, is any kind of unsupervised learning, whether it's done by a machine or not. It's a term that is generally used as a catch-all for things that we haven't figured out yet which we consider 'smart' – like learning, communicating, knowing and the ability to reason (like humans or dolphins or any other random classification of 'intelligence' that humans have devised). The important thing to know is that we aren't there completely yet, but the aspects most relevant to understanding things we create (like images, signals, voice and text) are being decoded now. This year, a paper was published by German researchers from the University of Tubingen with the help from a neuroscientist at Baylor College of Medicine in Houston, sharing how they taught a neural network to paint like Van Gogh (and other artists) by modelling not only 'style' but the spatial relationship amongst the components of the image, broadly described as the 'content' of the image.[24]

Currently, the most common application of data-mining techniques in marketing include targeted marketing and cross-selling (in e-mail and online advertising), consumer segmentation based on behaviours and engagement, and the fusion of first-party customer data with second-party social media data. Establishing this baseline of analytics is outlined in the case study chapters. There are several partners and vendors who are applying machine learning to data to improve the relevance of their analytic insights, and these can be found in our supplemental online material on Kogan Page's website.

It is important to understand data science even if you never plan to do it yourself. At best, you will have cross-functional teammates that will need you to speak the same language to move towards shared understanding and common goals. At worst, your company may be faced with competition that has announced new services around data and analytics and you'll need to be able to assess if it's a meaningful innovation in your category, or just hype.

3.3 The analytic process for insight generation

3.3.1 Phase 1: Identify the goal of the insight

The transformation from a business problem to a data-analytic problem involves four steps. The first is to evaluate the context in which you are looking to use data – if you're answering a business question, then make sure what is being asked is a business question (How do we increase marketing effectiveness? How do we decrease customer attrition?), and that you challenge the data team to give you the answer in a sentence.

3.3.2 *Phase 2: Choosing analytic approaches*

After understanding the business problem, the data science team must identify the best analytic technique, or combination of techniques, to solve the problem. This includes setting the problem in the context of statistical or machine learning techniques for modelling/calculation. It is important for the marketer to understand the basics of the analytic approach but not necessarily the specifics of each technique. Below is a list of techniques with a brief description to help facilitate dialogue.

As a marketer, if you're looking to analyse data that's relatively straight-forward and easy to manipulate, you may just use Excel. However, there are a number of advanced algorithms (all of which have commercial applications) that you might find more suitable for analysing large amounts of data.

3.3.2.1 Descriptive analytics

This is the phase we normally think of as the 'analysis' phase – when the proper source data is prepared.

In this step, analysis techniques are applied that help describe the data in summary form or, in some cases, organize the data into groups. Here is where data literacy turns into data fluency. For each of the types of marketing metrics listed in the previous sections, we will describe the type of data techniques that would be considered for each. This is meant to help aid dialogue on the process.

1 Aggregation analytics is a class of techniques used to summarize data including basic statistics, such as mean and weighted averages, medians and standard deviation. Other aggregation techniques include probability distribution fitting (the repeated measurement of variable phenomena and tried and true plotting points on a graph).

2 Regression analysis is a common way to predict the future based on the past by exploring spatial relationships. There are many types of regression techniques, but all share the common goal of predicting the value of a dependent variable where partial related variables are available, or estimating effects of an explanatory variable on the dependent variable – this is most common in forecasting (ie how much money will that customer be worth?).

3 Classification models are algorithms used to identify to which category or subpopulation a data point belongs. When speaking about classifications, you must be careful to also identify the discipline you are

speaking about. Statisticians use the term differently than practitioners of machine learning. For example, who amongst my group of customers will respond to my program? Common data science algorithms for regression and classification tasks are C4.5, k-means, CART and SVM.[25]

4 Clustering is a technique the goal of which is to group a set of data points so that the ones with the most in common are closest together. Importantly, clustering is not a specific formula; it is accomplished by using a series of algorithms. And it is almost always an iterative process. Common data science algorithms for clustering analysis are k-means, kNN and expectation-maximization (EM).

5 Similarity matching refers to the ability to identify similar people based on the data known about them – this is useful for product recommendations. A common data science algorithm for similarity matching is Apriori.

6 Co-occurrence grouping attempts to find associations between entities based on a transaction (something that is happening to them) – for example, do certain products get sold together?

7 Profiling attempts to characterize the typical behaviour of a group – for example, what is the typical mobile app usage for 18- to 24-year-olds?

8 Data reduction attempts to prune a large data set into a smaller data set for easier analysis.

3.3.2.2 Predictive analytics

Predictive analytics is focused on the prediction of future probabilities and the extrapolation of these probabilities into trends.

1 Simulation – a set of techniques used to create a simulated environment for testing predictive models. This includes models like agent-based modelling.

2 Optimization – a wide-ranging tool set for making optimal selections from a set of alternatives. This is commonly used to help set pricing for products and maximize yield.

3 Link prediction – this attempts to predict connections between data items – for example, connection requests on LinkedIn are powered by these types of algorithms. A common data science algorithm for link prediction is RankBrain/PageRank.

4 Causal modelling – this attempts to help us understand what events or actions actually influence others by looking at the difference between the situation if the influencing event were to happen and if it did not.

3.3.3 Phase 3: Data preparation

Sourcing and collecting information is a deliberate process. Several factors come into play when considering how to collect data – the fidelity, ability to link, perishability, classification of data, who needs to see the data and to what depth. These factors can make data collection quite expensive even when there's a desire to collect everything. The biggest challenges are as follows: not all data is stored in one place, stored in the same or compatible formats, or even relevant to answering the business question. The process, then, must evolve at its own pace to create robust, useful, usable data sets. Often, you and your data members won't know that another data source is needed until you iterate your modelling a few times based on the business problem.

A data scientist can help with data collection by using tools that crawl web pages. Common programming languages like Mechanization or Python might be reasonable starting points for your data scientist. They help you navigate to different web pages, enter data in forms, simulate clicks of Submit buttons, and collect the data.

Other methods of gathering data might include purchasing data from vendors that has been collected and cleaned, and has been treated for missing values, normalizing and standardizing data. Vendors include NPD for sales data or social data like GNIP. Another source of data includes open-source data sets provided by the government, universities, and from large open-source data projects like Microsoft Bing's earth data.

With the amounts of data now available, it is now imperative for companies in nearly every sector to leverage both internal data and external data offered by partners in the form of social, purchase, third-party advertising etc, to remain competitive. The 'research' departments of large companies might hire statisticians and analysts while smaller companies might hire consultants to comb through reams of data to find insights. The volume and velocity of data (in addition to veracity and variety) has outstripped the ability of individuals and their client workstations to process it, and so many businesses and consultancies have sprung up to assist marketers in the application of data science principles and data-mining techniques.

3.3.4 Phase 4: Data processing

The next step is processing the data. Also known as data wrangling, this includes the necessary steps of cleaning, discovery and structuring the data. You will almost certainly need to understand parsing libraries for XML, JSON, CSV and HTML. One of the most important and efficient tools while working with data is the Regular Expression available in Python or MathLab, or any type of data science tool.

A type of processing includes enrichment, which is a set of techniques employed to add information to, or fill gaps in, a data set. Examples might include appending purchase data or credit scores, or standardizing prefixes or suffixes.

Some top-level understanding of processing data might include the following:

1 converting data to tabular format;

2 cleansing by removing or inferring missing values;

3 normalizing and scaling data;

4 enriching for data completeness;

5 transforming unstructured to structured – applying metadata to help search data more efficiently.

This is also a time for discovery, ie what does the data have to offer from a business perspective? In some cases, visualization techniques can help the analyst understand the data content, quality and any collection issues.

3.3.5 Phase 5: Validation and publication

Validating is the action that surfaces data quality and consistency issues, or verifies that they have been properly addressed by applied transformations. For example, when looking at birthday data, does the distribution of dates look uniform across the year? Or for competitive media spend, is the data too consistent in each quarter or does it ebb and flow seasonally (implying that someone may have arbitrarily distributed the spend per quarter in equal amounts)? Marketers should check for data completeness (do all customer records have a transaction amount attached to them?) as well as data recency (when was the last update of the data?).

Publishing refers to planning for and delivering the output of your data wrangling efforts for downstream project needs (like loading the data in a particular analysis package) or for future project needs (like documenting and archiving the logic used to transform the data for use by other data scientists and analysts.)

This data doesn't necessarily end in reports. It can also be published in a computer readable output.

3.3.6 Phase 6: Data visualization

Data visualization is a term used to describe the outcome of the ways that data can be arranged in a visual format to make it (and the story it tells) more accessible. Data visualization is not the same as storytelling. Void of language, data visualizations do not have the necessary power to provide the emotional impact that makes the insights memorable, provocative or sharable. However, data visualization is a crucial part of telling a story when metrics are part of that story.

Metrics are a good way to get all stakeholders on the same page. When starting a data group in marketing, the first analyst will be in charge of gathering data from disparate sources like sales, media and operations, and may spend upwards of 80 per cent of their time doing so. Over time, with the investment of the proper technology to scale data analysis and visualization to help centralize sourcing of data including Excel reports, Google Analytics and custom relational databases like MYSQL, a company will invest in BI (Business Intelligence) tools (a type of data visualization) that help create clear, standardized reports. This might include a platform like Tableau or Spotfire. These tools allow a large number of data rows to be visualized for flexibility purposes. These might be in-memory analytics tools that load the data into your computer's memory to allow you to manipulate the data in real time. Occasionally, you'll need to enhance your data with additional data sets to help create the necessary dimensions and measures for good visualization. Data visualization is also very effective in demonstrating segmentations in the data.

Data visualization software can help marketers tell a story about data through meaningful diagrams. Our brains process visual data 60,000 times faster than text, making visualization one of the most efficient means of communication.[26] Business communication is not just about proving a point with scientific rigour. It's also about convincing your audience and getting them to relate to the point you are trying to make.

Chapter 6 will cover the technologies and service providers that codify and provide the tools and services necessary to help facilitate the data-creativity process. As part of a growing field, data scientists today come with a core competency. If that core competency is technical, that is an acceptable addition as long as there's a process to facilitate dialogue – one that should ideally be driven by the marketer. It is the responsibility of an organization's leadership to extend itself to welcome and clarify the process as it exists, and to set priorities and goals that a combined data and creativity team can accomplish together.

Notes

1 Tukey, John W (1980) We need both explanatory and confirmatory, *The American Statistician*, **34** (1), Taylor & Francis, Ltd, Oxfordshire

2 Thank you to all those who assisted in this process, including Tye Rattenbury (Trifacta), Luuk Derksen and Denise Xifara (Decoded), Mark Kelly (Verizon), Frank Speiser (SocialFlow), Nathaniel Watson (Brandwatch)

3 Dezyre, '100 Data science interview questions and answers (general) for 2016', 1 December 2015 [online] https://www.dezyre.com/article/100-data-science-interview-questions-and-answers-general-for-2016/184 [accessed 1 May 2016]

4 Twose, Dominic and Jones, Polly Wyn, 'Creative effectiveness', *Millward Brown*, November 2011 [online] http://www.millwardbrown.com/docs/default-source/insight-documents/articles-and-reports/MillwardBrown_AdMap_CreativeEffectiveness_11_2011.pdf [accessed 1 May 2016]

5 Reinartz, Werner and Saffert, Peter, 'Creativity in advertising: when it works and when it doesn't', *Harvard Business Review*, June 2013 [online] https://hbr.org/2013/06/creativity-in-advertising-when-it-works-and-when-it-doesnt [accessed 1 May 2016]

6 McDonald, Malcolm and Mouncey, Peter (2009) *Marketing Accountability: How to measure marketing effectiveness*, Kogan Page, London

7 Ibid.

8 Ibid.

9 Ibid.

10 Ibid.

11 Ibid.

12 O'Toole, Mike, 'Small Business Saturday turns five: how American Express and local retailers have changed business culture', *Forbes*, 24 November 2014 [online] http://www.forbes.com/sites/mikeotoole/2014/11/24/small-business-saturday-turns-five-how-american-express-and-local-retailers-have-changed-business-culture/#5636b25c4d31 [accessed 1 May 2016]

13 Business Wire, 'Small Business Saturday® results: shoppers provide encouraging start to the holiday shopping season' 30 November 2015 [online] http://www.businesswire.com/news/home/20151130005359/en/Small-Business-Saturday%C2%AE-Results-Shoppers-Provide-Encouraging [accessed 1 May 2016]

14 McDonald, Malcolm and Mouncey, Peter (2009) *Marketing Accountability: How to measure marketing effectiveness*, Kogan Page, London

5   Reinartz, Werner and Saffert, Peter. 'Creativity in advertising: when it works and when it doesn't', *Harvard Business Review*, June 2013 [online] https://hbr.org/2013/06/creativity-in-advertising-when-it-works-and-when-it-doesnt [accessed 1 May 2016]

16   Christensen, Clayton (2011) *The Innovator's Dilemma: The revolutionary book that will change the way you do business*, Harper Business

17   Nielsen, 'Nielsen PRIZM' 2016 [online] https://segmentationsolutions.nielsen.com/mybestsegments/Default.jsp?ID=70 [accessed 1 May 2016]

18   Christensen, Clayton M, Raynor, Michael and McDonald, Rory, 'What is disruptive innovation?' *Harvard Business Review,* **93** (12) (December 2015) pp. 44–53

19   Simmons, 'Our Products' [Online] https://simmonsresearch.com/product-portfolio/#ProductPortfolio [accessed 1 May 2016]

20   IBM Big Data and Analytics Hub, 'The Four Vs of Big Data' [online] http://www.ibmbigdatahub.com/infographic/four-vs-big-data [accessed 1 May 2016]

21   Hawkins, Jeff and Dubinsky, Donna, 'What is machine intelligence vs. machine learning vs. deep learning vs. artificial intelligence (AI)?' *Numenta*, 11 January 2016 [online] http://numenta.com/blog/2016/01/11/machine-intelligence-machine-learning-deep-learning-artificial-intelligence/ [accessed 1 May 2016]

22   Shah, Khushbu, '5 best machine learning APIs for data science' 2015, *KDnuggets* [online] http://www.kdnuggets.com/2015/11/machine-learning-apis-data-science.html [accessed 1 May 2016]

23   Ibid.

24   Gatys, Leon A, Ecker, Alexander S and Bethge, Matthias, 'A neural algorithm of artistic style', 2 September 2015 [online] http://arxiv.org/pdf/1508.06576.pdf [accessed 1 May 2016]

25   Li, Ray, 'Top 10 data mining algorithms in plain English', 2 May 2015 [online] http://rayli.net/blog/data/top-10-data-mining-algorithms-in-plain-english/ [accessed 1 May 2016]

26   O'Connor, Chad, 'The power of visual storytelling', 8 March 2014 [online] http://archive.boston.com/business/blogs/global-business-hub/2014/03/the_power_of_vi.html [accessed 1 May 2016]

New mental models for marketing   04

The idea that business is strictly a numbers affair has always struck me as preposterous. For one thing, I've never been particularly good at numbers, but I think I've done a reasonable job with feelings. And I'm convinced that it is feelings – and feelings alone – that account for the success of the Virgin brand in all of its myriad forms. RICHARD BRANSON[1]

4.1 What are mental models?

In today's marketing zeitgeist, the dynamic changes driven by technology innovation, social media and data have forced many of us to reconsider what it is that we know and what we know to be true in marketing. Mental models help people make sense of the world – to interpret their environment and understand themselves. Mental models include categories, concepts, identities, prototypes, stereotypes, causal narratives (if this, then that) and worldviews. Mental models play a decisive role when it comes to cooperating and coordinating team activities in complex environments and contexts.

Mental models are neither good nor bad. They are meant to facilitate decision making. In fact, as marketers, we aim to create brands by leveraging existing mental models about value (premium = quality), status (this is desirable – buy now!) and meaning (green is authentic) to encourage consumer purchase.[2]

Best practices have evolved into 'next practices'; prevailing theories on market dynamics must now be re-configured into hypotheses that need to be tested in market, and customer loyalty isn't just about repeat purchase. Yet, we have some deep-seated ideas about how consumers think and how marketing works that might also require some evolution. We might know consciously that they aren't true, but we still operate with that programming when it comes to our decision-making process.

For example, some marketers may have the belief that measurability comes from the sound bites we've passed around for a long time ('which half is effective'). These soundbites can create the misleading assumption that advertising and other forms of marketing aren't measurable, when actually this is no longer the case. Yet still agencies are challenged to help develop the 'Big Idea' (discussed in more detail in the following section), whilst too many marketers still labour under the belief that the most important brand question is 'How does it make them feel?' rather than also considering the equally vital questions of 'Does it work as promised?' or 'Will they remember?' Even a well-quoted, dynamic entrepreneur and successful businessman like Richard Branson tells us that brilliant business moves only come from the gut. But is that true today?

This kind of thinking typifies the way we think about marketing today and how we see the world. As John Adams once said, 'Facts are stubborn things',[3] but upon a closer look, the things we consider facts may no longer hold true because we can observe more through data. A person's decision-making process is informed by:

1 the (incomplete) information they have available;
2 the (finite) processing power of their brain;
3 the (limited) amount of time they have to decide/act.[4]

We do this because as humans, we can't process every single piece of information that comes to us. Instead, we need to construct mental models that simplify the world for our understanding. Simplifying for our mind doesn't simplify the world, so we must continue to adjust how we look at the world to stay close to the truth. This is not only true in marketing, but also in every area of our lives.

There are, of course, limits to mental models. The effectiveness of mental models can be limited by the very simplifications that underlie them. Oversimplification can lead to systematic errors of judgment, logic and forecasting. For example, an online marketer who assumes that consumers are going to continue to provide data about their habits, practices and desires for free is making an assumption that could easily turn out to be incorrect. Already some marketers are beginning to see that for relatively small fees they can circumvent major potential privacy liability.

Recall we previously mentioned Godel's Incompleteness Theory, which proved that no system can be both complete and consistent and that the errors inherent in mental models are inevitable.[5] That is why those using

Figure 4.1 How mental models are formed

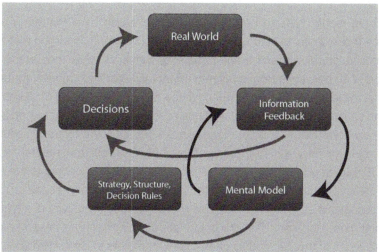

mental models must be aware of their potential limitations and find ways to reduce the consequences of those limitations.

They can also be improperly used. When the environment becomes truly complex, decision makers fail to respond appropriately by constructing new mental models. Instead, they seem to revert to older, simpler models (source). Decision makers, for example, often forecast by averaging past values and extrapolating past trends rather than rethinking the forces at work in the industry and imaging how they might play out. Yet such complex relationships are increasingly common in the wired world of the internet.

To the extent that mental models are inaccurate, they lead directly to risk (although it is often hidden risk, since the model does not alert the modeller to it). This is exemplified today by the pressures on the music industry since the advent of downloading, the bankruptcy of Kodak by the growth of camera phones, and the pressure on taxis from competitors like Uber.

It is imperative that marketers shift their mindset to one of growth from a perspective of asking questions rather than one of risk aversion from a perspective of seeking only validation of what they already know. This chapter aims to lay out useful mental models, mental models to watch out for, and new mental models in marketing that can leverage the most out of what data has to offer the creative process and vice versa.

4.2 Current mental models in marketing

We have many types of hero in marketing. We also have heroes in business – those captains of industry who have built a brand so strong that they command premiums and market share by virtue of what they stand for. Encoded in messages from a revered savvy marketer and creative entrepreneur is the idea that creativity trumps data – in fact, that the role of 'numbers' doesn't have much of a role at all in business success. A sophisticated audience can see that it's a point of view, not a 100 per cent factually accurate statement of how Mr. Branson runs his business, but the mental model that RINGS true (but may not actually be true) for many people is the idea that creativity is the human-generated 'feelings' that might precede an idea, and success is attributed to that. This message about creativity is a type of mental model (or story) that the only true decision making is based on gut. These types of mental models often cause marketers to lag in implementing data systems that work for them, or to not support the initiative fully despite the organizational need, and there's a quantifiable business impact because of that. According to a 2014 global survey of 395 C-level executives by the Economist Intelligence Unit, the majority of marketing executives agree that big data will play a valuable role in the organization's future; 48 per cent of those surveyed believe big data is a useful tool, and 23 per cent say big data will revolutionize the way businesses are managed.[6] Yet in the same survey, only 27 per cent of respondents described their big data initiatives as 'successful' and only 8 per cent described them as 'very successful'. In fact, organizations were found to be struggling even with their Proof-of-Concepts (PoCs), with an average success rate of only 38 per cent. Many marketers and IT departments that support them cite that 'top-level' management support is vital, and much of the disconnect between implementation and results lies in the ability to interpret the results in a way that illuminates a path for senior management. These are mental models that are ripe for disruption.

4.2.1 The 4 Ps of marketing

The most common framework in marketing has been the 4 Ps. Many marketing mix models that help marketers calculate ROI still rely on this idea that the main inputs in marketing are the 'product', 'promotion', 'placement' and 'price'. Today, with the availability of data and technology in more user-friendly formats, we now have eight or more Ps in marketing, including people, participation, personalization, process, pay, partner, purpose, physical evidence and more.[7]

4.2.2 Consumer attitudes and usage vs. measured consumer behaviour

This is a result of the cognitive bias called self-reported bias, which often comes from the consumer wishing to portray themselves in a more favourable light. Despite this, we can learn a lot from ethnographic research as long as we consider the possibility that both interviews and data are reasonable but imperfect ways of understanding human behaviour and motivations.

4.2.3 A homogenous customer vs. a target audience of one

In marketing, we often focus on a target audience that shares similar characteristics. We have the ability to shift this from characteristics, attitude and usage to a dialogue related to right time, right place, right message – we're no longer beholden to a generalized message. Building loyalty, however, requires a dedication to brand building, and that requires an understanding of what makes us human and what brings us together. As marketers, we need to do well with both target markets as well as target audiences.

4.2.4 Marketing owns the customer interaction

To truly engage customers for whom our traditional ways of reaching them (30-second spots (interruptive TV ads), out-of-home advertising (OOH), radio ads, digital web banners) companies must create superior products, digital experiences and service touchpoints. Customers expect this. And to deliver these experiences, we need to engage internal departments like customer service, partnerships, operations, product teams and the executive suite.

4.2.5 Big data vs. smart data

'Big data', for marketers, has been tamed in some aspects (social media listening and insights tools), but completely untouched in other respects (user data, device data, connecting users to social data). Small data, in contrast, refers to small, usable chunks of data that can be processed by the human mind without additional analytical or technical assistance (web analytics, social listening, business intelligence tools). The use of big data is a function of both the company size (to generate unique insights from first-party consumer or product data) as well as what the services market has to offer in terms of tools to process 'big data' for consumption.

4.2.6 Analogue dollars vs. the digital dimes (and the mobile pennies)

Coined by NBCUniversal's Jeff Zucker, the phrase 'analogue dollars to digital dimes' describes the shift of media dollars from traditional channels like TV, OOH and radio to digital display to digital and mobile advertising.[8] As the number of units of display has exponentially increased, the value (and effectiveness) of these units has decreased. We need to shift beyond our current means of valuing communication and marketing effectiveness on metrics such as viewability and impressions to new ways of reaching consumers (this might include partnership marketing, direct engagement through personalization, and opt-in marketing).

4.3 Current mental models in advertising

Advertising, as a subcategory of marketing, also requires a review of what ways of thinking can help communicate the brand message and purpose.

4.3.1 The Big Idea

'The "Great (Big) Idea" in advertising is far more than the sum of the recognition scores, the ratings and all the other superficial indicators of its success,' said Leo Bogart, an American media and marketing expert, 'it's in the realm of myth, to which measurements cannot apply.'[9]

In advertising, the Big Idea (or, as Leo refers to it, the 'Great Idea') is the 'homerun' experience that agencies strive to hit for any work. Agencies describe it as the alchemy of the brand purpose, culture (a word used to describe the range between a trend for the moment or a lasting meme embedded in a world's consciousness for years to come) and an idea that a consumer can grab onto to help redefine themselves. It's a concept so amorphous, so big (and, according to Bogart, so mythic) that when the 'Big Idea' doesn't deliver on business goals, we play into the mental model that creativity's true impact cannot be measured.

The 'Big Idea' still matters, but it's not always possible to break through the many things that compete for consumer attention that are not a branded product or service. As a result, the 'Big Idea' may shift into several smaller 'Ideas' on what a consumer might need in the course of their day and as a result, agencies must think differently in order to break through.

4.3.2 Lateral vs. analytical thinking

Creative agencies today still operate under the either/or proposition of lateral (creative) or analytical (analyst) thinking.

Lateral thinking is a type of thinking developed by Edward De Bono.[10] It involves stimulus or frameworks that help start new thinking by recognizing and transcending certain established patterns. By moving from concept to concept, it tries to establish several different directions to go in. Lateral thinking involves solving problems through an indirect and creative approach, using reasoning that is not immediately obvious and involving ideas that may not be obtainable by using only traditional step-by-step logic or simple analysis.

Analytical thinking is a process or skill in which an individual has the ability to scrutinize and break down facts and thoughts into their strengths and weaknesses. It involves thinking in thoughtful, discerning ways in order to solve problems, analyse data, and recall and use information.

4.3.3 Storytelling is the most important type of creative

People process information best from stories. That's because stories transmit information to their listeners in a form that emphasizes meaning rather than details. That emphasis comes through creating emotional responses from the story – instilling fear, excitement, sadness or suspense in the audience. In advertising, marketers attempt to do the same to make their brand name memorable. The challenge, though, is that we're bombarded with stories all the time now, not just from other brands, but from the entertainment and media industries. Storytelling is effective, but there are other ways of creating positive brand affinity and spurring purchasing action, including superior customer service through social media or an intuitive service design that requires a systematic way of thinking creatively (rather than narratively).

4.3.4 Thinking vs. feeling in advertising

Some studies suggest we care more about rational ads for things we need, like medicine, and are more receptive to emotional ads for things we simply want, like clothes. Another study showed that while younger consumers prefer emotional ads for 'identity and fun' products (beer and cologne) and fact-based ads for 'utilitarian' products (pain relievers and investment plans), older consumers prefer emotional ads for just about everything.[11] Regardless, the research industry is split on testing, and therefore market-ers needs to embrace a spirit of experimentation to know what works best for their consumers and audience. It is not an either/or proposition anymore.

4.3.5 Roles of channels and mass media

Great marketing is not only a function of paid channels. And while social media has now evolved into a paid channel (through Facebook and Instagram targeted advertising, promoted pins on Pinterest, promoted tweets on Twitter, and more), making sharable content IS a marketing strat-egy. Not all strong promotion comes from paid marketing. The combined realms of data and creativity can help us understand this other world.

4.4 Current mental models in business

Some success stories are press worthy. Leaders like Jack Dorsey (CEO of Twitter and Square) and Tony Hsieh (CEO of Zappos and co-founder of LinkExchange), by virtue of their technology-driven businesses, are consid-ered brilliant business minds who have leveraged data. We understand them to be creative entrepreneurs with technical and data savvy to grow companies astronomically quickly. This does not just apply to technology companies. There are many creative entrepreneurs with phenomenal success who continue to build their empires by leveraging the combined effect of data and creativity in innovative ways, like Russell Simmons, Ralph Lauren and others.[12] Russell Simmons (hip hop mogul), through his agency Narrative, has leveraged a combined relationship between Universal Music and Samsung to create ADD Music, a label harnessing the power of data by creating a music discovery platform to help decide the next big act.[13] These entrepreneurs often fly in the face of old 'ideas' about business. Below are a few new mental models embraced by a new wave of entrepreneurs.

4.4.1 Business decisions are based on intuition and data

Large organizations get large because they optimize. The pursuit of opti-mization, however, can stifle creativity that often needs to take a less direct path, but there are many organizations that are proving otherwise. Companies like IBM and GE have proven that large organizations stay relevant by embracing the application of creativity to business processes as innovation. These large organizations had to clear their own mental models of how growth can be achieved and sustained.

4.4.2 Marketing as an investment

In 2009, American Express adopted a new mindset to recognize marketing events as long-term investments rather than expenditures.[14] Rather than focusing on optimizing the traditional 4 Ps, they focused in on broad consumer and cultural analysis, selected a focused target market, and made strategic investments as a means of finding and retaining customers. As a result, their strategic partnerships and marketing innovation groups created programmes such as AMEX Offers through Social, Small Business Saturday and Open Forum – all programmes that American Express has initiated through their big data efforts to deliver on the idea of 'marketing as service'.

4.4.3 Embracing uncertainty as a creative opportunity

In 1921, Frank Knight wrote a book called *Risk, Uncertainty and Profit*.[15] He describes two types of uncertainty: one where we know the potential outcomes in advance and the probability of each (uncertainty risk), and another where we don't even know the possible outcomes in advance, let alone the probabilities (genuine uncertainty). He points out that real opportunities for profit exist in the face of genuine uncertainty. We have often used data to help us quantify uncertainty risk, but data can be used to help generate possible outcomes by aggregating data, experimenting, testing and learning, and can create an environment where it's okay to fail.

Some prevailing mental models about the role of data in the creative process stymie the possibilities that can be unlocked. We must rethink our mental models in the research, theory and practice of marketing to actualize the innovation promises that data and creativity can deliver on.

Our stories (our mental models) are merely hypotheses of how the world works. But we see them as reality and they influence what data we collect, how we collect it and the meaning we glean from it.

4.5 Biases that arise from mental models

More than half of marketers believe that to stay competitive, their enterprises must be committed to innovation. But even companies revered for their dedication to continuous learning and applied creativity find it difficult to always practise what they preach.

Consider Volkswagen: innovation and technology are pillars of their brand in both their business and marketing. After serious problems arose this year with their existing technology, their leaders confessed that their quest for market share had compromised their devotion to their other key pillar of consumer safety.[16] How did this happen?

Through research conducted by experts in organizational behaviour, psychology and business, they reached a conclusion that biases can cause people to focus too much on a single factor (success, dominance, consumer wants vs. consumer needs), take action too quickly, try too hard to fit in, and depend too much on experts. This is the same challenge that can happen now if a marketing organization is too focused on one modality over another.

From our mental models, certain biases can take effect. These biases can come from any number of mental models, so to test if a model works in a way that creates opportunities (instead of limiting the world), we must see if the result of our model forms these biases.

To be able to balance the importance of data and creativity, it is important to extend beyond the jargon, whiz-bang techniques and seemingly straightforward results of data as well as the emotionally sweeping, gut feel that creativity brings to the table.

Below is a list of biases to look out for when working with both analysts and creative. By familiarizing themselves with it, CMOs can ask smart questions to keep the process on track. Biases that result from the desire to create a story:[17]

Functional bias (fixed mindset). People will believe things more easily that fit their pre-existing mindset. Marketers might assume ways a customer might behave that is contradictory to the insight generated from data.

Outcome bias. People decide first, then rationalize. If people are stuck with something, they will like it more over time.

Survivorship bias. Introduced when we only look at the 'survivor' data, ie only data that's available from still-existing companies or experiments. This often happens when people write books analysing 'winning strategies' – it doesn't account for the risks and threats that non-surviving companies endured. In marketing, this could be analysis on churn without accounting for a website failure that caused people to cancel their subscriptions.

Anchoring bias. People make judgments by comparison/anchoring. Sometimes the conditions are not the same for proper comparison. It is important to consider more comparisons than simply past performance.

Pattern bias. We seek patterns that might not be there. When marketers and analysts run into this challenge, a helpful tie-breaker is to seek more data.

Representativeness bias. People tend to over-weigh recent information and deemphasize core marketing changes or prior feature changes.

Conservatism bias. Data can sometimes reveal emerging trends, for example about customers and their habits, that are so unexpected and counter to past behaviour that they are difficult to accept.

Confirmation bias. When people look at data to confirm their prior hypothesis; this sometimes happens when creative leads data.

Availability heuristic. Proper test protocols are important; people often rely only on pre-collected data and do not conduct randomized controlled experiments.

Bandwagon effect. People (marketers and data folks) may have heard of a particular phenomenon (say, the wrong shade of blue causing people to abandon a website) and try to reproduce it to validate it.

Blind-spot bias. It's important to develop several different hypotheses around a theory about consumer behaviour; we often end up focusing on one or two rather than developing a sufficient number of quality hypotheses.

Clustering illusion. Sometimes the data shows that there is a correlation in the data. It's important to test these hypotheses over time to see if they hold true.

Information bias. Marketers should expend time and energy only when there is a possibility of producing an actionable result and not based on distorted evaluations of information.

Overconfidence. Marketers may understand a lot about their domain, but they may not understand everything.

Social proof. People look to other people's decisions when reaching a conclusion. We often do that in relation to our marketing peers.

The Von Restorff effect. Objects that stand out against their peers are more memorable. Often, marketers might see press coverage of new campaigns as an indicator of superior performance.

Biases that result from the desire to simplify data analysis are biases that analysts might have when presenting data to their fellow marketing team members: [18,19]

Overfitting data. Data folks too often commit the sin of overfitting data – in other words, finding something out of nothing. Sometimes, marketers test too many hypotheses without proper statistical control until they happen to find something interesting and report it.

Placebo effect. In a UX A/B comparison, a data scientist needs to ensure the test population of users is unaware which is the 'old' and which is the 'new', or worse, if the test users are internal, which option is preferred by their manager or CEO.

Pro-innovation bias. If an analyst comes up with an actionable result, the marketer should ensure a quantitative benefit can be established for taking that action. This often comes into question when new technology vendors offer a new way of engaging users, but it might not fit into the overall marketing plan.

Recency bias. When an anomaly occurs, a marketer and the analyst need to assess the relevance and causes more deeply than the action that immediately preceded the occurrence (such as last touch attribution modelling.)

Stereotyping. If doing customer segmentation, stereotyping can actually help the marketer form hypotheses (eg households with children may be more likely to purchase toys), but these hypotheses need to be tested (those without children in the house, such as grandparents, may also purchase toys).

Zero-risk bias. A marketer should not gravitate toward a high-confidence, low-impact actionable result over a medium-confidence, high-impact actionable result. Instead, the team should work on increasing the confidence or redefining the hypotheses.

Selection bias. This occurs in a survey or experimental data, when the selection of data points isn't sufficiently random to draw a general conclusion. If selection bias isn't accounted for or acknowledged, and the results are claimed to be widely applicable, it is known as the spotlight fallacy. Selective perception manifests itself as selective reception.

4.6 New mental models to consider

4.6.1 The right questions

We need to evolve the marketing department's (and hopefully the entire company's) culture to support experimentation, conversation and a future based on a shared purpose. This allows us to add the capabilities provided by data analytics with creative data strategists.

4.6.2 Organizations are hypothesis driven, not data driven[20]

For all the hype about 'data-driven marketing', we are not driven by data or even by whim. Instead, we are driven by our understanding of phenomena that we observe, and those hypotheses should not be confused with theories. Data enters our organizations, our spreadsheets and our analytics programs through the lens of mental models that cause us to filter and fit data to those models. Therefore, we must be clear that we are moving towards truth and understanding, not necessarily results.

4.6.3 Scientific method IS design thinking

Design thinking, a term coined and popularized by IDEO's David Kelly, describes the process of creativity that has been introduced into corporate environments.[21,22] However, it has remained in the realm of process and is light on the inclusion of data, big and small. Design thinking is the scientific method applied to marketing.

4.6.4 Understand the relationship between data, phenomena, and theories

In 1989, Jim Bogen and James Woodward published a paper called 'Saving the Phenomena', delineating the distinctions between data, phenomena, and theories.[23] According to them, data are typically the kind of things that are observable or measurable (more people than average click to purchase items when there is an advertisement of a sale). Phenomena, on the other hand, are physical processes that are typically unobservable (people buy when things go on sale). Theories, then, are utilized to systematically explain and predict phenomena, not data (coupons drive sales). The relationship between theories and data is not direct, as we often skip the step of articulating phenomena and move straight to theory. However, without making this distinction, we often make assumptions and leap to conclusions (those who purchase on sale are not the target demographic or the target only purchase when there is a sale.)

4.6.5 Measure what matters

'We still talk about share of voice,' said president of PepsiCo's global beverage division, Brad Jakeman, at the 2015 ANA Masters of Marketing Convention, 'which is a television metric.'[24] The industry is still run by outdated measurement systems like Nielsen TV ratings and CTR benchmarks because we still view marketing performance as a function of paid advertising while ignoring the shifts in consumer behaviour as it relates to social media. Today, we are looking for drivers of purchase behaviour of the target market and the ways to drive influence and conversation with the target audience.

4.6.6 Look beyond the pattern and trends to the individual outliers

The vernacular of big data analysis with words such as trends, correlations and inferences shows that we tend to look to the summary and generalization of behaviour. However, for a marketer, it's those that diverge from the trend over time that might be the most significant.

4.6.7 Context matters

To 'get it right' with data science and analysis, we have to dig into the details. We need to 'unpack' the aggregate-level views that we compile like we 'unpack' briefs to help understand the dynamics occurring below the surface. We need to dig more deeply and to focus on the specific context of the data, as well as the other micro-details surrounding it.

The massive increase in and accessibility to computing power allows us to model the world like never before, but knowledge discovery is a human endeavour that is not replaceable by machines. We should do our best to model how the world actually works rather than how we see the world in our minds.

4.6.8 Embrace uncertainty and ambiguity

Even with data, there is uncertainty and risk. Business analysts and marketing teams are navigating completely new terrain. Success, to an extent, will come from throwing darts in the dark to understand how to interpret the data and what the data represents.

4.6.9 Purpose, focus, and perspective for data

In his *HBR* article 'A Predictive Analytics Primer', Tom Davenport does a nice job of laying out the three basic components that underlie predictive analytics:[25]

1 The data: Google's chief economist Hal Varian was famous for saying that Google doesn't have better models; it just has more data. Beware that more is not always better, but the dependency between relevant data and useful models is important.

2 The statistics: this is the set of mathematical techniques, ranging from basic to advanced, that are applied to the data to derive inference, meaning and insight. The most common statistical technique used in predictive analytics is linear regression, which the author nicely describes as the iterative process of selecting and testing the impact of variables on the outcome.

3 The assumptions: these are the things that are presumed to be true, with the most common being that the future will continue to be like the past.

To get the most out of data in the process, we must define the following things when we go about collecting and interrogating the data:

1 A purpose for data – particularly related to its collection and storage.

2 A perspective on data – data collection, analysis, how much, from where – what is the 'full' data perspective?

3 A focus for data – particularly as it relates to analysis, strategy and recommendations.

4.6.10 Collect data with purpose

Currently, companies who have embraced the access to and availability of data are often buried under an avalanche of data from social login tools, customer logs and marketing automation tools. In other words, they may or may not be collecting the right information, but they are most likely not storing it in a way that's useful in creating helpful customer profiles. Businesses are collecting information as a byproduct of their core business functions – often before they have an analytical plan in place.

The data collection process needs to be more purposeful. A great example is the US Census, which relies upon teams of statisticians to develop sophisticated planning and sampling methodologies. The US Census Bureau, knowing exactly which research questions it's aiming to answer, designs studies around very specific goals.

4.6.11 Critical thinking

Critical Thinking consists of mental processes of discernment, analysis and evaluation, especially as they relate to what we hear by way of points that are raised or issues that are put forward for discussion. It includes the process of reflecting upon a tangible or intangible item in order to form a sound judgment that reconciles scientific evidence with common sense. Hence, Critical Thinking is most successful when it effectively blends our natural senses or feelings with our logic and intuition, all applied in a systematic manner. Obviously, humans possess tools like imagination, empathy and creativity. While these faculties may be uniquely human, tools that support and empower these synthetic activities are emerging. Just as machine-based analytical tools support the analytical mindset, machine-based synthetic tools support a synthetic mindset, powering our imaginations and our hypothesis setting.

Marketing is an industry that relies upon new replacing the old, be it a new product, new campaign, or new channel. And there are already many encouraging conferences, online publications and conversations within marketing, as well as with other business practices like technology, operations and finance. These actions and activities are starting to bridge and break down the walls that divide theory, practice, and 'experience'. New is not always better, but it's important to have a way to continually challenge what is considered the right way to do things. We need to conduct more experiments in marketing and data, and creativity can help us navigate.

Notes

1   The Marketing Imagination, 'Brand development: re-imagine your business to differentiate your brand', 14 May 2015 [online] http://themarketingimagination.com/2015/05/brand-development-re-imagine-your-business-to-differentiate-your-brand/ [accessed 1 May 2016]

2 McVagh, Andrew, 'The Charlie Munger reading list', *My Mental Models*, 17 January 2016[online] http://www.mymentalmodels.info/charlie-munger-reading-list/ [accessed 1 May 2016]

3 Adams, John (2004) *The Portable John Adams.* Penguin Classics

4 Simon, Herbert (1957) A behavioral model of rational choice, in *Models of Man, Social and Rational: Mathematical essays on rational human behavior in a social setting*, Wiley, New York

5 Creative Advantage, 'Mental model' [online] http://www.createadvantage.com/glossary/mental-model [accessed 1 May 2016]

6 The Economist Intelligence Unit, 'Who's big on Big Data?', 2014 [online] http://www.bigonbigdata.eiu.com/static/pdf/EIU_Platfora_Whos_Big_on_Big_Data.pdf [accessed 1 May 2016]

7 Meyer, Robert, 'Wharton Marketing: changing the world of business' [online] [https://marketing.wharton.upenn.edu/files/%3Fwhdmsaction%3Dpublic:main.file%26fileID%3D330+&cd=1&hl=en&ct=clnk&gl=us [accessed 1 May 2016]

8 Satell, Greg, 'Is big media trading digital dollars for analogue dimes?' *Forbes*, 19 August 2013 [online] http://www.forbes.com/sites/gregsatell/2013/08/19/is-big-media-trading-digital-dollars-for-analog-dimes/ [accessed 1 May 2016]

9 Carducci, Vince, 'The Great Idea in advertising is far more than the sum of the recognition scores, the ratings and all the other superficial indicators of its success; it is in the realm of myth, to which measurements cannot apply', *Popmatters*, 1 March 2005 [online] http://www.popmatters.com/review/how-brands-become-icons/ [accessed 1 May 2016]

10 Turner, Travis N, 'Lateral Thinking by Edward De Bono', *Creative Leader*, 15 June 2012 [online] http://www.creativeleader.com/lateral-thinking/ [accessed 1 May 2016]

11 Drolet, Aimee, Williams, Patti and Lau-Gesk, Loraine, 'Age-related differences in responses to affective vs. rational ads for hedonic vs. utilitarian products', 9 April 2007 [online] https://marketing.wharton.upenn.edu/files/?whdmsaction=public:main.file&fileID=585 [accessed 1 May 2016]

12 Marr, Bernard, 'Ralph Lauren is using data to revolutionize fashion', *LinkedIn*, 2 July 2015 [online] https://www.linkedin.com/pulse/ralph-lauren-big-data-smart-shirt-future-fashion-bernard-marr [accessed 1 May 2016]

13 Kaye, Kate 'Data helps Russell Simmons' label pluck stars from obscurity', *AdAge*, 28 January 2015 [online] http://adage.com/article/datadriven-marketing/data-helps-russell-simmons-label-pluck-stars-obscurity/296755/ [accessed 1 May 2016]

14 Neisser, Drew, 'Why American Express continues to dominate in service', *psfk*, 28 January 2014 [online] http://www.psfk.com/2014/01/american-express-marketing-prowess.html [accessed 1 May 2016]

15 Knight, Frank H (2008) *Risk, Uncertainty, and Profit,* Evergreen Books (Kindle edition) [online] https://www.amazon.com/Uncertainty-Profit-Illustrated-Frank-Knight-ebook/dp/B004GKLYGE?ie=UTF8&btkr=1&ref_=dp-kindle-redirect [accessed 1 May 2016]

16 Levin, Doron, 'Fallout from the Volkswagen scandal is hitting consumers and the courts', *Fortune*, 8 October 2015 [online] http://fortune.com/2015/10/08/volkswagen-scandal-fallout/ [accessed 1 May 2016]

17 Dvorski, George, 'The 12 cognitive biases that prevent you from being rational', Gizmodo, 9 January 2013 [online] http://io9.gizmodo.com/5974468/the-most-common-cognitive-biases-that-prevent-you-from-being-rational [accessed 1 May 2016]

18 Piatetsky, Gregory and Rajpurohit, Anmol, 'The cardinal sin of data mining and data science: overfitting', *KDnuggets* [online] http://www.kdnuggets.com/2014/06/cardinal-sin-data-mining-data-science.html [accessed 1 May 2016]

19 Personal Excellence, 'How to stop analysis paralysis and make (great) decisions quickly' [online] http://personalexcellence.co/blog/analysis-paralysis/ [accessed 1 May 2016]

20 Hostyn, Joyce, 'Better human understanding, not big data, is the future of business', *CMS Wire*, 7 November 2013 [online] http://www.cmswire.com/cms/customer-experience/better-human-understanding-not-big-data-is-the-future-of-business-023088.php [accessed 1 May 2016]

21 Kelley, David and Kelley, Tom, *Creative Confidence: Unleashing the creative potential within us all,* Fletcher & Company

22 Miemis, Venessa, 'What is design thinking really?' *Emergent by Design*, 14 January 2010] [online] http://emergentbydesign.com/2010/01/14/what-is-design-thinking-really/ [accessed 1 May 2016]

23 Bogen, Jim and Woodward, James (1988) Saving the phenomena, *The Philosophical Review,* **97** (3) [online] http://www.pitt.edu/~rtjbog/bogen/saving.pdf [accessed 1 May 2016]

24 Schultz, E J 'PepsiCo exec has tough words for agencies', *AdAge*, 15 October 2015 [online] http://adage.com/article/special-report-ana-annual-meeting-2015/agencies-fire-ana-convention/300942/ [accessed 1 May 2016]

25 Davenport, Tom. 'A predictive analytics primer', *Harvard Business Review*, 2 September 2014 [online] https://hbr.org/2014/09/a-predictive-analytics-primer [accessed 1 May 2016]

Building a customer-centric organization using creativity and data

05

Transformation is not a single decision, process or outcome. Like success, how we define transformation largely depends on our goals and what achievement looks like. And like success, it does not come overnight. And most of all, like success, transformation is a mindset.

In 2006, Burberry was underperforming relative to its sector. At a time where growth for luxury goods was experiencing the highs of an internet boom at 12–13 per cent, Burberry's growth was hovering at around 2 per cent.[1] Competition was coming in all forms from traditional luxury goods retailers in Germany and France. Angela Ahrendts had recently taken the helm as CEO and had to focus the vision around their unique strengths and opportunities. Ahrendts and her management team identified several strengths, such as their heritage in London and famous trench coat (both very strong brand pillars), plus an opportunity in a new market none of their competition was targeting: millennials.[2] Ahrendts describes their decision to embrace digital transformation as one driven by a need to communicate with their new target. And while digital transformation requires a lot more than savvy in new marketing channels, the need for understanding customer needs, personalizing experiences through the use of data, and leveraging data for creative purposes was exactly what the 100-year-old company need in order to begin its transformation into a customer-centric organization.

The process of transformation to a digital, customer-centric organization requires an investment in data resources and a commitment to have them work with creativity – especially in a creative company. This commitment, for Burberry, started with a desire to reach new customers – essentially, a marketing function. This is not a unique pathway toward transformation. According to Tye Rattenbury, the director of data science and learning at Salesforce, the analytic function in most enterprises generally starts in the marketing group.[3] Most analytics that happen on the business level don't store consumer data on an individual level. Most analytics for business are specifically about the business. Marketing departments generally start with a few analysts that focus on reporting. In fact, a majority of the time, reporting is often not about the report itself, but about collating and organizing information. In the process, marketing analysts spend very little time analysing, but rather executing summary statistics and then circulating them to respective stakeholders. Over time, savvier analysts begin to automate the process, either through an informal friendship with someone in IT or through their own self-learning, to automate the extraction of data from internal reports or external sources. Oftentimes, when the reporting becomes something that senior leadership embraces, this is when the analytic function regarding customer data remains at the marketing analyst level, but the collation, collection and preparation of data moves to the domain of the CTO/CIO.[4] Rattenbury also shares that his teams, while working with marketing clients, find it rare that algorithms and data reveal something wholly new about the customer or the consumer journey. They may reveal something that optimizes our understanding of the customer, but rarely reveal anything shocking. However, when they do, it's often where certain response biases obscure the truth that exists between what we believe and how we as consumers actually behave. It also provides visibility into the mundane aspects of our day that our memories are simply not optimized to store for retrieval.[5] As we mentioned in Chapter 4, our brains encode for meaning, which is often connected to life, death, and certain firsts and lasts that are unexpected and emotionally packed. And our traditional understanding of creativity, the ability to tell stories that touch upon those mystical elements, is a human capability. But data has the ability to point us in the direction of the new, changed and unobserved. From my perspective, however, there are revelations that data can make about things that we find it difficult to see for ourselves. These could be things that happen over long periods of time (for example, changes in our preferences in content), socially sensitive topics (how often Americans have sex in a year) or things that happen too quickly for the human eye (the application of machine learning to sports to improve athlete performance).[6] This is consumer understanding that affects everything from insurance to entertainment. And that's a lot more that we as marketers can use to help build products and communications to deliver value.

In this chapter, we distil the practices to help steer the course of this complex journey of creating a robust data and creative process, team and technology stack in the marketing group. This journey attempts to cover large and small marketing departments.

5.1 The process overview

5.1.1 Building awareness and assessing capabilities

1a Build awareness of the opportunities for this type of thinking and how it can serve marketing.

1b Find allies in other groups (technology, operations, etc.) who might want to share this vision and who can benefit from it.

1c Assess where you are to create compelling consumer experiences.

1d Create the strategic plan with milestones and benchmarks.

1e Engage senior leadership.

5.1.2 Progressive investment of people, process, data, and technology

2a Hiring.

2b Analytics as a starting function – the first quick win.

2c Evolution to automation.

2d Evolution to insights.

2e Technology and data resources.

2f Buy or build.

5.1.3 Creating a culture of data and creativity to work together

3a Focus on shared interests

3b Focus on storytelling.

3c Focus on agility.

3d Culture.

3e New marketing roles.

3f Set up new ways of decision making, accountability and staffing.

5.1.4 Sustain the environment

4a Encouraging adoption

4b Measurement of the programme.

4c Iterate.

5.2 The process in detail

5.2.1 *Step 1: Building awareness and assessing capabilities*

The investment in data in a creative environment requires more than a person. Building awareness starts with a few key points. Consider three concentric spheres of influence and interests. In the first sphere (innermost circle), it is important to get the people who report to you directly on board. They will, by and large, be the ones experiencing the most change. The second sphere, your colleagues in other groups, are meant to help carry momentum once programmes are established. To this audience, you can begin to identify allies with a shared vision for a centralized customer experience powered by data. The CMO Council's yearly survey has shown that marketing's influence on corporate strategy development has increased by 20 percentage points from 2006 to 2013.[7] The third sphere is the top leaders in your organization. The goal is to help them understand the potential threats and opportunities from data and gain a sense of urgency for beginning the initiative now.

An emphasis on more easily quantified goal setting, improved business performance, and more opportunity for engaged customers can help build the case. For senior management especially, it's important to provide them with several pieces of information and experiences to help convey the urgency.

a Education – groups like Decoded or Hyper Island do a great job of educating the senior suite. With day-long seminars and interactive courses, these types of learning leaders can help provide environments that best suit the senior management style and needs in terms of understanding the impact and helping to define goals for the data program.

b A clear strategy and well-articulated initiatives and benchmarks for success – the strategy is often aligned with business goals such as a better relationship with customers, improved business performance, as well as other initiatives, such as how data can be a way to create shared understanding (and therefore better alignment) among global teams.

To create this, it's important to first assess the internal state of data affairs by asking questions that help gauge the ability of the data, technology and leadership to handle change. This is also an opportunity to assess data assets such as access to data, completeness of existing data and quality of data. This assessment cannot always rely on what the holder of data says, and often requires a third party to help assess quality. Another type of asset is the current competencies and knowledge of existing teams. For example, frontline employees may know a lot about existing customer preferences and that knowledge must be transformed into data. Yet another type of asset is physical, including offices, branches, retail footprint, distribution networks like satellite offices or partner spaces – anything that can be used to affix counting technology to help start the measurement process.

c   Align data goals within marketing with business goals – marketers that strive to create or maintain a tight relationship with the CEO will make certain that data needs for marketing help support company goals and bridge organizational silos by integrating the creative and data process in marketing in service of other disciplines.

When marketing demonstrates that it is fighting for the same business objectives as its peers, trust and communication strengthen across all functions and enable the collaboration required for the gains of this process to be realized.

5.2.2 Step 2: Progressive investment of people, process, and technology

5.2.2.1 Hiring

For companies taking their first steps in analytics, it's possible to get started with software and services from providers, generate some successes and insight, then a year or two later reassess and determine if they want to build their own data science or analytics team.

Initial hires are critical in setting the tone at the department. Look for a core of people with a breadth of skills. People with a broad range of expertise can come together nicely in a company, especially if collaboration is already a pillar of your brand.

Many organizations ask where analytics teams should be placed – whether they should be centralized or disbursed within a company. Blend the two models. There are advantages to centralizing – especially as teams grow – such as sharing skills, tools, methodology, and scale. However, with advanced analytics, it is critical to be close to the business and understand the decisions that are being made. The value of the centralized vs. distributed model of analytics has been a topic of debate, but, like all recommendations, the best configuration depends on the company.[8] Some companies have analytics groups that report to a CIO or the CTO to centralize the function. A larger majority report to various lines of business – the CFO, CMO, chief data officer, operations, strategy and planning, the chief risk officer, the head of engineering, and more. If a company chooses to decentralize, keep everyone in touch. Often, analytics groups within the same company lose contact. They gain a great deal by comparing projects and sharing ideas.

When hiring, it's important to hire for two qualities in your broadly skilled individuals: curiosity for the business and a knack for storytelling. Graham Douglas, former chief creative officer of the recommendation mobile app REX, asks his analytics team to share their insights using sentences to help package the data in a way anyone would understand.[9] What often results is a framing discussion such as context for data that helps make the data useful.

Really great analytics people can bring an incredibly high-powered, abstract way of thinking to the creative process – whether it be applied against promotional copy, new product ideas or strategic directions.

The data scientist is hired after the first set of easy wins. More on the illusive data scientists later in the chapter.

A word on data scientists

If you look at the evolution of the 'data scientist' in the past 10 years, you'll come to understand the trends and the evolving values surrounding data.

In the late 1990s, the internet was seeing its heyday of ill-conceived applications to traditional businesses like grocery shopping (webvan. com) dying violently on the stock market. The need for analytical skills was independent from any creative function. The marketing analyst was a business intelligence (BI) developer who knew how to use a range of different reporting tools (SSRS, MicroStrategy, QlikView, etc.) to look backward at progress and frame success as an improvement on historical performance.

Then, in 2008, the first job title of 'data science' appeared on LinkedIn.[10] The 'science' part made data seem scary. It became a formal science, full of physicists, mathematicians and computer scientists. The emergence of cheaper storage, faster RAM and software platforms that codified models made it possible to do more and so we did more – without understanding what we were doing.

The shift to advanced analytics has been driven by organizations' understanding that data has exponential commercial value in predicting future (and analysing current) consumer behaviour patterns. This is applicable across nearly every industry but is most pronounced in the banking, financial services, insurance, pharma, telco and fast-moving consumer goods sectors.

There's been a rise in a new kind of role – one anecdotally reflected upon by recruiters and predicted by the 2013 McKinsey study on big data; that of data interpreter.[11] A data interpreter is usually someone from a business or technical background, who is used to communicating between business and IT, and understands and communicates well the needs of both. Typical roles here would be data strategy or data solutions experts.

And yet, in the specific field of marketing, there is a needed role that communicates between the creative teams and the specific subset of IT that includes data analysis and programming. In the future, it may be these very people who make the marketing decisions, not because of the skills learned to do well in both, but the mental models that each discipline needs in order to make decisions in the ever-changing landscape.

5.2.2.2 Analytics as a starting function – the first quick win

You can't manage what you can't measure, so make sure you always have a clear picture of how aware your organization is that data analytics is the most critical capability required to support the evolution of a corporate strategy. Measurement is a way to begin harnessing the power of knowledge within the organization.

Many times, whether it be in an industrial or consumer products company, large or small, marketing departments start with one or two analysts to begin the measurement process.

An important issue for analytics teams is handing off a finished project – how do you make sure your new concept works in practice? Sometimes you embed your analytics in the everyday software used throughout the company. Sometimes, though, you have to ensure buy-in first.

5.2.2.3 Evolution to automation

Self-service data analytics, business intelligence or data science enable a point-and-click approach to data exploration, visualization and analysis. Self-service refers to the opportunity for business users and analysts to work with data, whether they have a background in statistics, data mining or technology.[12] It's gaining ground for several reasons:

1 Direct access to data means faster time to insights. When a marketer has to channel data reporting requests through a data team, it can take days for that request to be fulfilled. Data bureaucracy is eliminated with self-service tools that put data at the fingertips of users.

2 Easy access to data means wider adoption. When data is hard to get, or requires a knowledge of programming language (like SQL) to query, it informs fewer decisions. Conversely, when data is readily available, it becomes a natural part of more decision paths.

3 Web-based tools promote collaboration. When data is hidden in data-bases that only high data priests can access, and a static data set is provided as an Excel file, collaboration can be difficult. Web-based tools mean a URL about a successful campaign can be shared with a colleague, who in turn can take the analysis one step further. Collaboration and web-based software go hand in hand.

4 The best data is fresh data. When data reports are pulled and shared via e-mail, they – and the insights that are based on them – can quickly become out of date. Web-based interfaces offer the promise of being connected to live, continuously updated data – and the ability to set alerts with triggers. As marketing continues to go real-time, knowing within minutes that a digital campaign is in a nosedive translates into meaningful dollars.

To evolve into automation, there are both vendor partners and implementation partners to help provide software, interfaces and processes to turn the reporting function into an automated one. This can often reduce the workload of your analysts by 80 per cent, from gathering, standardizing and augmenting data to simply focusing on analysis.

There is a well-known article on *Medium* (online publication for self-published long-form articles) by Robert Chang that quotes Michael Hochster's elegant summary of the types of data specialists in the field. In this, he describes them as 'data scientists' but these descriptions can also apply to analysts.[13] In many cases, analysts become scientists should they display an aptitude for programming and storytelling.

Type A data scientist vs. Type B data scientist:

> The Type A (A is for Analysis) data scientist is very similar to a statistician but knows the practical details of working with data that aren't taught in the statistics curriculum: data cleaning, methods for dealing with large data sets, visualization, deep knowledge of a particular domain, writing well about data, and so on.[14]

Type B are very different:

> Type B (B is for Building) data scientists share some statistical background with Type A, but they are also very strong coders and may be trained software engineers. They build models which interact with users, often serving recommendations (products, people you may know, ads, movies, search results).[15]

Depending on which stage a company is at in their data practice, there is a different emphasis for their data function as it relates to automation.

Early on in the lifecycle of a company's analytics group, the primary analytic focus is to implement logging, to build ETL (extract, transform, and load) processes, to model data and design schemas so data can be tracked and stored. The goal here is focused on building the analytics foundation rather than analysis itself.

In the mid-stage of the analytics group's growth, much analytics work is around defining KPI, attributing growth, and finding the next opportunities to grow for their data.

When established, companies leverage data to create or maintain competitive edge. Search results need to be better, recommendations need to be more relevant, logistics or operations need to be more efficient – this is the time where specialist like machine learning engineers, optimization experts and experimentation designers can play a huge role in stepping up the game.

Data scientists frequently come from computer science and engineering backgrounds (although not always). They are graduates who are highly skilled programmers who become expert developers and technologists. But engineering is only part of the data science equation. To be impactful, data science projects need to tell an overarching business story. At the end of the day, metrics are tools that help organizations solve problems – which is why every organization is going to need a team of data storytellers.[16]

These roles, while grounded in technology, will require little-to-no programming experience. They will, however, require proficiency with statistics, communication with developers and writing about data.

5.2.2.4 Evolution to insights

The evolution into insights is where the rewards of a data-driven approach are reaped. What's important to define in insight generation (whether it be about the business or about the customer) is how to help imagine the category or cultural context that makes the data meaningful.

A great recommendation for this type of collaboration comes from Tony Clement, VP of analytics at Big Spaceship.[17] He believes that reporting is meant to be a launchpad for discussion. And within analytical teams, he attempts to create a collective consciousness among the team by meeting daily for 15 minutes to drill context for the different problems team members are trying to solve. Like the agile development process used by technologies, the drills include review of all manners of analytics outputs, such as research findings or a measurement framework. This daily meeting is meant to force people out of their analytical thinking and to contribute first (and often best) thoughts to a new problem.

5.2.2.5 Build, partner or buy?

The leap to a self-sufficient data process internally requires marketers and their technology counterparts to bridge the following challenges, according to Cap Gemini consulting:[18]

1 Scattered data lying in silos across the organization, including a lack of robust processes for data capture, curation, validation and retention.

2 Absence of clear business case for data investment (or it is not aligned with the vision).

3 Ineffective coordination across the analytic teams.

4 Dependency on legacy systems for data management.

The power of data analysis comes when multiple data sets can be brought together – when media spend can be connected to CRM files and in-store purchases – as well as people and processes. Rarely are these data sets to be found from the same vendor or in the same internal department. Answering this question requires an internal digital (and data) transformation.

The question then evolves into whether to build these self-service tools internally, to buy them, or to partner with another organization with capabilities to leverage? Depending on the scale of data a company is working with, whether you or your partners already have a data warehouse or are looking for an end-to-end solution (from data to visualization), and the level of customization needed, there are a number of vendors to choose from: Tableau, SiSense, ZoomData, Looker, Spotfire, to name just a few. Fast, flexible user interfaces that enable visualization and analysis of data can be deceptively difficult to build. And while these tools are sexy to create, and thus make for appealing projects for internal engineering and product teams, they are rarely a company's core competency.

It's a far better choice to investigate existing vendors, consult with colleagues who have successfully deployed a self-service solution, and get something running within a few months. The alternative is to devote several quarters to a grand vision that is unlikely to succeed.

Remember, there's a difference between foundational, maintenance and innovation investments. A foundational investment might be a global content management platform to help track the performance of different types of content across business units. In these cases, some investments are shared with other investments (in this case, digital). Maintenance might be implementing analytics tag containers in your websites to control data collection for first-party and third-party purposes. When making those decisions to buy, build or partner, it's important to consider whether these investments help build corporate value through data assets.

5.2.3 Step 3: Creating the culture for creativity and data

5.2.3.1 Organize for experimentation

Edward de Bono, a psychologist, semiotician, author, and design-thinking expert shares this perspective: 'Most executives, many scientists, and almost all business school graduates believe that if you analyse data, this will give you new ideas. Unfortunately, this belief is totally wrong. The mind can only see what it is prepared to see.'[19]

As people, marketers, analysts and creatives are hypothesis-driven. We can often use our biases in our favour to help answer questions using data. This requires a commitment to experimental design in the process. Experimental design refers to how participants are allocated to the different conditions (or IV groups) in an experiment. However, in a creative context, this can be the premise for powerful campaigns, artwork, or the basis of a new business. For example, Nissan launched a campaign in 2014 using Oculus Rift, which enabled consumers to create their own cars. Then those selections were put to a public vote, to lay the groundwork for their next generation of products.[20]

5.2.3.2 Organize for communication

The ability to recognize an insight or finding within data that is really engaging and actionable is what will establish credibility for any data analytics program. That ability is one of the core attributes of a good communicator who knows how to identify and target an audience, craft a key message, and ensure quality in the delivery.

With data communications, you're trying to convey a larger message – and as with any good story, you're conveying that message in a way that offers a memorable insight or surprise. Service workers in Florida dislike their jobs more than any other region or type? A quarter of all video views on Facebook happen on Friday? Brendan Dawes, a well-known digital artist, recently said, 'Data is not enough, data needs poetry'.[21] Here are a few ways to organize for communications:

1 Figure out your purpose (hypotheses or questions) and then gather your data.

2 Encourage people to write their points in a sentence and not rely on charts.

3 For non-data-informed individuals, encourage them to work through charts and visualizations to help summarize the insight.

4 Separate data for insights from measures of success.

5.2.3.3 Organize for agility[22]

Today, marketing organizations must leverage global scale but also be nimble, able to plan and execute in a matter of months, weeks or, increasingly, instantaneously. Complex matrixed organizational structures are giving way to networked organizations characterized by flexible roles, fluid responsibilities and more relaxed sign-off processes designed for speed. The new structures allow leaders to tap talent as needed from across the organization and assemble teams for specific, often short-term, marketing initiatives. The teams may form, execute and disband in a matter of weeks or months, depending on the task. That means that teams need to be made up of specialized, T-shaped skilled individuals, but they must be given the ability to implement change.

5.2.3.4 Creating culture

The introduction of data will have an impact on company culture – it's up to the senior manager to make sure that impact is one of transparency, collaboration and experimentation rather than being punitive, with information hoarding and paralysis. Data is not meant to be used as another limited resource; rather, by setting up processes where data and analysis are available to everyone, conversation can begin to align groups within the organization around a shared goal.[23]

The introduction of analytical capabilities into an organization is also intertwined with the individuals you hire. It's important to bring in those with a sense of curiosity as well as those without what writer Merlin Mann describes as 'expectational debt'[24] – a crippling effect caused by overly ambitious goals or unrealistic expectations. This is often found in the millennial workforce; those who have grown up with digital resources who also don't have the mental models that can slow down a process. They can cut through the slow process that analytics has required until now. Millennial-minded data analysts are driving change and economic growth through fact-based decision making. The most successful companies in the new data-driven economy will be those that encourage a 'millennial' mindset and cultivate employees at all levels into modern data analysts.

On the panel held at the 2015 INFORMS Conference on Business Analytics and Operations Research, Brenda Dietrich, an IBM fellow and vice president, shared her view that many young analytics folks and operations researchers display this trait in the form of impatience.[25] She shares that they don't understand why, once a team has conceived a new product, the company can't rush to market within, say, a few weeks. What they don't understand is that corporations don't move that quickly. They need to test a product, evaluate its profit potential and engage everyone from manufacturing to marketing and PR. The balance lives in between.

5.2.3.5 New marketing roles

Many brands today are much more centrally organized than they were a few years ago. Companies are removing middle, often regional, layers and creating specialized 'centres of excellence' that guide strategy and share best practices while drawing on the necessary resources wherever, and at whatever level, they exist in the organization. As companies pursue this approach, roles and processes need to be adapted. Coca-Cola, Unilever and Shiseido have set up dedicated marketing academies to create a single marketing language and approach.

Marketing organizations traditionally have been populated by generalists but, particularly with the rise of social and digital marketing driven by data, a profusion of new specialist roles are emerging. There are those who apply analytic capabilities to the task, those that create through content and design, and those who empathize with customers to align the work to what we know and make. Oftentimes, though, it's helpful to have a mix of what I'd call 'culture hackers' (those who feel and do), analysts+ (those who think and feel), as well as specialists like data scientists (think) and designers and editors (do).[26]

5.2.3.6 Organize for new ways of decision making and accountability

There is a zen quote by Lao Tzu that says: 'change the way you look at things and the things you look at change.'[27] The digital era brought with it a huge proliferation of data sources and in turn a proliferation of technologies that help us collate, analyse and operationalize data.

Our role in data-centric agendas like e-commerce, digital marketing, insight generation and measurement now makes data central to how we operate, and as a result, it impacts how we staff, understand the quality of our work and make decisions.

Staffing is not a simple matter of hiring. We must build marketing organizations that are attractive to those who are technically minded, numerate and highly adept at analysis. We must ensure that these individuals will have a seat at the table to make an impact. Data has been described by some as the 'new oil' to power the new economy.[28] If so, then like any other natural resource it needs to be governed well and made accessible in a way that's useful and helpful to all.

Access to performance data, from Google Analytics to Facebook Insights, means that we expect instant analytics. New analytical techniques are closing historical knowledge gaps and we can now commercially evaluate parts of the marketing mix that previously defied measurement, such as TV. Marketers today are required to continually monitor and assess performance and to be able to effectively explain complex results to audiences who might not be data or digitally literate.

5.2.4 *Step 4: Sustaining the environment*

5.2.4.1 Encourage adoption

One of the best ways to encourage adoption is to inspire and evangelize at scale. One way to do this is to foster connections by putting marketing and other functions under a single leader. A year after Antonio Lucio was appointed CMO of Visa, he was invited to also lead HR and tighten the alignment between the company's strategy and how employees were recruited, developed, retained and rewarded. Keith Weed leads communications and sustainability, as well as marketing, at Unilever.[29] Another key to fostering adoption in the organization is to focus on inspiration and to do internally what marketing does best externally: create irresistible messages and programmes that get everyone on board. Companies like AOL and Unilever holds globally coordinated and locally delivered internal and external communications events to engage employees and opinion leaders companywide directly with the message of how data can transform their business through elevated customer experience. The idea is to keep evangelizing the insights and outcomes through corporate communications, during hackathons, brainstorms and events where disparate groups are brought together to problem-solve together.

Inspiration is so important that many companies, Unilever among them, have begun measuring employees' brand engagement as a key performance indicator. Google does this by assessing employees' 'Googliness' in performance appraisals to determine how fully people embrace the company's culture and purpose.[30]

Another key factor beyond inspiration is training. Whether through a training programme (for example Intel's Digital IQ training programme to teach social media) or a reverse-mentorship programme (employed by companies such as GE), training can be a social environment to bring about systematic change.[31,32]

And last, but certainly not least, is a close relationship with the IT leaders in the organization. These collaborative partners need to help implement and maintain your data vision. It requires agile learning and can either be forged through a top-down approach (if you have the support of your senior management team) or through a skunkworks project basis (ie projects completed in an unconventional way through an experimental team).

5.2.4.2 Measurement of programme

Successful companies are more likely to measure brands' success against key performance indicators such as revenue growth and profit, and to tie incentives at the local level directly to those KPIs. The first step is to set up a scorecard to help rate the progress toward the data goals for customer experience (and other data goals if you've also aligned operations, IT and sales). The next step is to ensure that the original business cases laid out in Step 1 are translated down to individuals and their departments and that the relevant KPIs are in place. For example, in customer service, have you seen an improvement in customer on-boarding based on answering the right questions? For marketing, have we seen better response toward content marketing? The third step is to ensure that the new business cases cascade 'up' to our broad business objectives.

5.2.4.3 Align incentives and rewards

If measurement and goals are a feedback loop, then the reward and incentives structure is the fuel that keeps us running in the loop. A great way to incentivize employees and leaders is to ensure that the right attitudes and actions are rewarded. The most important part of data is collaboration and sharing. Other actions to be rewarded are consistency in reporting and meeting and exceeding measurement goals. The type of incentives, of course, can vary from cash to intangibles like awards.

A word on leadership.

The role of a leader in a creative environment is challenging enough. Much of it has been written about in leadership books, though the literature on how to manage for it has been less populous. According to *Harvard Business Review*, the first priority of creative leadership is to engage the right people, at the right times and to the right degree in order to install the right culture for creativity. This is true of analytic teams as well.[33]

Leaders will need to seek out, hire and promote both creative and analytic talent. They'll also have to cross-train team members on the importance of both left-brain and right-brain skills. To further build trust between analytic teams and their creative counterparts, leaders can co-locate the two groups and create 'both-brain' teams that work together on multiple campaigns over time. And when both-brain collaboration works the way it should, they should highlight those campaigns and reward the individuals involved.

They will need to nourish both-brain skills with thoughtful training and incentives. This story about Google's process can also prove instructive for integrated teams. Google founders tracked the progress of ideas that they had backed versus ideas that had been executed in the ranks without support from above, and discovered a higher success rate in the latter category. The greatest successes can come from any level of contribution provided they are advocated and moved forward by workers' own initiatives.

The second priority is to shepherd the teams through the mapped process outlined in this chapter. By curating the right people to help generate hypotheses, there's an opportunity from the start to build the momentum of the process.

Marketers need to identify the specific decisions that could benefit from analytic insights, clarify the criteria used to make each decision, and only then gather the required data and perform the necessary analyses. To avoid turf wars, project or campaign leaders should assign clear roles to both analytic and creative team members for each of these key decisions. These leaders will themselves need to model the both-brain sensibility and serve as active liaisons between the two camps as necessary.

The third priority is to balance the drive for something higher – the brand purpose and how it exists in consumers' lives – with the very real need to commercialize an idea and bring it to market. It's hard to find that balance within a single individual, so stewardship of the combined analytic and data thinking must be managed by the right person.

The fourth priority is to provide an avenue for any and all team members to come to senior leadership and help unstop roadblocks. Tony Clement has this to share:[34]

When an artist puts a thumb up to their painting and looks for perspective, what they're doing is essentially doing what is called grounded theory. They spend hours and hours up front creating the painting, hundreds of strokes trying to get the hand perfect, then they step back and look at the painting with their thumb up; that's the kind of mindset when it comes to what it is you are talking about, eg creating relevant data-based strategies, with going through the data and then stepping back and looking at it. One person is kind of the unicorn who can do that and see that perspective, which is amazing, but really in the package what you're looking for is someone who can detail the hand and then for that analyst to be okay with showing that hand in its entirety to someone else. I see analysts as being kind of artistic in that sense, crafting their data and then giving it over to someone to critique. I think that's the process that needs to be embraced; the faster that cycle, the perspective created with the team that you're working with, the more ideas you're going to have. That comes down to trust. Building a person who can have an analytical skill set in an environment where they feel they're trusted and can share their work and art faster, is going to lead to more ideas and more excitement.

5.3 Working with partners

5.3.1 Working with agency partners (services)

Service partners can be strategic partners, creative partners, implementation partners, or a combination of all three. The goal of such experts is to help guide the combined analytic–creative process.

A great partner will take you through their process and outcomes. At Crossbeat, we talk about Big Ideas that Work. At Ogilvy, they emphasize the customer at the centre of the brand experience. At Epsilon UK, they emphasize the combined expertise of data analysts sitting with creatives.

Checklist questions for choosing an agency partner

In any form of the promised dream, there are several things to evaluate:

1 Can they lead you through the process?
2 Do they have strong relationships with data and technology vendors?
3 Does their internal process reflect respect for the process as well as outcomes?

4 What is their stance on testing?

5 Is their creative out of the box?

6 Is their implementation scalable, effective and efficient?

7 Do their creative lead, tech lead and business/data lead collaborate well?

8 Can they articulate a mapped process?

5.3.2 *Working with technology partners*

Technology partners are those who bundle software with their services. The first rule of thumb is to always meet them in person. Chemistry is incredibly important because very rarely is any solution turnkey. Also, ask your colleagues in the industry about their experiences. Be sure to ask both large and small customers – if they can't work with both types of customer, you'll have a hard time growing with them.

Checklist questions for choosing a technology partner

Here are the questions to guide the introduction and investigative step of the process.

1 Tell me about your product.

    a) Pay attention if they tell you what they do (we're an agency who helps evaluate and implement technologies in your digital transformation).

    b) Pay attention to what they say their stated value is (we are the most experienced, the cheapest).

2 Who are your competitors?

3 Do I need other technologies or internal expertise?

4 Can you show me where in the competitive ecosystem you sit?

5 Who are the other brands similar to me, or that have the same challenges I do?

Always ask them to follow up with your organization in six months. Most of these technologies are changing quickly. Depending on your needs, Forrester provides a comprehensive list, from self-service data preparation to business intelligences to visualization.[35] Additionally, the investment advisory firm Lumascapes also offers a comprehensive view of technologies that your service partners can help implement.[36]

5.3.3 Working with media partners – from Facebook to Buzzfeed

Today, media partners are a lot like technology partners. They do have a product they are selling in addition to all their data. These partners now offer targeted products that can work with your first-party and second-party data to help create models for better targeting, insights and personalization. The next chapter goes into depth on this evolving relationship.

Notes

1 Ahrendts, Angela, 'Digital leadership', *Capgemini Consulting*, 2012 [online] https://www.capgemini-consulting.com/resource-file-access/resource/pdf/DIGITAL_LEADERSHIP__An_interview_with_Angela_Ahrendts.pdf [accessed 1 May 2016]

2 Millington, Angela, 'Burberry looks to a "fundamentally different" way of using data across its business', *Marketing Week*, 20 May 2015 [online] https://www.marketingweek.com/2015/05/20/burberry-looks-to-build-customer-data-into-the-fabric-of-its-business/ [accessed 1 May 2016]

3 Interview with Salesforce director of data science and learning Tye Rattenbury. Personal interview, 10 November 2015

4 Brown, Brad, Court, David and Millmott, Paul, 'Mobilizing your C-suite for big-data analytics', *McKinsey*, November 2013 [online] http://www.mckinsey.com/business-functions/business-technology/our-insights/mobilizing-your-c-suite-for-big-data-analytics [accessed 1 May 2016]

5 Interview with Salesforce director of data science and learning Tye Rattenbury. Personal interview, 10 November 2015

6 The Conversation, 'Machine learning and big data is changing sports', *Science 2.0*, 18 May 2015 [online] http://www.science20.com/the_conversation/machine_learning_and_big_data_is_changing_sports-15562 [accessed 1 May 2016]

7 De Swaan Arons, Mark, Van Den Driest, Frank and Weed, Keith, 'The ultimate marketing machine', *Harvard Business Review*, July–August 2014 [online] https://hbr.org/2014/07/the-ultimate-marketing-machine [accessed 1 May 2016]

8 Franks, Bill, 'Do you know who owns analytics at your company?' *Harvard Business Review*, 23 Sep 2014 [online] https://hbr.org/2014/09/do-you-know-who-owns-analytics-at-your-company [accessed 1 May 2016]

9 Interview with (former) REX chief creative officer Graham Douglas. Personal interview, 10 October 2015

10 Jones, Matthew J, 'The evolution of the data scientist job title', *LinkedIn*, 28 January 2016 [online] https://www.linkedin.com/pulse/evolution-data-scientist-job-title-matthew-j-jones?forceNoSplash=true [accessed 1 May 2016]

11 Manyika, James, *et al.*, 'Big data: The next frontier for innovation, competition, and productivity', McKinsey, May 2011 [online] http://www.mckinsey.com/business-functions/business-technology/our-insights/big-data-the-next-frontier-for-innovation [accessed 1 May 2016]

12 Harris, Derek, 'The rise of Self-Service Analytics – in 3 charts', *Gigaom*, 13 Feb 2015 [online] https://gigaom.com/2015/02/13/the-rise-of-self-service-analytics-in-3-charts/ [accessed 1 May 2016]

13 Chang, Robert, 'Doing data science at Twitter', *Medium*, 20 June 2015 [online] https://medium.com/@rchang/my-two-year-journey-as-a-data-scientist-at-twitter-f0c13298aee6#.fhxc7h09d [accessed 1 May 2016]

14 Hochster, Michael, profile, *Quora* [online] https://www.quora.com/profile/Michael-Hochster [accessed 1 May 2016]

15 Ibid.

16 Samuel, Alexandra, 'The best data storytellers aren't always the numbers people', *Harvard Business Review*, 28 October 2015 [online] https://hbr.org/2015/10/the-best-data-storytellers-arent-always-the-numbers-people [accessed 1 May 2016]

17 Interview with Big Spaceship VP of analytics Tony Clement. Personal interview, 20 October 2015.

18 Capgemini Consulting, 'Cracking the data conundrum: how successful companies make big data operational' [online] https://www.capgemini-consulting.com/resource-file-access/resource/pdf/cracking_the_data_conundrum-big_data_pov_13-1-15_v2.pdf [accessed 1 May 2016]

19 De Bono, Edward (1992) *Serious Creativity: Using the power of lateral thinking to create new ideas,* Harpercollins http://www.amazon.com/Serious-Creativity-Lateral-Thinking-Create/dp/0887305660

20 Kingston, Howard, 'Experiential marketing is becoming a virtual reality', *Campaign*, 6 January 2015 [online] http://www.campaignlive.co.uk/-article/1329361/experiential-marketing-becoming-virtual-reality [accessed 1 May 2016]

21 Dawes, Brendan, TEDx talk: 'Data by itself is not enough, data needs poetry', *YouTube*, 5 December 2012 [online] https://www.youtube.com/watch?v=SUxBM03qHSs [accessed 1 May 2016]

22 McKinsey, interview: 'Eric Schmidt on business culture, technology, and social issues', May 2011 [online] http://www.mckinsey.com/insights/strategy/eric_schmidt_on_business_culture_technology_and_social_issues [accessed 1 May 2016]

23 Booz & Company, 'Benefiting from big data: a new approach for the telecom industry', *Strategy&*, 2013 [online] http://www.strategyand.pwc.com/reports/benefiting-big-data [accessed 1 May 2016]

24 Lonergan, Kevin, 'What data skills gap? We just aren't looking hard enough', *Information Age*, 7 November 2014 [online] http://www.information-age.com/what-data-skills-gap-we-just-arent-looking-hard-enough-123458613/ [accessed 7 October 2016]

25 Kart, Lisa 'Building a top performing analytics team: unicorns wanted', *DataInformed*, 7 May 2015 [online] http://data-informed.com/building-a-top-performing-analytics-team-unicorns-wanted/ [accessed 1 May 2016]

26 Li, Michael, 'The best data scientists know how to tell stories', *Harvard Business Review*, 13 October 2015 [online] https://hbr.org/2015/10/the-best-data-scientists-know-how-to-tell-stories [accessed 1 May 2016]

27 Ching Ni, Hua (1995) *The Complete Works of Lao Tzu: Tao Teh Ching and Hau Hu Ching*, Sevenstar Communications

28 Palmer, Michael, quoting Clive Humby, 'Data is the new oil', *ANA*, 3 November 2006 [online] http://ana.blogs.com/maestros/2006/11/data_is_the_new.html [accessed 1 May 2016]

29 De Swaan Arons, Mark, Van Den Driest, Frank and Weed, Keith, 'The ultimate marketing machine', *Harvard Business Review*, July–August 2014 [online] https://hbr.org/2014/07/the-ultimate-marketing-machine [accessed 1 May 2016]

30 Halzack, Sarah, 'An inside look at Google's data-driven job interview process', *Washington Post*, 4 September 2013 [online] https://www.washingtonpost.com/business/capitalbusiness/an-inside-look-at-googles-data-driven-job-interview-process/2013/09/03/648ea8b2-14bd-11e3-880b-7503237cc69d_story.html [accessed 1 May 2016]

31 Curran, Chris, Puthiyamadam, Tom and Wendin, Chrisie, 'Raising your digital IQ', *strategy+business*, 15 February 2016 [online] http://www.strategy-business.com/article/Raising-Your-Digital-IQ?gko=4b002 [accessed 1 May 2016]

32 Mooreman, Christine, 'Marketing in a technology company: GE's organizational platform for innovation', *Forbes*, 29 January 2013 [online] http://www.forbes.com/sites/christinemoorman/2013/01/29/marketing-in-a-technology-company-ges-organizational-platform-for-innovation/#5139e5ee62c9 [accessed 1 May 2016]

33 Amabile, Teresa and Khaire, Mukti, 'Creativity and the role of the leader', *Harvard Business Review*, October 2008 [online] https://hbr.org/2008/10/creativity-and-the-role-of-the-leader [accessed 1 May 2016]

34 Interview with Big Spaceship VP of analytics Tony Clement. Personal interview, 20 October 2015

35 Evelson, Boris, 'The Forrester Wave™: Enterprise business intelligence platforms, Q1 2015', *Forrester*, 27 March 2015 [online] https://www.sas.com/content/dam/SAS/en_us/doc/analystreport/the-forrester-wave-enterprise-bi-platforms-106893.pdf [accessed 1 May 2016]

36 Kawaja, Terence, 'Marketing Technology Lumascape' (presentation) 2016 [online]http://www.lumapartners.com/lumascapes/marketing-technology-lumascape/ [accessed 1 May 2016]

Media and tech partners that facilitate connections with consumers

06

This chapter will cover four ways in which media and technology partners have infused data into the creative process to work together with marketers:

1 in paid and earned advertising (including social media);

2 in brand-owned digital properties like websites, mobile apps and e-commerce;

3 in consumer research that drives personalization in consumer experience; and

4 in content creation.

None of this would be possible without strong technology partners to help maintain the ecosystem that has been built since the late '90s. Some of those technology partners are household names like Google, Facebook and Twitter. Beyond providing an application, they also provide data as a product. These external vendors help marketers observe the world through data, define the challenge, gather data on the target (and the challenge) into a holistic profile, generate insight, create targeted experiences including content creation and personalization, dialogue and reporting, and bring the metrics and learnings back to the holistic consumer profile. This is an overview of the types of technology vendors and data partners available as well as a perspective from their view in order to see, in aggregate, the evolution in the marketplace of data used for the creative development process. These vendors and partners all support a majority of the global brands today. Finally, this chapter also contains coverage of the importance of the input of a strong CTO and/or CIO to find the solution that's best for your organization.

6.1 Paid and earned advertising

6.1.1 Facebook, Google and Twitter

It's hard to know how and when 'the internet' (online, the web, social media) – and in a marketing context, consumer behaviour – went from being a single happy place that existed outside of the real world to the complex 'something-for-everyone' that's inseparable from our habits, our conversations and the way we function in life.[1] And while the typical consumer knows that the internet is made up of different things (news publishers, social media sites, commerce sites, chat rooms, online communities, blogs, forums, dating sites, etc.), they are hard pressed to know exactly where it is they learn and transact, except to often refer to it as 'the internet' – a word to describe this single, universal, monolithic thing, channel, entity, place or sometimes person. And even as we marketers see the internet as the wildly diverse place it is, with many vendors, partners and adversaries, when we become consumers, all reason goes out the door. As consumers, we see the internet as a singular destination with no regard to channels – we even talk about it that way. Scanning the search results for 'internet is obsessed with' reveals that venerated newspapers and journals like the *Guardian*, *New Republic* and the *Hollywood Reporter* do reflect an implication that the internet is a singular force from which we get our news, our entertainment, our facts, our gossip, our information, our misinformation and our friendships. But, we don't see it that way as marketers. As marketers, we are forced to see channels, types of content that only fit in certain forms, etc. because in the last 20 years that the internet has evolved, and so has the landscape of vendors, publishers and technology partners who have invested time, resources and energy in both understanding consumer behaviour and creating viable business models to deliver value to their marketing clients.

You'll remember that in Chapter 3 we discussed the importance of understanding PageRank (and now its next iteration, RankBrain), not only because it serves as the birth of online marketing, but because it reflects the human intelligence involved in judging relevance and the human effort involved in citing the right sources.[2] Before 2000, when Google became the de facto search engine and transformed marketing, the market was led by search engines like Lycos and Alta Vista. At the time, search engines would work on a comparative basis on terms, checking their entered search word with the database of terms they created to describe the page. The page that had text most similar was considered more relevant. But in 1998, Google founders Larry Page and Sergei Brin created an algorithm – dubbed PageRank after Page's last name – that managed to take into account both the number of links into a particular site and the number of links into each of the linking sites. By focusing on the relative importance and value of the information itself (what is important) as well as the importance and authority of the source (who is important), Google applied unsupervised machine learning to web pages (as data). And by doing so, they have also placed a premium on delivering the right content.[3]

Google has built a business model out of doing what any media channel would do – advertising. As the fundamental business model of the internet, Google, Facebook and Twitter all make money by collecting consumer data and offering advertisers an opportunity to market to you. Now, through its evolution of Adwords, its DoubleClick products and YouTube (amongst the many other hundreds of products servicing marketers and the consumer), Google knows exactly what someone's interested in and when she or he is interested, and Google remembers those things more accurately than people's brains are wired to do. And it remembers it like a machine, whether it's five minutes, five hours or five months ago.[4]

The marketing industry's evolution and success depends on how well it understands fast-changing consumer habits. Google, of course, represents the behemoth in the category. There are literally hundreds of thousands of possible vendors, tens of thousands with experience, thousands focused on the space of data and marketing, and perhaps several hundred that focus in on that soft spot of data and creativity in marketing. This chapter will focus in on those vendors and partners that enable the data and creativity process. Marketers, with their help, can continue to tell great, anthemic stories to the right audience and do this more quickly, with a broader spirit of experimentation.[5]

For example, Google introduced research in late 2015 on the consumer journey, specifically the notion of 'micro-moments'. In their words, they 'fractured the consumer journey into hundreds of real-time, intent-driven micro-moments'. This mapping has allowed marketers to enter a realm of 'moment marketing'[6] – where marketers can truly deliver the right message at the right time in a context that heightens recollection and creates an emotional connection (see Chapter 8's case study on British Airways' 'Magic of Flying' campaign). This is only made possible by the collection of data amassed through Google's intricate network of products including Gmail, Maps and Search, all collected under our 'sign-in' user IDs.

Another example includes the recent partnership between Facebook and Tesco's data business Dunnhumby.[7] Specifically, Dunnhumby data links Tesco's shopper information with Facebook's 37 million monthly users in the UK to help brands see the impact of Facebook creative on shopping behaviour. Not only will brands be able to see whether a consumer saw an ad, but exactly what segments were most responsive, which creative drove behaviour, and the right number of exposures to avoid wearout of creative. In one test case shared, Dunnhumby reported that while testing six different creative executions, one advertiser found that the right creative produced a 10 per cent sales lift. Another found that exposing users to two ads per week rather than one resulted in a 6–7 per cent lift.[8]

The reality is that a marketer today cannot navigate the magnitude of niche audiences and the varying tastes and preferences of their target customer without these data providers. How deeply they can go is mostly dependent on budget, will and the size of the company.

The marketing technology has evolved quite a bit since the early days of Google, Facebook and Twitter. For nearly two decades prior to the advertising capabilities offered by them, marketing technology, particularly ad tech, depended on third-party data, collected and aggregated data across multiple websites and/or non-digital sources like syndicated research. The creative process was not leveraging any of this data, though much of the creative was based on inferences about intended behaviour. Over time, these media giants (Google, Facebook, Twitter and more) began to collect first-party data on their users. As mentioned in Chapter 1, first-party data is data collected directly from customers, which is often more accurate, but much harder to plan, store, process, and interpret meaningfully. This data helped these giants provide their customers with personalized experiences delivered through these networks at the right time and with the right message.[9]

Now they are able to offer this data to companies in the form of second-party data. This is essentially someone else's first-party data. These are large 'internet' companies as well as publishers who have gathered first-party data themselves and sell this to marketers directly. This includes data collected by a website (or Facebook, e-commerce, etc.) and whose rights and terms are covered in a privacy policy that states that the data used can only be used to provide services by the company and its affiliates. All companies must maintain control of their data, adhering to consumer privacy best practices and addressing security concerns. Like third-party data, it can help amplify and extend the limited supply of first-party data.[10]

This access to and use of data to help marketers not only target better but create more compelling creative has allowed data providers to take on a bigger share of the media spend by marketers.

6.1.2 Publisher data

As a result, publishers have also sought ways to get a better understanding of their audiences, announcing partnerships to offer marketers data and technology solutions. Condé Nast recently bought a data company called 1010data to gather business analytics on behalf of their advertiser partners about their audiences.[11] In late 2015, a new alliance called the Pangaea Alliance was formed by bringing together the *Guardian*, CNN International, the *Financial Times*, Reuters, and the *Economist* to offer their advertising partners the ability to access data via a technology platform that integrates with existing ad tech buying and selling platforms.[12] The next section will cover the mechanics of ad tech. Prior to moving into data, publishers were offering native advertising and sponsored content to advertisers so that the advertiser message would be received more openly by the publisher's readership. This is still an important offering that these media technology companies like Google and Facebook cannot necessarily offer. The section after that will cover partners that help publishers ensure that their viewership experience, their content and the advertiser messages are well received.

6.1.3 Data management platforms (DMPs) and programmatic creative

To manage all these datasets in the context of advertising and marketing, an entire technology and data ecosystem has sprouted to help marketers/ advertisers leverage this data. In advertising technology (dubbed 'ad tech'), there are a number of areas of technology that fit together to deliver these services. The first area is data management platforms (DMPs). DMPs are essentially data warehouses that ingest, sort and store data. The types of data they store are things like cookie IDs and their related attributes such as visitors' site visit preferences, gender, location and more that are then used to sort audience segments (using some of the techniques described in Chapter 3).[13] These segments are used to target specific users with online ads. As the number of sites has exponentially increased, there are now additional ad tech companies that help to better target by providing more data or providing the right content, ie the 'suppliers' of ads like DSPs (data supply platforms), ad networks and exchanges (similar to the financial trading model of trading desks and exchanges, these are brokers that bring the buyers and sellers of media space together to make a 'trade' of media space viewed by a specific audience for money). The DMPs essentially tie all these technologies and the activity among them to help optimize future media buys and ad creative. This information is fed from a marketer's DMP to its DSP to help inform ad buying decisions. On the publisher/media side, DMPs can also be linked to supply-side platforms and other technologies that can help them sell their ads for more. In those cases, the DMP is storing publisher information on its readers. Agencies, publishers and marketers all use DMPs. Vendors that sell DMP technology to the digital media world currently include Adobe, Lotame, BlueKai, CoreAudience and X+1.[14]

More deeply, relating to creative work like banners or messages, companies such as PaperG, Persio and Spongecell offer programmatic creative services, including dynamic creative optimization (DCO) services, to help deliver multiple types of creative content or ads to help optimize for a specific action like click-through. Programmatic also covers creative management platforms (CMPs) that are focused more on enabling a designer to create and manipulate a large amount of creatives all at once, one at a time, or

Figure 6.1   DMP Programmatic and marketing cloud

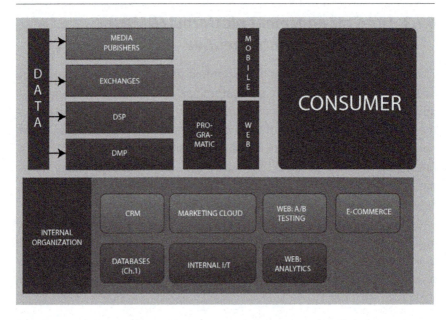

somewhere in between, rather than focusing purely on automation of the DCO.[15] In a nutshell, DMPs provide DCOs with the data about a consumer/audience member. The DCO takes the data from the DSPs (recall, the DSP is where campaigns are built to target inventory and audiences). The DCO then optimizes the creative for each individual audience user targeted in the inventory within the DSP's specifications about the advertiser's campaign, such as their audience reach goals, the creative inventory they have to share with each individual audience user, and other criteria like location or age.[16]

6.1.4 *Social and search targeting through data*

There are a number of other technology and content vendors that are helping to take this data from brands and providing functionality in content delivery that is powered by second-party data. SocialFlow is a technology solution provider that uses real-time data and business rules to determine what social media properties to publish and when for both owned and paid social posts.[17] Their newest product (as of late 2015), AttentionStream, provides brands with the ability to sponsor content on publisher social channel feeds. Rather than trying to compete with the clutter of brands fighting for attention on social, SocialFlow research found that publishers are, in fact, best placed to attract attention (not ad creative).[18] For example, a cable operator was looking to reach consumers at the right time. They were able to sponsor Entertainment Weekly's top-performing TV-related Facebook post during the season finale of a show. Without having to buy expensive TV media or know more than two hours ahead of time what the best-performing post would be, data helped to orchestrate a convergence of messages that did not interrupt the attention of the consumer. It is technologies like this that are cropping up to better serve the consumer and to help brands deliver value .[19]

6.1.5 *Marketing automation (also known as the Marketing Cloud)*

Data and technology drive more than advertising. There are now a whole host of solutions (individual components and full end-to-end workflow product suites) that help manage internal data on customers and creative assets for marketing purposes. Broadly described as 'marketing automation', these data and technology tools originally served to automate specific marketing tasks based on scenario (ie providing customer service representatives automated responses to customer queries on social media) and has since evolved to cover not just a single channel of client interaction, but the multiple channels that link with a broad array of connected, creative expressions and experiences to better serve customers.[20] Now that these tools are offered as web-based platforms that save and store marketer information in the Cloud, the terminology in the United States, has evolved to call it the 'Marketing Cloud'.

The core of marketing automation is a single view of the customer. A single customer view is essential, as is a connected approach between CRM (customer relationship management), content management, content marketing, social media tools and call centres.

CRM (customer relationship management) begins with access to data on the customer – both internal transaction systems and external data on customers and markets. To analyse all that data, marketers need to be comfortable with analytics and data science. Brian Harrington, executive vice president and chief marketing officer of Zipcar, shared:

> I want to get to a place where a copywriter has almost as much fluency around programmatic buying, for example, as the people who manage the campaign. If they want a career in marketing – to be a modern marketer, and add value in marketing – everyone has to have a base or deeper understanding of digital and analytics. We are blending art and science here, and everyone needs to know something about both.[22]

CRM is often tied to e-mail marketing capabilities and programs. Like ad tech, CRMs have capabilities to segment their customers to help marketers better target them. These CRMs may ingest data from call centres, many of which are also managed by automated tools. Some companies use partners like Bazaarvoice and Zendesk to help manage customer inquiries by providing online tools through their websites to answer questions or help customers answer questions for other customers.

Marketing automation also supports the workflow of the marketing staff. This provides a standardized method of collecting and creating data on compelling social content to help social media community managers create posts (vendors like Percolate and NewsCred provide these types of functionality).

The creation and distribution of creative assets is another significant area for marketing automation. Particularly important for global brands, the distribution of 'approved' content for different regions requires a single source for assets. Large companies like Adobe, GetChute, Expion and Contently tackle creation by offering tools in visual asset creation (Adobe and GetChute) as well as written copy creation (Expion and Contently).

Approvals of assets is often a concern for legal and compliance teams in organizations and has also become a considerable concern as copyright and privacy laws are more strongly enforced, particularly in Europe. Altimeter Group, a research group based in California, provides an excellent overview of the vendors listed here.

There are four components that every digital marketing cloud should be offering:[21]

1 Multi-channel marketing automation – for publishing and promoting content that helps marketers engage customers across several different channels, particularly mobile and social. It also needs automation for the intelligent algorithms that sequence how that engagement happens.

2 Content management tools – to create and manage the content and engagement tools that can be deployed across different channels.

3 Social media tools – for listening to and engaging with social media networks to tap into consumer conversations, responding with custom content, or social media advertising.

4 Analytics platform – to create profiles of consumers based on their online behaviour and evaluate which marketing campaigns are working and which aren't.

6.2 Content creation

Successful content marketing requires intention and purpose behind everything a marketer posts. The reality may be that an organization may not think it's a priority in communications or service, but it is where many consumers now turn to for opinions as well as entertainment. According to an Accenture report for 2015, nearly 87 per cent of Americans and 62 per cent of Europeans use their phones while watching TV.[23] On their phones, they spend nearly 80 per cent of their time, on average, on things like e-mail, social media and news.[24] Data is leveraged in a few key ways to help this content creation process.

6.2.1 Understanding the target audience

This is a common refrain within this book. Social media platforms like YouTube, Facebook and Twitter offer audience metrics, but there are other vendors that provide metrics not only on your existing audiences, but on your target audiences as well. These vendors like Adobe's Marketing Cloud, Percolate and Brandwatch have a multitude of clients for whom are able to provide benchmark data on how other categories are performing. Companies like CrowdTangle ingest the data of Facebook Pages (public), Twitter, Instagram and other social platforms and provide benchmark performance metrics on content. Specifically, they can, when looking across a multitude of public pages, see what types of entertainment content or posts by the category 'athletic gear providers' (for example) are performing well and how many likes, on average, they get.

6.2.2 Measurement

Few content strategies remain successful without a measurement strategy. Like advertising metrics, it is important to tie content marketing metrics to broader marketing goals. Is it to drive more awareness? Build an audience? Encourage people to convert? Reduce call centre expense by deflecting appropriate queries to a digital channel? Certain vendors such as SimplyMeasured or Unmetric are large global players in the space, along with Adobe and Brandwatch.

Content metrics should be outcome-based. For example, an increase in reach can show audience growth, but can also be the expected result of a promoted campaign. It is important to look at the audience growth in the context of engagement metrics (number of likes or shares). Are those metrics proportionally based on audience growth? If not, then reach is not a good metric for audience growth. Another example may be a video that is immensely popular, but after running some campaign tracking tests (a campaign tracking test is a random sampling of those who watch the video who may be served a 1–3-question survey asking if they recall the product, what the message was, and their purchase intent) you may reveal that no one recalls the social post's content. Vendors include Millward Brown or Kantar Digital, who provide measurement in-ad or in-social.

6.3 Website optimization, personalization, and e-commerce

Mike Linton, the chief marketing officer of Farmers Insurance, commented in an interview: 'Marketers still need creative skills without the aid of analytics or automation, but you can use those tools to test the creative after it's been developed.' He specifically suggests A/B testing to 'help determine the details around the creative – where it goes on the web page, and small decisions like colour and so forth. Over time, analytics and creative work together to make for improved impact in the marketplace and on the ROI.'[25]

6.3.1 Website optimization

A/B Testing reveals which alternative works better but it doesn't help creative or data teams to come up with new alternatives to try. There are many examples of A/B tests online (WhichTestWon is one, or vendors like Optimizely and KissMetrics provide solutions to assist). It's possible to find inspiration from award-winning sites like FWA or Dandad.org and Creativity, but many times, the most creative solutions come from focusing on the right definition of the problem. Data can help greatly with the proper problem definition by focusing in on questions like, 'Who is the audience?', 'What are they looking for?', 'Where have they come from?', 'When in their journey are they seeking us?' and 'Why would they behave this way?' Throwing creativity into the mix will solve this problem. Great solutions often come when trying to answer a specific problem, not relying on the data to test each step.[26]

The systematic use of A/B testing tends to give marketers a sense of which is the best conversion result possible without radically changing the design of the site. When A/B testing, marketers should avoid going one step at a time but this will not necessarily bring the big conversions and leaps resulting in the more radical changes that creativity can bring. This is covered in depth in Chapter 9, the Adore Me case study.

6.3.2 Personalization

The use of data in the right contexts can be incredibly powerful for the user experience on the organization's' website or e-commerce platforms. The user can be 'known' if they log in using either social sign-in (the button you click when the website asks 'Sign up with Facebook') or with a site-specific username and password. For example, for known users, it's possible to greet people by name when they first land on the page. This action alone has accounted for more than a 20 per cent increase in size of first-time sales.[27] For anonymous users, something as simple as location data is available to craft a path of content and products based on that information. In either case, sharing recommendations from specific friends (for known users) or what is popular for the area (for anonymous users) provides the social proof that is part of consumer behaviour.

6.3.3 E-commerce and mobile commerce

In e-commerce/retail businesses, cart abandonment is a common problem. With a robust marketing automation system, data can tell us a few things about what items are being abandoned and when. More importantly, the marketing cloud can often send a follow-up e-mail asking customers with registered e-mails to return to finish their purchase. For mobile e-commerce, conversion is still a major problem, as mobile check-out processes remain difficult.[28] Data can help to a certain point, but no one has cracked the usability code in terms of interfaces. As a result, many product design and digital groups are utilizing voice-activated interfaces. This means that users will be able to speak into the phone to add to carts for easier path to purchase. This is incredibly relevant, as data is now coming in the form of voice, which means that input must be translated from voice to text. This technology, while incredibly powerful, is not precise yet. In fact, many businesses are still collecting the data sets needed to train machine learning algorithms. Comcast found that young children's voices are the most difficult to translate, as are low-pitched voices. The use of NLP (natural language processing) in combination with machine learning is a major area of exploration of data and creativity (and is discussed further in Chapter 10).

6.4 Working with the CTO (or CIO)

A successful partnership among leadership in organizations is imperative to germinate and grow successful data and creative programmes in marketing. While Chapter 5 shared how to grow the internal marketing team, this section focuses on how to build a relationship to create the infrastructure to support the type of scale we have discussed in this chapter.

The important thing here is that there may be others in the organization seeking more information on the customer or the business, but it is often up to the marketing group to champion a customer-focused approach to data. As a result, the CMO or senior marketing leader must define the business goals, and use cases and specific requirements of any data or analytics initiative. The CTO (chief technology officer) or in some cases the

CIO (chief information officer) must define feasibility and cost of analytics to support specific use cases of the data for marketing. Here are four considerations when having the dialogue.

6.4.1 Share goals and shared language

According to the CMO of SAP, Jonathan Becher, 'Marketers and technology people speak very different languages, so there's a need on both sides to become bilingual.'[29] This means that not only do marketers need to understand data and technology at a high level, they must often be able to know when to ask questions. According to Luuk Derksen, a data scientist at DECODED, a pioneering educational organization focused on digital and data literacy amongst business and government executives in the UK and United States, a marketer can bring two things to the table: the ability to ask 'what does a classification model do and why is it important?' but to also share domain knowledge and give inspiration on consumer behaviour for him to model in the data. For CTOs, it's important to be sure to brief in person rather than relying on long technical documents or business requirements; oftentimes, the anecdotal details better describe what the CMO is trying to do than what the CMO thinks s/he is trying to do.

6.4.2 Clarify how decisions will be made (Data and Decision Governance)

According to the *Harvard Business Review*, a decision governance framework is vital to help decision making when things get tense.[30] It's often best to negotiate this like any document governing the start of the relationship – the intent is to be fair from the beginning so that when decisions are made, they are inclusive of everyone's best interests.

6.4.3 Hiring 'translators'

Another key suggestion from the *Harvard Business Review* is that those who do the work often best understand the day-to-day negotiations that have to happen. 'The CMO needs to hire someone who understands customers and business needs but 'speaks geek.'[31] The CTO needs to hire technical people with a strong grounding in marketing campaigns and the business.'

6.4.4 Work together on a few customer journeys that matter

Complex analytics can reveal often hundreds of opportunities to improve customer journeys, but the CMO and CTO can help prioritize them based on impact. To do that, there is no substitute for a team of marketing and operations people physically walking through a specific journey.

6.4.5 Complete transparency on budgets, work states, and progress

The CMO and CIO (and potentially the CTO) must bring complete transparency to the project and process. This is vital to building trust. Some journals recommend quarterly reviews, but a better option, particularly in the beginning, is monthly reviews to see progress. Implementation is the domain of the CIO, but being transparent across the board allows all parties to understand expectations and priorities and review with board members as necessary to jointly discuss progress, challenges and team findings.[32]

6.4.6 Celebrate successes

Great leaders identify, measure, recognize and reward meaningful efforts and achievements – and celebrate often with the people involved. This is vital for new and nascent projects of this sort, but particularly for one in which several different disciplines come together.

Notes

1   Alang, Navneet 'The internet isn't obsessed with Jennifer Lawrence. "The internet" doesn't exist', *New Republic*, 7 January 2016 [online] https://newrepublic.com/article/127208/internet-isnt-obsessed-jennifer-lawrence-the-internet-doesnt-exist [accessed 1 May 2016]

2   Hornby, Tom, 'The rise of Google: beating Yahoo at its own game', *Low End Mac*, 15 August 2013 [online] http://lowendmac.com/2013/the-rise-of-google-beating-yahoo-at-its-own-game/ [accessed 1 May 2016]

3   Poppick, Susie, '10 ways Google has changed the world', *Time*, 18 August 2014 [online] http://time.com/money/3117377/google-10-ways-changed-world/ [accessed 1 May 2016]

4 Poppick, Susie, 'Is my data safe?', *Time*, 18 August 2014 [online] http://time. com/money/873/is-my-data-safe/ [accessed 1 May 2016]

5 Gordon, Jonathan and Perrey, Jesko, 'The dawn of marketing's new golden age', *McKinsey*, February 2015 [online] http://www.mckinsey.com/ business-functions/marketing-and-sales/our-insights/the-dawn-of-marketings-new-golden-age [accessed 1 May 2016]

6 Think with Google, 'An introduction to micro-moments: what we've learned' [online] https://www.thinkwithgoogle.com/collections/micromoments.html [accessed 1 May 2016]

7 Netimperative, 'Social shopping: Facebook syncs ad data with Tesco's dunnhumby', 7 April 2016 [online] http://www.netimperative.com/2016/04/ social-shopping-facebook-syncs-ad-data-tescos-dunnhumby/ [accessed 1 May 2016]

8 Ibid.

9 Donovan, Bryan, ' Public versus private: the battle of the data ecosystems', 23 October 2015, acxiom [online] http://www.acxiom.com/public-versus-private-battle-data-ecosystems-2/ [accessed 1 May 2016]

10 Sands, Mike, 'Second-party data about to go mainstream', *ad exchanger*, 29 June 2015 [online] http://adexchanger.com/data-driven-thinking/second-party-data-about-to-go-mainstream/ [accessed 1 May 2016]

11 Sloane, Garrett, 'To compete with Facebook and Google, publishers step up their ad-targeting game', *Digiday*, 2 October 2015 [online] http://digiday.com/ publishers/advertisingweek2015-how-major-publishers-are-trying-to-target-ads-just-like-facebook-does/ [accessed 1 May 2016]

12 GNM Press Office, 'World's leading digital publishers launch new program-matic advertising alliance, Pangaea', *Guardian*, 18 March 2015 [online] http:// www.theguardian.com/gnm-press-office/2015/mar/18/worlds-leading-digital-publishers-launch-new-programmatic-advertising-alliance-pangaea [accessed 1 May 2016]

13 Brinker, Scott, 'Marketing technology landscape supergraphic (2015)', *Chief Marketing Executive*, 12 January 2015 [online] http://chiefmartec. com/2015/01/marketing-technology-landscape-supergraphic-2015/ [accessed 1 May 2016]

14 Luma Partners, 'Display Lumascape', *Slideshare* [online] http://www.slide-share.net/fullscreen/tkawaja/luma-display-ad-tech-landscape-2010-1231/1 [accessed 1 May 2016]

15 Point It Digital Marketing. 'Understanding Display Concepts: How a DCO, DSP and DMP can Work Together' [accessed 1 May 2016] [online] http://www.pointit.com/blog/understanding-display-concepts-how-a-dco-dsp-and-dmp-can-work-together/

16 Lennon, Rob, 'What display advertisers can learn about creative optimization from search and social', *Thunder Blog*, 5 May 2015 [online] http://blog.paperg.com/display-creative-optimization-learning-search-social/ [accessed 1 May 2016]

17 Tech Crunch, 'Socialflow raises $7.5 million to assist media corporations with social',7 December 2015 [online] https://techcrunch.com/2015/12/07/socialflow-raises-7-5-million-to-help-media-companies-with-social/[accessed 1 May 2016]

18 SocialFlow, 'SocialFlow's new AttentionStream ad unit gives brands access to top-quality, trending social content', 3 September 2015 [online] http://www.socialflow.com/socialflows-new-attentionstream-ad-unit-gives-brands-access-to-top-quality-trending-social-content/ [accessed 1 May 2016]

19 Interview with SocialFlow founder and chief product officer Frank Speiser. Personal interview, 10 December 2015

20 I-scoop, 'Marketing automation: strategy, practice, evolutions and vendors' [online] http://www.i-scoop.eu/marketing-automation/ [accessed 1 May 2016]

21 Adobe Target, 'Present the kinds of relevant and personal experiences that keep your customers coming back' [online] http://www.adobe.com/marketing-cloud/testing-targeting/optimization-capabilities.html [accessed 1 May 2016]

22 Davenport, Thomas, 'What automation will do to marketing and marketers', Wall Street Journal, 15 April 2015 [online] http://blogs.wsj.com/cio/2015/04/15/what-automation-will-do-to-marketing-and-marketers/ [accessed 7 October 2016]

23 Flomenbaum, Adam, 'Accenture report: 87% of consumers use second screen device while watching TV', *AdWeek*, 20 April 2015 [online] http://www.adweek.com/lostremote/accenture-report-87-of-consumers-use-second-screen-device-while-watching-tv/51698 [accessed 1 May 2016]

24 Nielsen, 'Screen wars: the battle for eye space in a TV-everywhere world', March 2015 [online] http://www.nielsen.com/content/dam/nielsenglobal/eu/nielseninsights/pdfs/Nielsen%20Global%20Digital%20Landscape%20Report%20March%202015.pdf [accessed 1 May 2016]

25 Davenport, Thomas, 'What automation will do to marketing and marketers', *Wall Street Journal,* 15 April 2015 [online] http://www.tomdavenport.com/wp-content/uploads/What-Automation-Will-Do-To-Marketing-and-Marketers.pdf [accessed 1 May 2016]

26 Cabot, Jordi, 'Creativity and A/B testing: friends or foes?' *Nelio*, 17 December 2014 [online] https://nelioabtesting.com/creativity-ab-testing-friends-foes/ [accessed 1 May 2016]

27 Interview with Salesforce director of data science and learning Tye Rattenbury. Personal interview, 10 November 2015

28 Milnes, Hilary, 'Where mobile commerce is going in 2016', *Digiday*, 5 January 2015 [online] http://digiday.com/brands/mobile-commerce-going-2016/ [accessed 1 May 2016]

29 Ariker, Matt, Harrysson, Martin and Perrey, Jesko, 'Getting the CMO and CIO to work as partners', *McKinsey*, August 2014 [online] http://www.mckinsey.com/business-functions/business-technology/our-insights/getting-the-cmo-and-cio-to-work-as-partners [accessed 1 May 2016]

30 Ariker, Matt and Perrey, Jesko, 'CMOs and CIOs need to get along to make big data work', *Harvard Business Review*, 4 February 2014 [online] https://hbr.org/2014/02/cmos-and-cios-need-to-get-along-to-make-big-data-work/ [accessed 1 May 2016]

31 Ibid.

32 Carey, Jim and Lancina, Gary, '2015 CMO digital benchmark study: findings and considerations to accelerate growth in the digital world', *Leapfrog Marketing Institute* [online] http://leapfrogmarketinginstitute.leapfrogonline.com/publications/2015-cmo-benchmark-study-findings-and-considerations-to-accelerate-growth-in-the-digital-world/ [accessed 1 May 2016]

Zappos: Creative and data marketing from the ground up

07

In the next three chapters of the book, we gain a perspective from eight executives from companies that are leaders in marketing, analytics, business units and strategic agency partners, to share perspectives on their experiences and biggest challenges. The question for each of them was not whether or not to implement analytics into a creative process, but how.

We spoke with marketers, digital marketers, CMOs, CEOs and agency and vendor partners to get a 360-degree view of the process of creating a new marketing department with the firepower, fluency and responsiveness to the uncertainty in business today.

All were the most senior executives with marketing, data or agency/vendor relationship responsibility in their companies, which included Zappos, Unilever, Adore Me, Facebook, SocialFlow, Brandwatch, Decoded, Salesforce and more. Their backgrounds varied, and included a head of digital marketing, a chief marketing officer, a head of business strategy and a data scientist.

We had seeded the discussion by asking each of them in advance about the burning issues they were facing. For these executives, the top five questions were:

1 What is your view of creativity and data?

2 What mental models have accelerated (or inhibited) your adoption?

3 What organizational models work best?

4 How does this play out in real business contexts for large corporations and small start-ups?

5 Why does this matter?

Zappos began in 1999 as a matter of convenience. The well-told tale is that founder Nick Swinmurn paced the aisles and walkways of stores and malls unable to find the right size, fit, colour and style of shoe. He brought his search to the internet, and found that there were mom and pop stores staking a claim online. Why wasn't there a single place within the online experience dedicated to shoes? That spark of insight led to the following vision statement:

- One day, 30 per cent of all retail transactions in the United States will be online.
- People will buy from the company with the best service and the best selection.
- Zappos.com will be that online store.[1]

7.1 Zappos.com website

Now, in 2016, Zappos is on a wholly different mission. Acquired in 2009 by Amazon, Zappos has navigated the shift from product to brand with financial success. Armed with a detailed understanding of their business and existing customers, they are setting out to find those customers who share their passion for great customer service and deliver them an experience that extends beyond shoes, and along the way generates double-digit returns.

How did Zappos get there? Its parent company, Amazon, is ranked as one of the favourite brands of millennials, thanks in no small part to Zappos.[2] A company that has made headlines for its dynamic and eccentric CEO Tony Hsieh with an 'offbeat worldview', Zappos has made strategic bets on its business, its people and its marketing that don't always seem obvious or 'data-driven'. However, the role of data in their organization is savvy, refined and core to their operations – especially in marketing.[3]

7.2 Living by 'measure everything meaningful'

Their commitment to their vision has led Zappos to single-handedly elevate the standards of service for both online retailers and brick and mortar stores by turning on their head some basic metrics that have ruled the traditional call centre.[4]

Zappos doesn't measure the performance of the Zappos customer loyalty team member by metrics that are optimized to getting customers off the phone quickly (such as low time to resolution or minimal call time). Instead, Zappos focuses on four other metrics: average call time, number of personal connection moments within the call, abandonment rate, and attendance rates. Each of these metrics was adapted from the traditional metrics in order to align with Zappos' brand promise of delivering happiness. By focusing on the percentage of time an agent spends on the phone, the company empowers its team to utilize their time by how they believe they can best promote customer loyalty. By quantifying the quality of time by measuring what are considered personal connection moments (PCM), Zappos is able to balance its culture and creativity with data. These moments might include metrics like the number of times someone might laugh or say 'thank you'.

Through this idea of 'measure everything meaningful' in customer service, by 2011, Hsieh had managed to create a strong brand promise with an infrastructure to deliver it while simultaneously driving sales of nearly $1 billion, with millions of customers. Now with the infrastructure of Amazon, a well-known, data-driven giant with a reputation for ruthless enforcement of rigorous metrics and expectations for growth, he had a balancing act between managing a brand, a culture of creativity, and growth. After rigorous integration, Hsieh found Zappos in a new market environment of retailers offering to customers the same services of free returns, same day shipping and friendly customer service. Zappos was in need of a strong strategy that would pass muster in its new parent company's rigorous adherence to data.

Zappos already had a robust set of data mining tasks to help reduce churn rate, increase profitability with existing customers and identify loyalty opportunities. Patrick Martin, the principal of business strategy for Zappos, shared six techniques that most commerce, insurance and mobile operators use to best leverage their data.

7.2.1 Affinity analysis

This analysis, done in-house at Zappos through its analytics team, looks at the items that a customer buys, which helps Zappos improve layouts and recommended or related products. Also known as 'basket analysis', this refers to what shoppers use when they are shopping.[5]

Keep in mind that this type of analysis makes the assumption that past performance can help predict future behaviour. This doesn't hold true 100 per cent of the time, but it does hold true for enough of a baseline of customers that it can deliver a return. It implies that there's a pattern to the data. Do people who buy one product also buy another product to accompany it? Does one product usually precede the purchase of another? Can you create bundled packages to capture that revenue right away rather than waiting for the customer to recognize their own pattern?

7.2.2 Sales forecasting

This looks at when customers bought, and tries to predict when they will buy again.

This also looks at the number of customers in your market and predicts how many will actually buy. For example, imagine if you are American Express and are helping your merchant restaurant partners to better understand their customers. Here are questions you might ask:

- How many people live or work within a mile of a restaurant?
- How often do they go and how much do they spend?
- How much do they tip? Do they tip more based on the restaurant, time of service, or a specific server (particularly if US-centric)?
- How many competitors are in that mile?

When it comes to forecasting sales, Zappos runs various types of scenario planning. Because its CRM data source is more accurate and complete, predictions may be more precise and relevant up to the minute.[6]

7.2.3 Merchandise planning

Merchandise planning links the consumer needs to the marketing to the buyers to help determine stocking options and inventory warehousing.

The right approach will lead to answers that can help you decide how to deal with the following issues:

- Inventory getting old – keeping information about inventory current or stocking up-to-date accessories for products.
- Selecting product – mining the Zappos database will help determine which products customers want, which should include intelligence on their competitors' merchandise.
- Balancing stock – database mining can also help you determine the right amount of stock throughout the year and buying seasons.

- Pricing – database mining can also help you determine the best price for products as Zappos uncovers customer sensitivity.[7]

7.2.4 Database marketing

By examining customer purchasing patterns and looking at the demographics and psychographics of customers to build profiles, you can create products that will sell themselves. Of course, for any marketer to get any value out of a database, the database must continue to grow and evolve. It requires additional database information beyond sales, including questionnaires, syndicated research and quantitative surveys.

For example, Zappos database has grown via the following means:

- Purchase records stored for individuals but anonymized by only listing city and state.
- Contests run to collect additional information about intention to purchase.
- E-mail newsletters that were used to update customers weekly were also used to send out surveys to collect additional information concerning new products and promotions.
- Twitter accounts that double as a flash promotion tool and customer service hub to listen to followers.[8]

7.2.4 Customer loyalty

Zappos' reputation for transparency, humour and personality seemed prescient of the upcoming social media revolution. Tony Hsieh was an investor in Twitter in the early days and was one of the first accounts to amass more than 1 million followers. Twitter was used as a communication channel AND a source of consumer insight. There are many tools that help provide consumer insight. Spigit, Brandwatch, Affinio and more use different data mining techniques from social media audiences to help acquire and retain customers.[9]

Some uses include the following:

- Employee innovation – a tool used to ask employees for their ideas on how to improve customer engagement, product development and future growth. Who says data mining is always customer-centric?[10]

- Facebook – through a technique called 'customer cluster', vendors use data from the audience on Facebook to generate ideas for improving brands, with the aim of satisfying more customers and increasing loyalty.

7.3 Zappos 'best customers strategy'

Zappos is not the first to employ a type of 'best customer' Strategy. Titled 'Best Customers' internally, the strategy has precedence in the consumer packaged goods category. In 2013, Velveeta, a Kraft brand of processed, unrefrigerated 'cheese food' did not see much growth for their business.[11] They could largely attribute this to the cultural shift toward organic and healthy eating across all target audience groups. To begin their strategic development process, Kraft ran big data analytics on supermarket scanner and consumer panel data and found that 10 per cent of their buyers accounted for 30–40 per cent of their revenue and more than 50 per cent of their profits. This insight led to several product innovations that facilitated more than $100 million in sales.[12]

Zappos, however, was a different story. Kraft's 'best customers strategy' made intuitive sense to Zappos, an analytically driven organization, but the data told a different story: those customers who valued and loved Zappos, who spent the most time with Zappos, weren't necessarily the 'best customers' in terms of net revenue.[13]

7.3.1 Reframing 'best customers'

The best customers, to Zappos, were not necessarily the most active on social media or those with the highest satisfaction survey results. Zappos specifically wanted to find the 'best customers' (high CLTV and affinity for the same brands) that also fit its brand essence. To find them, Zappos started from the outside in. On a qualitative level, they searched for brands they believed their 'best customers' would have an emotional connection to, and would find relevant to their lives. These brands, named 'resonant brands', ranged from traditional businesses to wildly popular experiences such as Whole Foods, Wanderlust the festival, Virgin America and Joie de Vivre Hotels.[14] What Zappos honed in on were the major players in the 'experience economy'.[15] Now began the quantitative process that required an equal amount of creativity and data. Leveraging social media and consumer panel data, Zappos extracted the brand values of each of these resonant brands and systematically began to construct a consumer journey through data, digital and experimentation.

7.3.2 Moving toward a new definition of 'best'

In parallel, another experiment with their target consumer was occurring. In August 2014, Zappos discontinued discounts.[16] This was a risky move. When they looked for patterns in their data around their 'best customers', they didn't find anything related to their best, but they did find a cohort that really enjoyed discounts. These bargain hunters did have a tell – they left items in the cart until they went on sale. What was a traditional metric of 'cart abandonment' was not really abandonment, but a holding place in one group's consumer journey. In its first day, Zappos lost more than a third of one day's gross revenue; however, another metric, net revenue, was positive.[17] In short, Zappos had discovered that those who were buying on sale were inordinately taxing the service infrastructure through returns and calls. Zappos began driving the 'discount customer' to their discount site, 6pm.com.

The data, then, was pointing to a need for acquisition of the 'right' type of customers. Technologies in place, such as remarketing based on visits, were in fact the wrong data-based technologies to leverage holistically. What they also discovered was that customers who did remain loyal to Zappos were willing to pay full price, and that insight wouldn't have been possible without the investment in a customer-centric data infrastructure built to Zappos' specification and maintained on their internal technology infrastructure.

The next step, then, was to better understand these remaining brand-loyal customers. Through a series of consumer panel surveys commissioned onsite, via phone survey and through e-mail experimentation with their customers, Zappos quantified those among its customer database – through a segmentation study – to find the 'best customers'. Surprisingly, in the traditional four-quadrant plotting of clients along an x-axis of customer lifetime value (CLTV) against a y-axis of loyalty, the analytics team found that the upper right quadrant of high value, high loyalty was a fractional amount (less than 10 per cent) of their entire active client base. They then compared the buying patterns of these best customers within their own database to build look-alike models through data management platforms that house third-party data, specifically Facebook's Lookalike Audience.[18]

Those in this 'best customers' cohort group had an order of magnitude higher spend than that of the average customer. That's powerful analytics within their database to discover and validate their new strategy.

7.3.3 Qualifying and quantifying the 'best customers'

Zappos' best customers were first identified by psychographics, then products purchased, and at the very last, demographics.

They valued their time more than money; they believed that experiences were more meaningful than products, and therefore wanted their products to deliver meaningful experiences. Most importantly, they stated that they were looking for consistent delivery of experiences and quick resolution of bad experiences, and that was the reason they liked Zappos. They were less interested in 'surprise and delight' (the marketing tactic of rewarding clients at random or for social media buzz) and were more interested in responsiveness to their needs and complaints. Many of them had families and children, although not more than 60 per cent. They identified with attitudes and psychographics such as 'success in life', 'a sense of belonging' and 'a sense of freedom' – all descriptive factors that Zappos felt it needed to recreate, not only in its imagery, but in its customer journey.[19]

This unprecedented level of understanding of the customer was wholly new for the team and in many ways began to test the executive and marketing teams' own stereotypes and prejudices about the retail category. Zappos wasn't simply seeing a new way to look at retail; it had an inside to track to understand how their brand was changing retail.

The first step of the journey to understanding consumer behaviour and focusing the target market is not something new. Market research to identify target markets isn't a new practice; however, it is now transformed by the availability of data. The collection of survey data itself isn't radically new, but the ability to leverage millions of anonymized data records on purchase patterns to identify a sample of potential participants in a survey and fusing the data sets together is a new capability that's only made possible by data and technology.

Data provides a lens to identify a target group that, before the advent of big data, wouldn't have been possible to find. Conventional wisdom was that the quickest, easiest path to growth was to identify light users or lapsed users, but our understanding of consumer behaviour through data allows us to not only challenge our pre-conceptions of 'best practices', but now empowers marketers to move into what *Contagious*, a magazine dedicated to innovation practices within the creative and marketing community, dubs the 'next practice'.

7.4 The creative work shaped by data

Armed with the knowledge of its best customers, Zappos applied this knowledge to its marketing strategy.

Zappos traced the customer journey backwards from who they were to what they do in their lives. Once Zappos identified who their best customers were, they thought about how the brand promise of 'Delivering Happiness' would live in their world.[20]

7.4.1 Remaking the catalogue

Like other online-only retailers, Zappos had mastered the domain of direct response in digital form. Naturally, in looking to find new customers, they considered new communication channels. One was to find people in the traditional direct-marketing space. They discovered that a high-quality print piece is a powerful, and often necessary, creative element to stay at the forefront of their customers' minds. They also discovered that many people treated catalogues like magazines, keeping them for months at a time.

Zappos found that a high-impact direct-mail piece – from full-size catalogues to postcards – has become an effective means of ushering customers to their site.[21]

Traditionally, online marketers initially focused on e-mail as their primary retention tool, so they largely concentrated their direct-mail efforts on new customer acquisition. Over time, while maxing out their e-mail marketing efforts (increasing to almost daily contacts and focusing on different e-mail-capture initiatives), they rediscovered direct mail not only as an effective acquisition and retention tool, but as a piece of brand work.

The key for Zappos in building a meaningful direct-mail campaign that delivered positive ROI was a fine balance between who is mailed (the customer/prospect mix), the creative imagery and copy, and the overall marketing costs. Each step in the process is equally critical, including campaign strategy, circulation planning, design and production, mail execution, and results analysis.[22]

The catalogue is nothing new to retail and Zappos has been producing one for nearly six years. To align this visually alluring vehicle to capture an audience and present product, they used e-mail data to help build the catalogue. Zappos prioritized the imagery selected by their buyers based on their experience rather than data, so that the through line from marketing to product was evident. They made price and product front and centre, but featured them in the context of the customer's life to create an emotional connection for their best customers. Rather than featuring families as props for the products, creative reflected the aspiration of success in life and meaningful moments. The creative was also meant to select products not from a promotional perspective, but from a curated point of view that would communicate Zappos' brand attributes of service for the best customers: Zappos can help its best customers 'stand out in a crowd' and experience a 'sense of freedom'. These attributes are high-impact motivators that Zappos identified as drivers of consumer behaviour.

This new catalogue was one of the most successful drivers of web traffic for Zappos. There were a lot of factors for Zappos to consider when evaluating its place in their branding. To help calculate a true ROI, Zappos created a benchmark baseline of performance of those brands it considered to be resonant brands (and not just competitors). They reviewed how resonant brands leveraged mailers and catalogues by subscribing to their mailing lists to understand the number of touchpoints necessary for customer retention without wearout and by conducting a quantitative research survey asking customers of resonant brands for their reactions to the number of circulars they received. The prospective customer profile was driven in large part by an understanding of their prospective customer universe; therefore, they focused on the growth of the overlap with their current customer database (specifically, they prioritized profiles of customers who most recently purchased with strong revenue). ROI calculation also included cost and availability of creative assets, participation from product/merchandising, cost-per-piece, and square-inch goals.

It was critical for Zappos to accurately measure the impact direct mail has in the multi-channel mix, ensuring that demand from stores, websites and catalogues is allocated properly so that decisions on future advertising spend will be made as scientifically as possible based on source and results, the goal being to generate incremental sales from these direct-mail initiatives and not merely to cannibalize e-commerce revenue. One common method used to achieve this is known as 'matchback', where marketers analyse all mailed addresses and match back transactions across their web, phone, and retail channels for a defined period of time (often 60 days).

7.4.2 *Rethinking personalization*

Patrick Martin, the principal of business strategy for Zappos, shared his contrarian view of the personalization conversation.[23] Personalization, at least experienced by most online shoppers, is the recommendation carousel that appears when browsing, selecting and checking out. True personalization, in his view, is more than recommendation. The true offering of personalization is knowing exactly who that person is at that exact moment in time and what you as a company can deliver to that person in terms of experience. This is one better than product recommendation. Here's a powerful example.

A consumer has a history of buying size 9 Clarks brand shoes. A true personalization experience would know that a 9 in Clarks is a 9.5 in Merrill's and recommend the right shoe size rather than additional products a person can buy. By understanding the context in which a person buys shoes (they buy hiking boots twice a year, in different sizes), Zappos can focus the customer experience on the thrill of anticipation in shoe shopping, not on the logistics of size, transaction and delivery. This type of combined analytic and creative thinking has led to next-generation test programmes for their best customers beyond Zappos.com, including ideas as far ranging as virtual reality, personalized samples through monthly subscription, and experiential activations in the places best customers would be receptive to Zappos. Activations included sponsored activities such as providing shoe care or ease of purchase at hotels, fitness gyms and festivals. This coordinated 1-2-3 strategy has paid off for Zappos; in the past 15 months, Zappos has doubled the number of best customers as well as capturing a larger share of their spending power. These best customers now buy everything from them beyond shoes.

7.5 The process: store internal data and build custom analytics

Building an organization that supports data and creativity in its marketing function requires an investment in time, technology, and most importantly, people and process. Brands need to connect customer relationship management (CRM) and media more than ever before, as well as understanding changing habits, trends and opinions of their target audience. Without a joined-up approach to collecting, managing and interpreting data across all touchpoints, brands will suffer against a competitor who has this in place.

Zappos built much of their analytics platform in-house, starting in 2011.[24] Working with a third-party technology firm, they made a decision to link together various analytics providers and create their own layer of business intelligence (BI). This decision was driven by their desire to have 'clean' sales data. They realized, though, that using third-party web analytics data alone made it difficult to connect individual transaction records to their pathway through the platform. Through custom development, they were able to access individualized data without compromising any concerns regarding privacy and personally identifiable information (PII). Individualized data is necessary to better understand a customer's path to purchase. This data platform also provides valuable intelligence for their buyers and their merchandisers. Their internal system has become a true end-to-end supply chain platform. They believe their platform is so robust that it could go toe-to-toe with many supply chain management platforms. Zappos currently does not leverage a DMP (Data Management Platform) to combine their first-party data with other data sets from second-party or third-party vendors, although they do a substantial amount of social and digital ad buying with Facebook, Google and other publishers.[25] They have made this decision for data privacy reasons. In this case, Zappos has made a strategic decision based on brand and customer service to refrain from reaping the benefits of full 'data-driven' marketing.

7.6 The people process: collaboration

A critical component of their culture of collaboration is their commitment to socializing the data internally. Data is not held only for business planning or merchandising purposes. Like the previously cited Clive Humby quote that 'data is the new oil',[26] the politics that can happen around reporting in organizations are much like those of oil. Data manipulation is sometimes restricted to certain departments or, more frequently, data teams are siloed so that they only serve the interests of those who control the data. At Zappos, the product, marketing and operations teams have access not only to each department's data, but are encouraged to ask teams to help collect information to support each other. For example, the business strategy team often shows the marketing data including inbound web traffic to the lead buyer so that they can merchandise better. A lead buyer may wish to sell inventory, but rather than using the web team to simply 'drive sales' to a specific product, the buyer can have their inventory placed in the right area of the site based on customer purchase patterns. Then, the traffic manager (the internal term they use for their in-house media buyers) is engaged to find the right media partner to help get the word out. The creative imagery was not selected by the advertising agency or the marketing group, but by buyers who spotted the trend in shoes in the first place. This type of collaboration amongst analytics and business people has a track record of delivering results.

The internal teams at Zappos revere Tony Hsieh as a major brand builder. There is a firmly grounded internal culture that numbers aren't the truth, but are the beginning of the insight. To truly understand the customer, Zappos must recognize the context that the consumer lives in and shops in, and that this context is established by data. Zappos prizes empathy and has trained these team members to be intuitive. That intuition has developed based on the business expertise of Hsieh, Fred Mossler, Steve Hill and others as to WHY the data is doing what it's doing. The data and marketing teams come together to not just paint a picture of the consumer and the sellers, but also to explain how they interact and how to make that interaction better through the Zappos experience.[27]

7.7 Assessment of Zappos' success

Data has had a major impact on Zappos' internal culture. In fact, data is reflective of Zappos' culture in evolving the brand purpose from delivering happiness to delivering the best customer experience. The Zappos team believe that data is a natural output of curiosity – that unless they are asking questions, they don't generate the meaningful data necessary to answer them. Data is necessary to meet human nature's desire for answers. The growth of big data is a direct result of our insatiable curiosity to know – about ourselves and about others. That's helpful, especially when talking about Zappos customers vs. Zappos Best Customers. Their insight that just because someone loves their brand it doesn't necessarily translate to a thriving business allows them to break free of the constraints of looking at the available data in front of them. By challenging 'best practices' and focusing on their 'next practice', they were able to create a new data plan, marketing plan, and business strategy to support growth.

The use of analytics to support delivery on the brand purpose is not unique to Zappos. Many service-based organizations in finance, healthcare and even CPG have made 'Happiness' and 'Service' central tenets of their brand actions. What makes Zappos stand out in the sea of service companies is its desire to align the brand's actions (including a corporate mandate to answer any question that is thrown to their customer service department) and to know their customer better. However, brand building is successful when Zappos breaks through in culture, and delivering excellent customer service is no longer something that generates cultural relevance. The focus of Zappos' analysis needs to move to understanding the culture outside their core audience in their next cycle of business innovation focused on growth.

The 'Best Customer' strategy, however, has begun to pay off in both dollars and certain brand-building initiatives. Specifically, in 2016, the business is the healthiest it has been since they began the process in 2011, and the brand is on track to continue to grow in terms of brand awareness, fiscal health and strength of vendor relationships. Zappos' business teams believe that data has enabled a continued environment of entrepreneurship and empowering self-governance.

Zappos now has the ability to treat customers more personally. In their view, data has allowed them to work with more variations, more choices, and to help create more opportunities for connection and serendipity with their customers, both on the platform and in their customers' lives. Data has given them licence to create new types of interactions with their customers – to charge retail price for the experience, to listen more closely, and to make customers feel special.[28]

Notes

1   Hsieh, Tony (2013) *Delivering Happiness: A path to profits, passion, and purpose*, Grand Central Publishing

2   Moosylvania. 'A labour of like: Millennials 2015 favorite brands ranking report', 2015 [online] http://moosylvania.com/millennials/Moosylvania_Millennial_Study_2015.pdf [accessed 1 May 2016]

3   Bercovici, Jeff, 'Zappos CEO Tony Hsieh on Google, Snapchat, Burning Man and more', *Forbes*, 16 April 2014 [online] http://www.forbes.com/sites/jeffbercovici/2014/04/16/zappos-founder-tony-hsieh-on-google-snapchat-burning-man-and-more/#c3f21201b3c5 [accessed 1 May 2016]

4   Verrill, Ashley, 'A Zappos lesson in customer service metrics', *CSI*, 7 June 2012 [online] http://csi.softwareadvice.com/a-zappos-lesson-in-customer-service-metrics-1101029/ [accessed 1 May 2016]

5   Interview with Zappos head of business strategy Patrick Martin. Personal interview, 4 November 2015

6   Ibid.

7 Ibid.

8 Ibid.

9 Ibid.

10 Larson, Troy, '5 Tips to creating an awesome corporate culture', *Mindjet*, 21 December 2012 [online] http://blog.mindjet.com/2012/12/5-tips-to-creating-an-awesome-corporate-culture/ [accessed 1 May 2016]

11 Yoon, Eddie, Carlotti, Steve and Moore, Dennis, 'Make your best customers even better', *Harvard Business Review*, March 2014 [online] https://hbr.org/2014/03/make-your-best-customers-even-better [accessed 1 May 2016]

12 Ibid.

13 Interview with Zappos head of business strategy Patrick Martin. Personal interview, 4 November 2015

14 Ibid

15 Pine, Joseph and Gilmore, James (2011) *The Experience Economy*, Harvard Business Review Press

16 Interview with Zappos head of business strategy Patrick Martin. Personal interview, 4 November 2015

17 Ibid.

18 Ibid.

19 Ibid.

20 Ibid.

21 Ibid.

22 Practical Ecommerce. 'Quick query: Zappos exec on benefits of printed catalogs', 19 May 2009 [online] http://www.practicalecommerce.com/articles/1108-Quick-Query-Zappos-Exec-on-Benefits-of-Printed-Catalogs [accessed 1 May 2016]

23 Interview with Zappos head of business strategy Patrick Martin. Personal interview, 4 November 2015

24 Ibid.

25 Ibid.

26 Palmer, Michael (quoting Clive Humby), 'Data is the new oil', *ANA*, 3 November 2006 [online] http://ana.blogs.com/maestros/2006/11/data_is_the_new.html [accessed 1 May 2016]

27 Interview with Zappos head of business strategy Patrick Martin. Personal interview, 4 November 2015

28 Nahman, Haley, 'I made Zappos my personal assistant for a week', *Man Repeller*, 26 April 2016 [online] http://www.manrepeller.com/2016/04/zappos-customer-service.html [accessed 1 May 2016]

Creative agency relationship: a new model

08

Creative agencies have always been a place where new ideas are incepted, adopted and evolved, especially as they relate to marketing practices. Creative agencies employ a broad range of creative talent and for that reason, a place where experimentation and technique development can occur.

The emphasis on creativity in advertising is new, relative to the history of advertising. Through the first half of the 20th century, advertising consisted of written copy about product introductions, features and benefits that explained value and were later laid out by a designer. In 1960, creative agency DDB & Co launched Volkswagen's iconic 'Think Small' campaign under the creative leadership of copywriter Julian Koenig and art director George Lois.[1] The campaign, voted as one of the most influential campaigns of the 20th century by AdAge, would usher in and define a new entire era of marketing called the 'Creative Revolution'.[2] This revolution focused on a lifestyle rather than a product, a personality rather than a thing, and an idea about how to live rather than mere consumption.

Now, nearly 60 years later, we are in the deep waters of the next wave of the creative revolution; one which not only requires marketers to find new ways of talking to and engaging consumers, but to develop a new way of working with agencies to apply creativity to the diverse set of problems marketers face today.

Of course, marketing departments are not creative advertising agencies, so to get the best out of the relationship between marketing and their creative partners, marketers and agencies must both bring a process to the collection and use of data in the creative process. Marketing departments are built to deliver more than creative ideas. They are built to make decisions, provide reporting and collaborate with an understanding of other organizational needs.

As a result, a marketing department's job is not to come up with the best creative ideas for all elements of the marketing mix, but to create the conditions for creativity that will flourish in their organization, impact business goals, resonate with consumers and build the brand.

The ambition to help marketers become more creative is as important a goal as becoming more data literate. It's important, though, to understand the 'how' and 'why' of both. By improving creative skills, marketers will cultivate the ability to evaluate creative work and create the conditions of good creative work. By improving data skills, marketers will cultivate the ability to give both insight and context to creative work and create a shared understanding with other stakeholders within the organization who are impacted by marketing.

'The difference between the forgettable and the enduring is artistry', says Bill Bernbach, one of the founders of DDB & Co.[3] Therefore, the use of data should maintain the high principle of 'art' to stay effective. To do so, marketers can follow the steps below and introduce data in the right ways:

1 Define measurable goals for advertising in support of marketing.

2 Create the right brief.

3 Cultivate insights with creative partners and provide guidance on the actionability of the strategy based on the insight.

4 Create the right alchemy of people to collide and interact (cross-functional teams between agency and organization).

5 Foster a 'feedback loop' for creating and evaluating work with organizational departments like technology, data/insights and operations.

6 Implement the right measurement system among strategy, production and media that aligns target, message and channel.

7 Set the tone for reporting to emphasize shared understanding amongst stakeholders.

8.1 Defining measurable goals for advertising

The most important step in any endeavour is goal definition. As covered in Chapter 3, marketing goals are measurable statements of what needs to be achieved to meet business objectives like growth, expanding market share or increasing profits, specifically related to brand, customers and product features. Advertising, then, is concerned primarily with the customer and how communication of the brand and the experience of the product affect the customer. This is an evolution of the traditional understanding of advertising. As recently as March 2016, Maurice Levy, Chairman of Publicis Worldwide, one of the largest advertising holding companies, publicly stated, that they were 'no longer in the advertising business'. They are in the data-driven communication business.[4] As a result, goal definition for advertising is imperative. Some goal statements might include the following:

- **Increasing awareness**. Awareness may be measured using a brand tracking study, a survey of a random sample by phone or online, or the number of mentions of the brand on social media. These metrics help marketers understanding if consumers have heard of the brand/ product.

- **Establishing comprehension**. Comprehension may also be tracked using a brand tracking study on social media, by measuring brand mentions with other keywords to describe it (do consumers or prospects mention the same key features, benefits or brand imagery the brand intended?), or using sophisticated biometrics systems like eye tracking to see if consumers understand what the offering is and how it will benefit them.

- **Creating conviction in purchase intent**. This may be tracked with surveys like brand tracking or visits to the website to serve as a proxy that consumers want to buy the product. Purchase intent is driven by the emotional elements of the work and the timing of the communication to specific consumer needs. This might mean changing our perceptions of the brand or introducing new programmes that make the product easier to use or access (for example, Delta Airlines' introduction of digital applications to demonstrate their commitment to technology and accessibility).

- **Generating Action**. Action can be measured as number of online purchases, sign-up for additional information, or any number of proxies for purchase.

The overall objective, however, should be clear and singular. Too many objectives can muddy the water.

8.2 Crafting the right brief

When crafting the right brief for creative teams, it's important to define the target audience in ways that your internal organization understands across the board. The call to action (and/or key message takeaway) must also be defined clearly. It is also important to attach all relevant and salient information including access to data and available research. Often, marketing research and data is on the existing consumer or on attitudes and usage. The research may not have a sense of the cultural forces that impact our customers and help to create an emotional connection.[5]

8.3 Cultivating insights

8.3.1 Understanding what's happening now

You can use data in the insights process to think about 'what happened?' as well as 'what's happening'. Descriptive analytics (summary statistics that may tell us things like number of clicks or visitors during a specific period of time) can reveal what's happening in real time, for example 'what are people saying about a product?' and 'who are the celebrities and cultural tastemakers our consumers and potential market are listening to?' Whether an output of Google Analytics or social listening, we can also get a historical view of what's happened and, in some cases, a real-time view of a very specific question being answered. Data can tell us interesting things when we ask it interesting questions, including monitoring trends in people's behaviour through 'big data', surveying their attitudes through 'small data', or analysing systems impacting behaviour, such as e-mail traffic or insights through 'in-between data' – regardless of the size, it's generally a survey of what's happened and what's happening. Data is often thought to be a precise and accurate representation of the world, although both precision and accuracy are functions of the right collection, storage and interpretation of data. With that data, it's possible not only to look at what's happened and what's happening now, but also to start looking at trends and patterns to help predict and infer things about the future. This is already evident in sites like Amazon, GoodReads, Netflix – essentially any site powered by a recommendation engine.

Recommendation engines are a product of an 'algorithm' that has taken the data of existing preferences to extrapolate new data. That ability is unlocked with the use of algorithmic and modelling techniques including agent-based modelling, predictive analytics, machine learning applied to natural language processing, and more, which make it possible to answer very specific questions about the future of very tightly defined 'agents' like consumers, sharers or audience. Applying these techniques makes it possible to hypothesize and imagine possibilities that go beyond the first degree of the data attributes ('if you like this movie, you'll like this other movie') to something wider ('based on what books you read, here's a dating recommendation for you'). In other words, recommendation engines make an inference about something that is arguably in a completely different realm from the data you have, but looking to do it with some sort of reliability in the way that one piece of data kind of informs on another. Starting to infer relationships beyond the primary (or even secondary) data or even, arguably, some of the forecasting techniques, is very much at the cutting edge of data technology today.

In Chapter 9, we'll explore how Adore Me is a shining example of today's upcoming superstar consumer product start-up. By leveraging data, they have reduced the risk associated with upfront costs of inventory and use real-time data analysis to see what products, images and communications are needed to support marketing and sales. We'll examine application of this data and creative process in the form of growth hacking.

8.3.2 Finding a target audience

Companies aren't always sure where their next markets are going be, but reading what others are saying about products on social media can sometimes help give them ideas.

Take the example of a safety boot manufacturer in the middle of a turnaround.

The company had been using traditional market intelligence techniques, but it knew it needed to do a better job with social media.

The challenge was how to pick the thousand or so conversations worth reading out of the hundreds of thousands of conversations mentioning the company's products.

Nexalogy, brought in to help the company, understood that marketers needed the context of the conversations as well as the conversations themselves. They needed to use that context to help them focus in on the most relevant conversations.[6] Their social data analysis system involved the analysis of people's different interests to develop an interest graph. This analysis involved doing millions of correlations to identify and help cluster the conversations (for example, conversations around style, colour, and in some cases, status symbols).

It selected the relevant conversations that mentioned the product and the marketers were surprised to see conversations of buyers who saw the boots as fashion statements.

For this case, the tool displayed results in two different maps: a lexical (text) map to show the links between topics so they could focus in on the relevant conversations, and a publisher map to help focus in on the influencers, bloggers and publications posting about the boots.

By calculating the correlation between the lexical and publisher map, it is possible to see who is leading the generation of buzz and conversation. By then appending demographic and location data to the publisher data, it became possible to understand the consumer in multiple dimensions.

Additional tools by Nexalogy also include an aspect analysis tool developed in part by leveraging machine learning algorithms based on research out of the University of Texas and the University of Auckland.[7] The aspect analysis tool analyses conversations and maps them against topics and categories according to the results of the learning algorithm. For example, it will recognize a tweet that reads, 'Ready for the breakfast of champions' as a topic about the daily practices of our day rather than a feeling about a topic. This type of categorization is helpful to understand the ways in which people use social media. The work by Nexalogy reflects the ever-shifting landscape (what is popular in December may only be popular in December) of the semantic web. Never content to map only once, Nexalogy refreshes its lexical maps using statistical inference methods and advanced clustering algorithms to infer context instead of static ontologies to better reflect the way human language and topics of interest shift.

8.3.3 Consumer journey

The core principle of customer relationship management (CRM) is that by understanding the customer holistically, a business can engage better and with more purpose. Understanding customers is critical in anticipating their needs and making predictions about their motivations and behaviours relative to a business's services and product strategies. This can be accomplished by harnessing the online and social data set, and by modelling, managing and moving it from the generic aggregate to a map of individual and social experiences.

The customer journey represents different touch points that characterize a person's interaction with a brand, product or service of interest. Customer journeys can be 'cradle to grave', looking at the entire arc of engagement from one brand or product to the next. At other times, journey maps are used to look at very specific experiences in the customer–company interactions such as the elegant and simple 'out-of-the-box' product set up or customer support experience.

All too often, these journey and experience maps are developed from an organization-centric point of view that assumes customer journeys are linear, and fails to take into account that customers and potential customers enact their own versions of the journey.

Another thing organizations tend to overlook is that in the digital world the customer journey is no long influenced only by the messaging, promotion and advertising that brands create but also heavily by social media conversations. Customers often rely on these conversations when they are evaluating a product to help make their decision. According to Mintel's American Lifestyles 2015 survey, 69 per cent of Americans seek out advice and opinions on products before purchasing. Of those who seek out advice, 70 per cent visit user review or independent review sites like message boards, Amazon and Yelp for that counsel.[8] These conversations influence the touchpoints along the journey and are rarely manifested into a single touchpoint or experience. Instead, the customer accumulates a rich mixture of impressions that inform their conscious and subconscious decisions to purchase or build brand affinity.

8.3.3.1 The social experience of travel

During the early days of social listening, Droga5 was tasked by the travel and perks division of a financial services company to better understand a traveller's entire journey, from inspiration to returning home. Using Crimson Hexagon, a social analytics tool known for its easy-to-use interface (which implements machine learning algorithms to better classify conversations on social media), the data strategy team began classifying the consumer journey based over a 12-month period. The data strategy team listed several assumptions: that travel is seasonal, that travel was booked at least four weeks in advance, and that the distribution of conversation participants had to match the demographic profile of the brand's target consumer: more female than male, affluent, and based in the United States. By mapping at least 200 conversations in each phase of travel for four seasons and four big events (including summer vacation, holidays, time off from school, and a celebratory personal event like a birthday or anniversary). Leveraging nearly 1,000 different individuals, they were able to map the customer journey and experience stages:

- Discovery.
- Booking.
- Planning.

- Travel to.

- Experience.

The team discovered points of tension in the experience such as the 'Travel to' and the 'Discovery' stages. The majority of people complained most often about the time and experience of the travel to a destination. This finding, completely unexpected, opened the door to ways in which the brand, founded on service, could bring their product to the forefront of consumer lives.

The team also discovered that, based on the rigours of the data collection process, they were also able to quantify the amount of conversation to help prioritize the degrees of impact of providing service in this area (ie how prevalent were these points of tension amongst service users, and how significant were they deemed to be?). The quantitative data, including web analytics based on social traffic, then allowed them to follow the signposts for movement and behaviours of interest on the branded experience.[9]

8.4 The right team

It's important to create the right alchemy of people to collide and interact (cross-functional teams) to facilitate creativity and data analysis. Big Spaceship, a creative agency that has worked with such diverse brands as Chobani, Google Play, HBO, Axe Body Spray and Hewlett-Packard, has a robust data and analytics team that works side-by-side with their creatives and strategists.[10] Within the analytics team, Big Spaceship leverages the mental model of 'warrior cultures'. Historically, the elite warrior cultures in societies like the Spartans would function in self-contained units to navigate situations of chaos and uncertainty in an effective manner. Today, groups like the Navy Seals and Special Forces use many of the same principles to operate toward accomplishing their mission. These principles include the ability to adapt very quickly to their environment in a team formation.

Tony Clement, VP of analytics at Big Spaceship, likes to use the model that operates within the Green Berets, a special division of the military. In his words:

> The Green Berets set up their teams in units of 12. Each person in the corps has a specialty, but every other person is also trained in the basic capabilities

of the other specialties, so if you have two medics and they both go down, everyone is trained in first aid. In building the analytics practice at Big Spaceship, one of the things that I've done is really ensure that everyone has a specialty, but also the base understanding of other people's skill sets, which allows us scalability and flexibility in any process that's put around us.[11]

He also described that when working with creatives and strategists, the analytics teams leverage research as a starting-off point to dialogue. Together, they engage in a process of 'Discovery', not to help ideate campaign ideas, but rather to construct questions to drive the creative process. This process of asking and answering questions is the 'Feedback Loop' of the next step. When working with clients, the combined data and analytic teams work with their counterparts in the client organizations to ensure that all information is flowing back to their counterparts in ways each department understands.

8.5 Feedback loops between different groups

Feedback loops are all about flow of communication. Traditionally speaking, a feedback loop is used to describe a situation where the output of a process is used as input into another process. In this case, feedback loops refer to the method by which advertising and marketing programs can be initiated and improved upon by different departments, by turning the output of one department process into input for another. It is not always reasonable to believe that all stakeholders and individuals in the creative process can be available and present for each stage of creative development (that would be a very expensive process), but at critical moments it's important that teams meet to discuss specific topics, not just for hand-offs, but for improved creative work.

8.5.1 Between insights and creative

Historically, strategy has briefed creative by cultivating a single creative brief. However, a better process includes a large group session to hypothesize a list of questions for insights teams to search for quantifiable results, and for creative teams to search for inspiration to answer those questions. For example, this might include asking the question of how people discover new music. Insights groups may source studies, run surveys, or use social media data to source the links shared online to help map a consumer journey of music discovery. Creative teams may cultivate their top 10 lists based on personal experience or ways in which people share music in the more personal moments of their lives.

8.5.2 Between creative and technology

Historically, creative concepts an idea and hands it off to production for the physical creation. However, a better process includes creative and technology both receiving a brief from strategy and insights groups. Technology can often bring to the table possibilities that may not have existed three months ago.[12]

8.5.3 Between media, agency and analytics

Historically, analytics was considered a reporting function to report on effectiveness. Now effectiveness is a function of proper interest targeting that's defined before campaign ads are delivered through DMPs that enhance consumer data with second-party data from research groups and media partners like Google or Facebook.

8.5.4 Between agency and the entire marketing group

Another important part of the practice of creating a feedback loop is the measurement of effectiveness of content. Many clients' work is about creating value on a brand basis (rather than customer acquisition), so they look at benchmarks in terms of engagement.

One brand working with agency MRY, in financial services, was looking at how they compared in engagement metrics with others in the same category. Although they fared well in the traditional category, they also chose to benchmark themselves against lifestyle brands like Disney. Even though they found that they couldn't beat Disney's content metrics, they found their metrics to be in the same league.[13]

8.6 Creative development

The 2015 Cannes Lions international advertising festival saw the introduction of 'Creative Data', a new category meant to give data its place within the creative process. In its first year, there were no Titanium winners.

The definition of Titanium for the purpose of Cannes Lions is creative ideas that point to a new direction for the industry and redefine the creative landscape. Titanium Lions will be awarded to 'game changing', breakthrough ideas that open new doors, change the world of creativity and inform new ways of thinking.[14]

This lack of distinction reflects the nascent relationship data and creativity have with one another.

One area that has seen considerable progress is that of user experience. The importance of interface in marketing is relatively new as a concept. Interfaces have more often than not been designed from an engineering approach – what was the least amount of work for the most functional use. As interfaces became consumer facing, elements of beauty and design were necessary. As the practice of user experience matures, techniques are quickly being developed, though best practice is still very much evolving.

8.6.1 Creative development: campaigns

An application of creativity around data is largely situated around whether data can tell you something that's interesting in the world. It can often serve as the hook between a brand purpose and the demonstration of that brand purpose in someone's life. It's an illustration about life that makes us catch our breath.

A classic illustration: in the UK, there's a prominent data point that's transformed national legislation. If a child is hit by a car at 40 miles per hour, they're 80 per cent likely to die. If they're hit at 30 miles per hour, 10 miles per hour less, they're 80 per cent likely to survive.[15]

That's a powerful, illustrative story. It doesn't require a beginning, middle, or end. It doesn't require a how-to guide for the general public on road safety, such as keep your eyes open, don't use your mobile phone, don't drive distractedly, drive 10 miles an hour slower – the data just speaks for itself.

8.6.2 Creative development: user experience

Traditionally, user experience design as a practice has focused on the user. Inherent in its name, this gives a laser focus to what would be best for the individual user based on their specific needs. But what if the goal of the creative work is to be dynamic and help anticipate a user's need?[16] Different types of thinking (including systems thinking) allow creatives to think about problems and solutions in multiple dimensions. Also known as 'service design thinking', systems thinking can help architect solutions to consumers' needs that work on several levels. System thinking leverages a lot of terms from narrative storytelling, such as 'actors', 'sequences' and 'interplays and relationships' and is helpful in thinking about a consumer's journey. For example, when mapping out how content might be shared, one might start with mapping a single consumer (actor) who might share their photos online; it may not simply originate as a camera image to upload on Facebook. Our consumer might take a photo, share it on their Apple iPhone iCloud stream and invite users to the group (sequence). They might then realize that a member of the group they wanted to share it with does not have an Apple device and so switch to storing the files on Dropbox (interplay). On Dropbox, another user might take that photo and upload it on social media, but may also decide to alter it with a funny quote and place it on their Snapchat or Instagram. A friend may decide that's compelling content and share it with another user, tagging it with the name of another friend, who might source it for a blog (relationship).

8.6.3 *Creative development: content and content strategy*

The creativity, then, for a marketer is not only to ask how these emerging data-based technologies can be used effectively, but how they can be used in novel ways to accomplish their specific business goals and how they can help construct a marketing programme that generates the right kind of attention that leads to customer loyalty.

The true application of creativity to data extends beyond using the evidence to create compelling brand narratives that resonate with consumers. For example, Prudential launched an entire advertising campaign focused on educating people on how our own brain tricks us when it comes to saving for retirement. The multi-channel campaign, driven by data and research from the University of Michigan, behaviour scientists like Daniel Kahneman, and psychologists like Dan Ariely, used this research to bring to the attention of the audience the fact that there are many forces working against them for healthy retirement savings, and encouraged them to work with experts like Prudential to help achieve a new understanding and experience of retirement.[17]

At Facebook, much research has been done on what kind of content people share and how. A former data scientist, Tye Rattenbury, shared his discoveries on the mechanics of how people interact with one another.[18] In his view, Rattenbury was able to model the different networks and the kind of content that went through to each network to which an individual user (and advertising consumer) belonged.

Facebook found that a good portion of the personal content created was not with the intent and purpose of reaching a small network of people.[19] However, an even larger amount of content was individuals sharing from the direct source or sharing opinions. Political news, sports news, entertainment news – each of these were proxies for the identity that humans engage in when they communicate with one another.[20]

8.6.4 Creative development: digital products

The power of being able to gather, identify, understand and execute upon patterns of data is critical for the long-term success of companies. Companies, beyond their marketing departments, must systematically make sense of data, extract meaning from that data, and ensure its quality and security. Data does not just improve existing products, but creates new competitive advantage and even leads to the rise of data itself as a product, including building applications around the data sets and providing customers with real-time responses. For example, airlines and government transportation agencies now share required information about flight times, but can also integrate that data with additional relevant data like the weather in a customer's arrival destination and access to transportation services when on the ground.

Perhaps one of the best-known fitness training product is Nike's Fuelband – an idea first put forward by their marketing team. The Fuelband, an activity tracker worn on the wrist used in conjunction with an Apple iPhone, iPad or Android device, launched in January 2012. Beyond tracking physical movements, it also directs relevant feedback to users on how well they perform those physical actions and what to do next.

Rattenbury has observed that this type of 'data as a product' innovation is happening around those activities and needs based around identity (goods that help us learn about ourselves), because affluent consumers are willing to pay for that reflection of self and status.[21] There are more and more opportunities in marketing to use data to inform people about their identities in ways that have never really been possible before.

While companies like Intuit (which acquired personal finance management company Mint.com in 2009 at the height of its popularity and insights on consumer spending) and GE are building B2B products, these products that answer a specific consumer need are now creating the type of brand loyalty they have been seeking as an extension of their marketing practice.[22]

8.7 The right measurement system

Getty Images, after enjoying market leadership for many years, needed to engage in brand marketing. Unsure how to articulate value for brand initiatives, the Getty team needed help from a group that could bring together the 'art' of brand marketing with the 'science' that had been governing their digital ad buying and marketing budgets for years. They wanted help to understand and craft a 2016 marketing plan based on their previous performance and vast amounts of site and marketing data, and most importantly, a way to attribute the impact of creativity on their sales metrics.[23]

In order to craft a 2016 marketing plan of $75 million, Crossbeat leveraged social analytics and audited and organized Getty's internal data analytics and warehouses as well as introducing four additional data sources to help make decisions for better digital and brand marketing. By implementing a data management platform (DMP) and striking relationship with vendors with historical data available via APIs (Application Program Interface), Crossbeat was able to align their CMO and COO teams for the first time in 20 years.[24]

8.7.1 How to evaluate creative work

A technology and entertainment client of Big Spaceship wanted new ways to implement a brand health monitoring system using unprompted consumer feedback through social media mentions rather than the traditional means of survey questions.[25] Through a partnership with social insights vendor Brandwatch, Big Spaceship was able to create, in the simplest terms, a brand-tracker service that allowed them to understand what consumers were identifying as the brand attributes and characteristics that were meaningful to purchase decisions. It allowed both the client and Big Spaceship to reframe the characteristics of the brand.

That was Big Spaceship's first learning. The second one resulted from a comprehensive system of data queries with more than 500 different rules in place to categorize social mentions in real time to a dashboard which would visualize the brand health. This dashboard served as an intelligence alerting system for product features, self-reported behaviour, and breakout performance of communications for their client. By integrating this data with the existing Google Analytics and media spend data, Big Spaceship and their client partner were able to create a turnkey view of product, app, and PR performance, and their relationships with one another.

8.8 Reporting

In most organizations, reporting is a post-script. It's an obligatory exercise to prove industry, and often arranged to show results. Often, though, those results aren't contextualized. In an effective marketing environment, reporting can be used as a conversation starter that combines multi-disciplinary information in a cohesive fashion. Each team must be willing to contribute full, accurate, unedited data out of a spirit of collaboration.

Each individual team member sorts the best way these data sets can contextualize the contributions from their interdisciplinary colleagues. This is not often a clean process. Invariably, one team, such as operations, might underperform while another, like digital marketing, may outperform their benchmarks, and every team member has to work out how to best help bring the right amount of information to the conversation at the right time. By doing so, it's possible to flip the conventions of reporting for internal purposes into a role of content for people to gather around, share and contextualize. Data becomes a way for people to then start talking about, thinking about, and sharing ideas about consumer behaviour and context. From here, there is a natural progression from what was and is happening to what could happen. That creative transformation has nothing to do with the numbers and analysis within the report itself, and the report then becomes a backdrop. This is when the magic happens. Analysts and data scientists can then have a clear, articulate and creative voice and have a point of view about ideas in which people aren't territorial but collaborative.

8.9 Examples of creative data work in advertising

CASE STUDY GE and R/GA

General Electric worked with digital creative agency R/GA to create a data visualization of all world records in events held at the Summer Olympics.[26] R/GA researched existing published data sets and the latest event results from the individual sporting federations to create a single data set detailing the world records in each Olympic event. The data set had 3,400 records, from 152 events in 6 sports, representing 71 countries, dating back to 1900. (Some Olympic sports, like gymnastics, do not have world records.) R/GA explored the data to find outliers and trends to better understand what would make for the best visualizations, and then sliced the data with different presentations to reveal the stories and make them more accessible to users. The resulting visualization, leveraging a visualization library, presented the data in four ways: records by year, event, duration, and location. Each visualization presents dots arranged in different ways, which can be clicked on to gain information on specific events. Plus signs designate clickable points to learn interesting facts relevant to the particular visualization.

For GE, this was a special story around celebrating human physiology through their involvement with the Olympics for consumers and athletes alike. Because GE provides a range of health-related technology services, the visualization was meant to demonstrate their commitment to the things that support great achievements by great people.

CASE STUDY British Airways and OgilvyOneLondon

If a creative agency possesses technical know-how, solid processes for creative and data to work together and a willingness to work closely with media teams, the result could be something as powerful as British Airways' 'Magic of Flying.'[27] The insight was that to children, flying is magic. Could they inspire that same feeling in an advertisement?

To do so, they created digital OOH activations in Piccadilly Circus and on the M4 motorway leading to Heathrow that initiated an advertisement which, whenever a BA plane flew overhead, would interrupt any display media on the OOH display with a video of a child getting up and pointing up towards the plane. The activation required a careful orchestration of tracking technology that would sense when a BA aircraft flew above and would capture the data of the trip including the call sign and navigation information. That data was delivered to a custom-built application that would tell Clear Channel Media's billboards when to start the ad in time to create the illusion that the child in the ad saw the actual plane. The power lies in data's ability to coordinate actions that people could not do with the naked eye.

CASE STUDY   Sundance Film Festival and Crossbeat

SundanceTV was a major sponsor of the Sundance Film Festival, an annual film festival that selects the best in show.[28] SundanceTV wanted to drive more foot traffic to its headquarters on Main Street to support its role in the festival and its original programming. Using beacon technology, SundanceTV's agency leveraged Foursquare's geo-location technology, which is the backbone of its Swarm and Foursquare products, and their Foursquare Audience Network (FAN), which could target mobile ads to those in the Park City Area, to drive festival-goers in local areas towards the headquarters on Main Street. Upon landing, nearly 30,000 festival-goers received a welcome message from SundanceTV. And while walking through town, they received one of 200 pieces of social content on Foursquare based on their location and delivered through the FAN network. This content strategy received the attention of other brands looking to do location-based activations with relevant content and delivered more than 200,000 targeted impressions in 12 days before and during the festival with custom content about things to do in Park City.

CASE STUDY A start-up named REX

Another example is a new application in the marketplace called REX, a recommendation app launched at Sundance Film Festival in 2016.[29] REX's mission was to create a piece of technology that's new and improved on the outside, but that captures the fundamentally human action of word-of-mouth recommendations. Graham Douglas, their former chief creative officer, shared:

> To this day, if I was going to Mexico or I needed to find a bar to take my girlfriend to on a date tonight, I wouldn't ask Yelp or Google or Trip Advisor unless I didn't have anyone that I thought had a better answer. I would ask you, I would ask my brother, I would ask friends that had spent a lot of time in Tulum or wherever. I still think that the best recommendations come from people, and I think if you've ever been at a bar after work or to a dinner party, without fail the conversation turns to, "Oh my god, have you guys seen this movie? Have you read this book? Are you listening to the new *Serial*?"'

CASE STUDY Genome Projects

The idea of data as a product spans a range of different industries. In the music industry, Pandora was the first to create the music genome project upon which a start-up music technology company was born. In 2000, the words 'music', 'data' and 'digital' were just beginning to be used in the same sentence. By marrying the fields of music analysis and database technology, a gentleman named Gasser became the architect of the Music Genome – the extensive database of musical attributes that lets Pandora make recommendations of similar (and well-liked) music from analysing the songs and compositions a consumer picks.

Since then, additional Genome Projects have been made for art, architecture, and fashion, by companies such as Artsy and Stylefinder.[30] A handful of agencies are currently creating these proprietary systems for cataloguing the world's architecture, architectural products and services.

Notes

1   Levenson, Bob (1987) *Bill Bernbach's Book. A history of the advertising that changed the history of advertising*, Gillard

2   Hall, C Justin, '"Think Small" advertising campaign', 2014 [online] https://clas-pages.uncc.edu/visualrhetoric/projects/individual-projects/think-small-advertising-campaign/ [accessed 1 May 2016]

3   Quoted from interview with William Bernbach, printed in DDB Doyle Dane Bernbach News, June 1974

4   Coffee, Patrick, 'Sir Martin makes it official: "we're not in the advertising business anymore"', *Adweek*, 25 March 2016 [online] http://www.adweek.com/agencyspy/sir-martin-makes-it-official-were-not-in-the-advertising-business-anymore/105255 [accessed 1 May 2016]

5   The Financial Brand, '8 steps to crafting killer creative strategies', 7 February 2013 [online] http://thefinancialbrand.com/27428/writing-effective-creative-briefs/ [accessed 1 May 2016]

6   PricewaterhouseCoopers, 'Technology forecast: reshaping the workforce with the new analytics', [online] http://www.pwc.com/us/en/technology-forecast/2012/issue1.html [accessed 1 May 2016]

7   Interview with Nexalogy founder and CEO Claude Theoret. Personal interview, 17 September 2015

8   Mintel, 'Seven in 10 Americans seek out opinions before making purchases', 3 June 2015 [online] http://www.mintel.com/press-centre/social-and-lifestyle/seven-in-10-americans-seek-out-opinions-before-making-purchases [accessed 1 May 2016]

9   Interview with (former) executive technical director for Droga5, David Justus. Personal interview, 4 October 2015

10 Interview with Big Spaceship VP of analytics Tony Clement. Personal interview, 20 October 2015

11 Ibid.

12 Cinquegrani, Sam and Stevenson, David, 'Technologists must spearhead the next creative revolution in marketing', *CMO*, 17 November 2015 [online] http://www.cmo.com/articles/2015/11/4/technologists-must-spearhead-the-next-creative-revolution-in-marketing-.html [accessed 1 May 2016]

13 Benkoil, Dorian, 'How hating the word "content" made MRY's CMO a better marketer', *Contently*, 15 October 2015 [online] https://contently.com/strategist/2015/10/15/how-hating-the-word-content-made-mrys-cmo-a-better-marketer/ [accessed 1 May 2016]

14 Barth, Chris, 'Cannes Lions/Innovation and Creative Data Winners', *Contagious*, 26 June 2015 [online] http://www.contagious.com/blogs/news-and-views/34780357-cannes-lions-innovation-and-creative-data-winners [accessed 1 May 2016]

15 UK PSA Campaign, https://www.youtube.com/watch?v=HeUX6LABCEA, from interview with Brandwatch CMO Will McInnes. Personal interview, 18 December 2015

16 Stone, Randall, 'The experience is the brand', *Economist*, 24 September 2014 [online] http://www.economistgroup.com/marketingunbound/collabora-tors/lippincott-experience-is-the-brand/ [accessed 1 May 2016]

17 Interview with (former) executive technical director for Droga5, David Justus. Personal interview, 4 October 2015

18 Interview with Salesforce director of data science and learning Tye Rattenbury. Personal interview, 10 November 2015

19 Facebook IQ, 'Creative strategies with topic data', 22 October 2015 [online] http://insights.fb.com/2015/10/22/creative-strategies-with-topic-data/ [accessed 1 May 2016]

20 Interview with Salesforce director of data science and learning Tye Rattenbury. Personal interview, 10 November 2015

21 Ibid.

22 Intuit, 'Intuit completes acquisition of Mint.com', 2 November 2009 [online] http://about.intuit.com/about_intuit/press_room/press_release/articles/2009/IntuitCompletesAcquisitionofMint.com [accessed 1 May 2016]

23 Interview with Getty VP of integrated marketing Monica Bloom. Personal interview, 13 January 2016

24 Interview with (former) executive technical director for Droga5, David Justus. Personal interview, 4 October 2015

25 Interview with Big Spaceship VP of analytics Tony Clement. Personal interview, 20 October 2015

26 Huerta, James, 'GE visualizes sporting world records (created by R/GA)', *R/GA*, 8 August 2012 [online] https://futurevision.rga.com/2012/08/ge-visualizes-sporting-world-records-created-by-rga/ [accessed 1 May 2016]

27 D & AD, 'Case Study: Magic of Flying', 2014 [accessed 1 May 2016] [online] http://www.dandad.org/en/d-ad-magic-of-flying-case-study-outdoor-ad/

28 Interview with Crossbeat founder and CTO David Justus. Personal interview, 4 October 2015

29 Interview with (former) REX chief creative officer Graham Douglas. Personal interview, 10 October 2015

30 Wikipedia, 'The Art Genome Project', 12 January 2015 [online] https://en.wikipedia.org/wiki/The_Art_Genome_Project [accessed 1 May 2016]

Adore Me: Growth hacking and crowdsourcing

09

Did you know:

- Women are more inclined to buy bras modelled by brunettes than by blondes?
- Plus-size models sell more lingerie than petite-sized?
- Raw, untouched images are more popular on Facebook and Instagram (and as a result, catalogue images) than glossy, retouched images?[1]

Deep insights about human behaviour and social interaction are often the driving force behind creative ideas in business and marketing. They force us to stretch our imagination because they introduce a novel perspective of where our mental models might hold us. These are also the types of insights that can be the cornerstone of a campaign, a new product or a brand refresh. For lingerie brand Adore Me, their insights came from a robust analytic and creative marketing process designed from the ground up by their founder and CEO, Morgan Hermand-Waiche.

Adore Me, launched in 2011, is an online boutique that offers women's lingerie at affordable prices, and attributes its phenomenal growth to its relentless commitment to being a customer-first company. Hermand-Waiche attributes both his start and his success to his fanatical commitment to an analytic-creative process. In a 2015 *Fortune* article, he shares that the inspiration for his business was a failed attempted at buying lingerie on a budget as a birthday gift for his girlfriend:

> I realized the lingerie market was underserviced, and saw a venture opportunity there. As a guy who had never shopped for lingerie before, I had absolutely no knowledge of the market, so I did what I do best: looked for data.[2]

While doing so, he found that the category of lingerie was ripe for disruption: a single player, high barrier to entry (due to manufacturing and logistics management), and full of failures from large retail incumbents like Abercrombie & Fitch and the now-deceased Fredericks of Hollywood.[3] Because he did not come from the world of fashion, he saw things that others in fashion don't see. He believed that the current retail businesses of 'the Ralph Laurens and Hilfigers of the world' were miles away from what's relevant today in modern culture and for the modern consumer.

In traditional retail, starting a brand with the diversity of styles to compete with someone as big as Victoria's Secret would require an investment of $10–$15 million before the first sale happened. Like many start-ups, Adore Me did not have access to the funds to finance a large marketing campaign or existing brand equity to leverage. They also had to achieve significant market share on limited budgets, plus the business uncertainty that often accompanies start-ups. Because of these differences from larger companies with large budgets and more established brands, start-ups like Adore Me have had to utilize analytical thinking, product engineering and creativity to significantly increase their company's core metric(s). Known as 'Growth Hacking', this type of marketing focuses on rapid growth by thinking outside the box.

9.1 Growth hacking

Growth hacking, first introduced in Chapter 3, is the application of different tactics and strategies aimed at unlocking growth at scale. This growth is achieved systematically by creating hypotheses on where target audiences are, testing messages and offers on these platforms to learn, optimize the acquisition methodology and hope/expect/plan for an exponential increase in sales, customer acquisition, views or visits.[4] Start-ups (and smart brands) that have embraced the tenets of growth hacking have discipline and dedication to data, understand customer behaviour outside of purchase path, measure everything, and have an ability to think creatively with a sense of curiosity and experimentation. In short, they code, launch, repeat, and with those findings, enlist and enrol other departments to help.

Though this approach has often been criticized as ignoring brand building, it's arguably the case that quality brand building requires an agreement on a set of principles that guide more than just marketing, sales and growth. If, as a company, the value of authenticity is important, then finding the influencers (people, publishers and communities) to support the messaging is necessary to stay in alignment with that value.

The key, of course, is to be smarter (the strategic part) and not use a single method, but rather a set of methods (the hacker part). The skills necessary to be successful are a hybrid skill set of creativity, analytical thinking and a bit of coding. The benefit, of course, is that relative to traditional marketing and channel partnerships, growth hacking is relatively cost-effective in terms of value, and less competitive. The tools of the trade that helped many start-ups, including Facebook, have, in the words of Hermand-Waiche, 'fostered a bubble' that has driven many marketers to other channels, including TV.[5] In the past, Facebook offered disruptive solutions based on data. First, it was the initial platform that allowed marketers to accurately measure results in real time. Second, while other platforms like Pinterest and Twitter offer those analytics in point one, they haven't developed real-time ad support that includes precise targeting. By combining those two, scaling could happen very quickly. But the influx of big brand dollars has made important events (like Christmas, Valentine's Day, birthdays and other retail occasions) cost prohibitive and they no longer offer the same opportunity to get clear signals on supply and demand. For example, from Jan 2014 to Jan 2015, Adore Me's cost per click went up over 170 per cent and conversions went down just from the inundation of content competing for audience attention.[6] However, the lessons below are applicable to both start-ups and big brands. The key to growth hacking is to understand the principles of how the process works, but to continue seeking new tactics to achieve this growth. The tactics change as new start-ups (and now many brands) enter the channel. The stages of the process are as follows: [7]

Acquisition. This stage describes when a potential customer sees advertising or hears about the brand that brings him/her to the website or joins the subscriber list. Sample metrics may include cost per acquisition (how much was spent on the buy per qualified visitor, who might be defined as someone in the demographic or interest target), user growth month over month, or number of visits to the site from a specific channel per number of impressions per channel.

Activation. This stage describes when a potential customer does more than visit, including engaging with content, and stays with the brand longer than a few seconds. Sample metrics might include number of visits to a landing page per month, webpage views/visits greater than two, time on site greater than 10 seconds, or clicking more than twice on the site. The important thing to note is that the pathway from

Figure 9.1 Growth hacking hypothesis

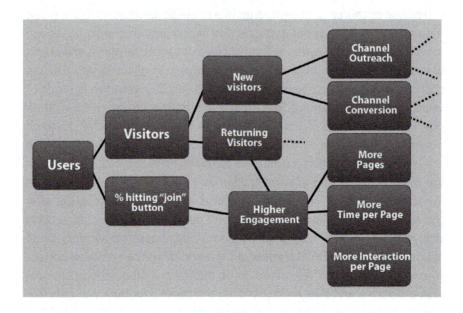

acquisition to activation must be clear, and that there are a number of vendors who can help with the attribution of this incoming channel traffic to internal traffic. Tools like Google Analytics allow analysts to create segments and goals to help track specific groups of visitors who meet these criteria.

Retention. This stage describes when a person signs up for an e-mail newsletter or follows on social media. Metrics might include the number of e-mail newsletter sign-ups or number of social follows or number of repeat visitors in a 30-day period.

Revenue. This stage describes when a customer makes a purchase. Metrics might also include the number of users who make a minimum revenue purchase that covers the cost of acquisition of a customer up to an average number that might equal the calculated customer lifetime value.

Referral. This stage describes when a customer recommends the brand to another. Metrics include average number of referrals for all customers, average number of referrals from top-buying customers, or average number of referrals from top-referring customers. These metrics help to create benchmarks for future performance as well as to understand the top drivers of the business.

In Adore Me's case, customers saw custom stories in their Facebook feed or e-mail referrals from other customers (acquisition).[8] Other ways include content marketing like videos through syndicated channels (like influencers and lifestyle bloggers), and rigorous PR. In fact, 76 per cent of marketers say that their brand leverages content marketing to drive awareness.[9] Many of those brands then use retargeting on Adwords and Facebook to bring potential customers to the site. Overall, 66 per cent of marketers said that Facebook proved effective as a vehicle for driving awareness through content.[10] Studies show that advertisers have learned over the years that Facebook works best in retargeting circumstances. Recently, they have been using Google Play to target customers to download the app.

To activate, Adore Me has designed their mobile app to push users to continually purchase.[11] They alert users to sales and discounts only for app users when their monthly showroom is ready. By keeping the notifications minimal but relevant, users continue to make in-app purchases. The key role of creativity is to make sure the user experience is simple and that customers are onboarded easily with a beginner walkthrough of how to use the app.

To retain, Adore Me sends out e-mails to first-time prospects who may have visited the site but not returned or completed their purchase. Additional e-mail questionnaires also come out 15 days after purchase to

Figure 9.2 Growth hacking testing

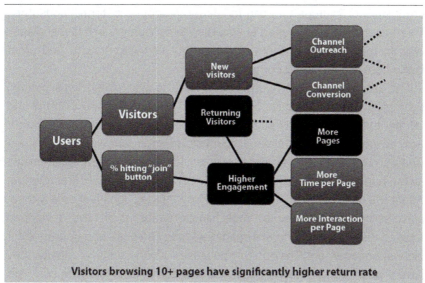

Visitors browsing 10+ pages have significantly higher return rate

ask about experience, and then are followed by trend recommendations to keep purchasers abreast of trends.[12] Adore Me also encourages users to sign up for a VIP membership. This practice is vital for understanding their 'best customer', and helps Adore Me reward their top customers and gather more data on purchase patterns and activity. Members are sent a new set of lingerie each month at a discounted price of $25 for the first order, then a $10 discount on sets, which typically sell for $50. Every sixth set is free. Members can opt out of monthly orders or cancel at any time.[13] This strikes a balance between collecting data tied to a single user and providing an experience that Adore Me members can use in the context of their own lives. In another example, using Facebook Insights, Adore Me saw a correlation between sign-ups and sorority membership. To increase referral, Adore Me gave sorority members a $15 credit if the referral signs up. Referring a friend underlines the power of recommendation, but it also serves a dual purpose by dramatically reducing cost of acquisition while offering a scaling opportunity that is not just limitless, but most importantly proprietary to Adore Me.[14] The following sections delve more deeply into the components of acquisition, retention and referral.

9.1.1 Leveraging APIs for acquisition: test and learn at scale

APIs are used by marketers to automate the transfer of data between separate software systems and platforms. By leveraging APIs, marketers can easily and effectively post or download large amounts of data from other sites or sources that can tell us more about a potential consumer. This information can be used to advertise to consumers in a fast and easy way. In the early days, there was no 'API' for customers to find other customers in an existing community.

For example, AirBnB figured out a way to hack Craigslist's posting submission process to drive bookings from Craigslist to AirBnb in the first 18 months.[15] In the early days of YouTube, they found that by making it easy to post videos on MySpace, musicians and fans would host their video on YouTube and share it on Facebook. Facebook has been a favourite for many start-ups, including Adore Me. In their technical infrastructure, Adore Me has built every tool internally so that they don't rely on any third-party software. To better leverage Facebook ads, they have developed tools to test as many different images as they can post, and optimized for highest engagement. They do this because, like any digital company, they have a very strong IT team. There also is a dearth of tailor-made software for what they require. They needed to connect their social media actions to first-party transaction data and, as an extension, business metrics.

Cost per acquisition (CPA) is a metric that many CMOs live and die by. It is an incredibly important measure when understanding the benefit and impact of creative work. Many young start-ups like Dropbox, Living Social, Uber and AirBnb incentivized sharing by giving away free services and products in exchange for word-of-mouth referrals or activations of new accounts.[16] For Adore Me, they offered several benefits to their members, including referral discounts and gifts to those members that refer a friend. This has accounted for a large part of their first-customer acquisition through e-mail. The CPA for Adore Me is the cost of the referral discount for each new sign-up.

The company worked with a market automation partner, Nanigans, to sharpen their targeting in time for Black Friday, the American tradition of shopping after Thanksgiving Day (the last Thursday of November each year).[17] Using Nanigans' Affinity Analysis tool and Facebook's Audience Insights tool, they uncovered a correlation between sorority membership and sign-ups as well as the relevance of relationship and gender targeting to find the right audience for their message. In this case, Nanigans leveraged Facebook's API to make the comparison.

Adore Me had their own coding to do: they created custom landing pages specifically for Cyber Monday (the online shopping day on the Monday after Thanksgiving) and Black Friday. They launched all-new copy, promotions and creative, focused on discounts, limited time offers, sale comparisons and matching. Again working with Nanigans, they were able to iterate thousands of ads, and automatically allocate budgets to those ads in order to optimize for engagement.

9.1.2 Paid media and search

Adore Me has embraced a combination of analytical thinking, creativity and social metrics to achieve growth of customers, sales or usage, particularly in newer social channels like Pinterest, by creating images specifically for Pinterest to broaden their lifestyle appeal.

They have also combined these with old-school tactics in order to maximize growth. In January of 2015, Adore Me began a television campaign, with spots on networks like Bravo, Lifetime and MTV, but their approach was very quantitatively driven.[18] For their campaign, they ran three ads: one with blonde models, one with a plus-size brunette model and one with multiple brunette models, and rotated through the media buy. This is a form of A/B testing, a process of showing a consumer several differ-ent options to gauge response. When Adore Me began its television campaign, it used some of the information it had gleaned from social media and testing to determine what ads to show on what networks, and when. And then they allowed TV to do what it does most – promote lift awareness and increase overall search and visits to the site.

9.2 Creative practices to increase activation and retention

9.2.1 Content marketing

While Adore Me relies on social listening platforms to monitor chatter, it is not their first line of defence with regard to feedback. Because Adore Me has placed such a large emphasis on customer interaction, most of the information they find about themselves they already know, including what kind of content their members and customers like. Adore Me sends and receives a good amount of e-mails and conduct its own customer surveys.

In order to encourage users to share branded content, it's important to make sure that what's created and tested is right for the platform. Former Facebook data scientist Tye Rattenbury shared with us that often on Instagram, it isn't the beautiful picture alone that wins, but the story beneath coupled with the picture. The goal of awareness requires differ-ent focus on metrics and methodology when compared to the goal of acquisition. In other goals, sharing is the mechanism by which to best grow.[19] Aaron Isaksen, Professor at NYU'S Game Innovation Lab, clarified six reasons why people share:[20]

a Social currency – we share what makes us look good.

b Triggers – we share things that remind us of something meaningful to us.

c Emotions – we share things that inspire awe, excitement, laughter and anger (but not sadness).

d Public/ease of use – we share things that are accessible and easy to use.

e Practical – we share things we think others might get value from.

f Stories – we share stories, not facts.

For Adore Me, sharable content includes bra fitting guides, how-to videos of their process, as well as polls, quizzes and interviews.

Says Hermand-Waiche:

> We have a lot of creativity going around the photo shoots, yet we want to make sure that the image we put forward is the right one. What we do is we let artistic people express their point of view through different sets, shoot concepts, product positioning, and lifestyle vs. product campaigns. Then we maybe A/B test each picture.

> In product design, we use a lot of data to guide the creative. By combining the history of sales, colour testing data with our customers, we were able to create the right kind of black balcony with a sexy cut.[21]

As a visual company, Adore Me allows the brand to speak through its rich imagery on social media. Unconcerned with the traditional problem of content piracy, they try as many different ads on social networks to see which ads receive the most clicks or drive the highest engagement.

9.2.2 User experience: create new interfaces

In the practice of growth hacking, activating more users, converting more sales and/or top-of-funnel metrics like registering more visitors and views are often the goal. Activation happens when a visitor has taken action,

Figure 9.3   Micro-optimization example: More sign-ups

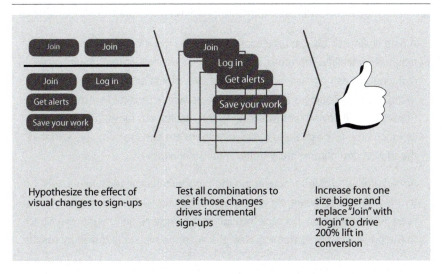

Hypothesize the effect of visual changes to sign-ups

Test all combinations to see if those changes drives incremental sign-ups

Increase font one size bigger and replace "Join" with "login" to drive 200% lift in conversion

large or small, that creates a relationship with the brand. This might include an e-mail sign-up, a social media follow, or making a purchase. To increase the conversion on the site, often brands must optimize the website experience to present information in a more comfortable and efficient way. This might mean changing a button colour, creating a clear call to action, or offering incentives that are easy to understand. These changes are often tests against each other (see the next session for A/B testing) with the most popular constantly tested against creative marketers' must-try new methods and techniques that provide some differentiating, exclusive or standout element compared to the competition.

9.2.3 A/B (or MV) test everything

In this stage, you implement tools like Google Analytics to help track website performance as well as platforms like KissMetrics that help serve different versions (A or B) of the page, button or object to be tested. A proper methodology for A/B testing and other types of experiments and optimizations is necessary to achieve optimal yet useful results. For most data-first analytical team members, their job is to ensure that the results are correct and follow proper protocol. However, a marketer's goal is to focus on results, growth and improvement. This divergence in goals does not always mean there has to be tension between data-analytic team members and marketing leads.

Kissmetrics, an optimization and analytics package that helps marketers improve on the metrics that matter, provides excellent advice on why A/B test results of marketers and scientists are different and where they can find middle ground. Consider the following example from KissMetrics:

> A data scientist's education teaches him/her to focus on data accuracy and result repeatability. Therefore, a data scientist will collect test results on as many people as necessary until a repeatable, statistically significant result is found, rarely choosing a variant that delivers worse results. This means that the scientist is paying less attention to the results, but rather giving the test as much time as possible to make sure there are enough samples, and that the results get incrementally better rather than worse.

> A marketer, who is less focused on the proper statistical techniques, will try new ideas too frequently (perhaps only waiting for 500 observations of a specific phenomenon like click-through or conversion), and might revert back to the original or try something else. Because the market is driven by results

and by growth, the marketer is looking for what works without isolating for randomness and time of the customer action.

A realist, a hybrid between the marketer and the scientist, will also want results, but doesn't wait until near certainty. In most cases, s/he might wait for 2,000 observations. In a sample run, the realist isn't looking for growth alone, but is looking to see which ideas increase or decrease conversion. This will result in the best results in the shortest amount of time.[22]

This type of testing, however, only evaluates the average visitor, and requires that brands serve weak as well as strong-performing content that takes longer, and therefore costs more money before any optimization can be done. More complex testing is now available through platforms such as Optimizely to deploy multi-variate testing (MVT). In MVT, analysts can test the combinatory effect of factors on a page. In the case of Adore Me, their marketing and social media team could test both the type of engagement copy ('What is your favourite style?' vs. 'Free shipping!') with the right call to action 'Share your favourite style' or 'Start your Xmas shopping now').

With multi-variate testing, software will enable analytics to see whether it was the longer text, the call to action, or perhaps the interaction effect of both switching to a longer text and call to action that was most successful. This in turn does require a larger amount of traffic to the website in order to reach a satisfactory level of statistical evidence for each variation.[23]

9.2.4 Referrals: influencers and partnerships marketing

For many young start-ups, the power of the influencer network can only be leveraged if it's coupled with an authentic connection with the influencer. T-shirt brand Private Party cracked the code by approaching celebrities with their distinctive bold-lettered T-shirts bearing catchy phrases like 'Netflix, Nachos and Naps' and 'Kate Moss Is a Capricorn' and photographing them. Their social following grew to 100,000 in a few months and has built them into a seven-figure brand.

By using tools like Affinio to leverage the 'social tribe' of influencers, brands can easily find the right influencer for the audience they wish to reach. Affinio aggregates hundreds of thousands of conversations and relationships between those having the conversation to detect a pattern in who influences who. For Adore Me, they focused on millennial celebrities on YouTube, not the traditional influencer.

9.3 Lessons in crowdsourcing

According to Sharon Klapka, VP of business and brand development at Adore Me, 'Crowdsourcing allows you to get a glimpse into the future. Seeing what shoppers are [going to be] interested in and then planning your inventory, planning your production and planning your designs accordingly.'[24] This type of philosophy requires a creative team that can embrace input from the customer and create a product. Hermand-Waiche eventually found Helen Mears, a former design director for Victoria's Secret with a willingness to embrace his spirit of balanced analytic-creative process.[25] As the current head of design, Mears receives reports on customer feedback to find out what consumers want before introducing their product lines. The company designs new styles based on the results of taking style quizzes and selling small test sets of bras and panties. The company also offers a wide range of sizes, from 30A to 46G. In fact, according to Hermand-Waiche, plus or petite sizes account for roughly a third of the US market and that share is growing. It's to this type of marketing, a type of crowdsourcing, that both Hermand-Waiche and Sharon Klapka attribute their customer devotion. The other, growth hacking through online advertising, social media and referrals to build its brand, has helped grow the business in size and in reputation, landing it near the top of *Inc.* magazine's Top 500 start-ups.

Coined by Jeff Howe in a 2006 *Wired* magazine article and made more viable today by tools like the internet and social media, the term 'crowdsourcing' refers to the method of outsourcing the generation of ideas, solutions or content to the public.[26] Also known as 'the wisdom of the crowds', it's an excellent way to provide a pool of data and brainstorm ideas to kick off and shape the creativity brief. For many brands, it's a popular method for a cost-effective yet sustainable approach to marketing. Crowdsourcing is a way to leverage new media to elevate the role of user-generated content as part of the broader marketing strategy. Klapka attributes a lot of Adore Me's growth and success to crowdsourcing: 'Crowdsourcing allows you to get a glimpse into the future. We see what shoppers are going to be interested in and then plan inventory, production and designs accordingly.'[27]

To gain this insight, Adore Me hosts a vote on its website and promotes the vote on social media (the company advertises on Facebook, Pandora and Spotify and at the time of writing is currently testing Instagram and Twitter). To encourage participation and increase traffic to their site, Adore

Me – which claims to have more than 800,000 followers on Facebook – also offers a promo code as a reward for voting. Klapka said that traffic to their site increases about 200 per cent when Adore Me promotes one of their polls.[28]

The first poll, which brought in 34,056 votes, asked consumers to choose between two corsets. Their latest was a vote for the favourite beach cover-up; it brought in 52,116 votes. 'I don't think it's coincidental that the items they vote for later become bestsellers', said Klapka.

'When you're launching 30 to 40 designs every month and you're a start-up and you're fuelling your growth, you want to know that the products you're choosing are really gonna sell strong,' she said, 'otherwise it's a waste of your time, it's a waste of your energy, it's a waste of money.' Adore Me uses several types of crowd voting, a form of crowdsourcing, although there are additional types that can be used to tackle marketing and advertising challenges.[29]

9.3.1 Crowd Voting

Crowd Voting, which is used by Adore Me, leverages the community's judgment to organize, filter and rank content (ie images posted by the Adore Me community or by Adore Me marketing). Jeff Howe cites the 1:10:89 Rule which states that out of 100 people:

- 1 per cent will create something valuable;
- 10 per cent will vote and rate submissions;
- 89 per cent will consume creation.[30]

This works well when the creative aspect of product development is over and there are a few elements of the product that become opportunities to better engage with the brand's biggest advocates.

9.3.2 Crowd Creation

Crowd Creation activities, the best-known forms of crowdsourcing, are 'creation' activities such as asking individuals to film TV commercials, perform language translation or solve challenging scientific problems. Research from Crowdtap, a crowdsourcing platform for marketers, and global research company Ipsos, has shown that people aged 18 to 36 now trust consumer-generated content more than non-consumer-generated content (50 per cent more). A well-executed example of this is the interactive project 'The Wilderness Downtown'. Soundtracked by the band Arcade Fire's 'We Used to Wait', the director Chris Milk, in collaboration with Google, invited fans to create a portion of the video project by submitting their home address and a drawing they would send to their 'childhood' selves.[31] Then, in real time, these images were rendered digitally via technology and crowd creation, and used on tour. The Johnny Cash Project, another crowd creative music video, was fashioned from drawings done by audiences to accompany Cash's 'Ain't No Grave' – his final studio recording.[32] Fans connected their smartphones to their webcams via a unique code on the video's site. By moving their smartphone around viewers could change the visual effects on the video, creating sprinkles of light and colour. The video, of course, was not the sole output of the crowd's actions without editing, directing, and packaging. By sourcing the material from the crowd, the creative became immediately personal for audiences.

9.3.3 Crowd Wisdom

The 'Wisdom of Crowds' principle harnesses many people's knowledge in order to solve problems, predict future outcomes, or help direct corporate strategy.[33] Howe states: 'Given the right set of conditions the crowd will almost always outperform any number of employees – a fact that many companies are increasingly attempting to exploit.' Studies by Caltech professor Scott E Page confirm that even concentrated groups of highly intelligent people are consistently outperformed by crowds. Examples include companies like CrowdMed, a site that allows patients to submit their medical cases to the site to be solved by a cadre of medical detectives from around the world.[34]

9.3.4 Crowd Funding (eg Indiegogo)

Crowd Funding circumvents the traditional corporate establishment to offer financing to individuals or groups that might otherwise be denied credit or opportunity. Kiva, a micro-lending portal, offers an example of crowdsourcing. Kiva provides a marketplace for aspiring entrepreneurs in developing nations to seek out project financing that is not readily available in their home markets.

Of course, crowdsourcing, particularly crowd wisdom, is far from infallible. The author of the 2005 book *The Wisdom of Crowds*, James Surowiecki, explained that one requirement for a good crowd judgement is that people's decisions are independent of one another.[35] If everyone let themselves be influenced by each other's guesses, there's more chance that the guesses will drift towards a misplaced response bias.

Platforms such as Crowdtap (a spin-off from the advertising agency MRY) and Indiegogo offer their brand clients an enterprise version of their platforms to crowdsource opinions on brand clients' new products or positioning. These platforms have figured out ways to keep their audience engaged without selling them out to those brands trying to reach them. By maintaining authenticity in the audience, those audience members are more forthcoming and honest in their feedback when they vote for their favourite flavour or colour.

Because crowdsourcing provides a wider supply of resources, businesses can fine-tune the ways they use Big Data, analytics, and data enhancement. Technology companies can use crowdsourcing for testing and finding glitches in apps and software. For example, the makers of the note-taking app Evernote use UserTesting.com to record users' actions and ask them questions – rather than exhaust their own resources conducting tests and compiling results.[36] Brick-and-mortar retailers could use the crowd for secret shopping to gain insight about their stores and employees. Some tasks for these crowdsourced workers could be scanning shelves for pricing mistakes or product misalignment. A retailer could also use crowdsourcing and cloud applications to launch a storefront makeover or website redesign, and solicit feedback from its target audience before a full launch.

9.4 How start-up growth hacking methods can benefit a big brand

Growth hacking and crowdsourcing are two methods of combining data and creativity that are still 'in progress'. These methods are certainly not without their critics or flaws. For some critics, growth hacking is not necessarily what builds brand equity over time, the way traditional marketing campaigns may. Crowdsourcing is not always 'statistically' representative of a brand's target segment. Still, as methods, they can deliver marginal-to-significant growth, particularly on limited budgets and in a competitive marketplace where barrier to entry is low and the attention of the consumer is fleeting. Marketers of new products or those targeting new segments should adopt some of these practices, especially in the face of uncertainty of the business division, the target market, or the long-term viability of the product. These methods, after all, were born out of necessity and as the saying goes, 'Necessity is the mother of invention'.[37]

When asked what advice he might have for a CMO of a large company who needs to launch a new product in today's marketing environment, or even a CMO of a small company, Hermand-Waiche replied:

> Be 'customer first'. Ultimately, when we have a disagreement or a challenge, we always think, 'Okay, what would make the customer feel better?' The reality is usually a mix of data and creativity. It's actually the biggest of our rules: put our customer first. I would tend to feel that it drives a lot of decisions inside the company. Just take an example of a conflict between my head of supply chain and my CFO. Supply chain is going to say, 'Hey, I talked to marketing, and we have this new, cool box in which we can ship our Christmas orders. There's a little mistletoe inside. It's super cute. It's going to be amazing, and customers are going to be super excited. Then Marketing is going to say, 'Oh, that's great. I love the suggestion', and operations may say, 'I can promote this on our website, to create more sales.'
>
> The financial officer is going to say, 'Look, it might create more sales, but it will obviously cost more money, and no one can, as of now, guarantee which volume of sales it's going to generate. Some things cost more. We're not sure it's going to bring more. I'd rather not do it.' We have a conflict of interest between the different people who want to do different things and ultimately this type of situation happens every day. Our rule is customer first, so we always do what we feel is best for the customer.[38]

For Hermand-Waiche, data is not only a tiebreaker that helps facilitate decision making and discussion, but stands as a proxy for the customer voice:

> When you think about combining data and creativity, internally you are actually saying something different to the world. In many ways, data becomes a language for the people, is what I'm hearing from what you're saying as well. I think that's a really powerful thing to remember, especially since it's a cultural trend that's happening for us now too; because technology has allowed us to democratize and access information in many things, it makes sense that it would seep into our cultural ideas.

In the world of traditional marketing, massive spending on distribution could compensate for sub-standard products. However, we now live and consume in a time and place where even the largest or the most creative product launches cannot create scalable, repeatable and sustainable business growth if the product is not a good market fit. The hard lesson to learn from upstarts is that product matters as much as promotion. This may be the single most important marketing innovation coming from those who have neither the marketing budgets nor the know-how. Established brands must now also compete on a product and distribution level like AirBNB, Dropbox and Uber.

Hermand-Waiche believes that 'Adore Me is really the brand by the people, for the people, that wants to be available and approachable by everyone, which means every wallet, every style, and every size', and while most fashion brands have built their image around sex appeal, Adore Me stands apart: 'We want to welcome everyone. We are really fundamentally differently rooted.' And this is a modern, global cultural value that consumers everywhere have embraced.

Notes

1 Klapka, Sharon, 'The future of retail and commerce marketing'. Session presented at AdWeekXII, October 2015, New York, NY

2 Hermand-Waiche, Morgan, 'Proof data can't always help you make decisions', *Fortune*, 6 December 2015 [online] http://fortune.com/2015/12/06/trust-gut-entrepreneurs-decisions/ [accessed 1 May 2016]

3 Interview with Adore Me founder and CEO Morgan Hermand-Waiche. Personal interview, 5 October 2015

4 Gooding, Liam, 'Growth hacking like a pirate, a beginner's guide to pirate metrics', *Trakio*, 15 January 2014 [online] http://blog.trak.io/growth-hacking-like-a-pirate-a-beginners-guide-to-pirate-metrics/ [accessed 1 May 2016]

5 Hermand-Waiche, Morgan, 'How The Facebook bubble is driving online startups into the arms of offline advertising', *Tech Crunch*, 17 April 2015 [online] http://techcrunch.com/2015/04/17/how-the-facebook-bubble-is-driving-online-startups-into-the-arms-of-offline-advertising/#.k6ziqqb:sVpb [accessed 1 May 2016]

6 Ibid.

7 StartitUp, 'Task: AARRR (startup metrics)' [online] http://startitup.co/guides/374/aarrr-startup-metrics [accessed 1 May 2016]

8 Nanigans, 'How online retailer Adore Me reached 1,500 new customers in 5 days' [online] http://www.nanigans.com/blog/fb/ecomm/how-online-retailer-adore-me-reached-1500-new-customers-in-5-days/ [accessed 1 May 2016]

9 Gerard, Michael, 'Content marketing statistics: the ultimate list', *Curata*, 8 October 2015 [online] http://www.curata.com/blog/content-marketing-statistics-the-ultimate-list/ [accessed 1 May 2016]

10 Toledano, Eyal, 'How to acquire customers when Facebook ads stop working', *Sociable Labs* [online] http://www.sociablelabs.com/blog/how-to-acquire-customers-when-facebook-ads-stop-working [accessed 1 May 2016]

11 James – Crush Campaigns, 'World-class growth hacks to drive mobile app installs', 18 January 2016 [online] http://www.crushcampaigns.com/growth-hacks-to-drive-mobile-app-installs/ [accessed 1 May 2016]

12 Schlossberg, Mallory, 'This company determined to kill Victoria's Secret is becoming a major force in the lingerie market', *Business Insider*, 10 October 2015 [online] http://www.businessinsider.com/how-adore-me-is-threatening-victorias-secret-2015-10 [accessed 1 May 2016]

13 Ibid.

14 Nanigans, 'How online retailer Adore Me reached 1,500 new customers in 5 days' [online] http://www.nanigans.com/blog/fb/ecomm/how-online-retailer-adore-me-reached-1500-new-customers-in-5-days/ [accessed 1 May 2016]

15 Yongfook, Jon, 'Growth hacking 101: your first 500,000 users', *Slideshare*, 2 May 2012 [online] http://www.slideshare.net/yongfook/growth-hacking-101-your-first-500000-users/19-Partnerships_An_incentivised_partner_sending [accessed 1 May 2016]

16 Meadows, Chris, 'The Dropbox cloud storage service as a disruptive innovation', *Teleread*, 26 February 2012 [online] http://www.teleread.com/the-dropbox-cloud-storage-service-as-a-disruptive-innovation/ [accessed 1 May 2016]

17 Nanigans, 'How online retailer Adore Me reached 1,500 new customers in 5 days' [online] http://www.nanigans.com/blog/fb/ecomm/how-online-retailer-adore-me-reached-1500-new-customers-in-5-days/ [accessed 1 May 2016]

18 O'Brien, Sara Ashley, 'Plus-size models sell more bras', *CNN*, 17 March 2015 [online] http://money.cnn.com/2015/03/17/technology/startup-adore-me/ [accessed 1 May 2016]

19 Interview with Salesforce director of data science and learning Tye Rattenbury. Personal interview, 05 November 2015

20 Bohemia, Erik, 'Leading innovation through design: proceedings of the DMI 2012 international research conference', 2012 [online] http://www.academia.edu/17373430/Leading_Innovation_through_Design_Proceedings_of_the_DMI_2012_International_Research_Conference [accessed 1 May 2016]

21 Interview with Adore Me founder and CEO Morgan Hermand-Waiche. Personal interview, 5 October 2015

22 Kurt, Will, 'Most of your A/B test results are illusory and that's okay', *Kissmetrics,* [online] https://blog.kissmetrics.com/your-ab-tests-are-illusory/ [accessed 1 May 2016]

23 Van Der Zee, Theo, 'A/B or MVT: when to choose which type of test?', *ConversionReview* [online] http://www.conversionreview.com/blog/ab-mvt/ [accessed 1 May 2016]

24 Klapka, Sharon, 'The future of retail and commerce marketing'. Session presented at AdWeekXII, October 2015, New York, NY

25 Interview with Adore Me founder and CEO Morgan Hermand-Waiche. Personal interview, 5 October 2015

26 Howe, Jeff, 'The rise of crowdsourcing', *Wired*, 6 January 2006 [online] http://www.wired.com/2006/06/crowds/ [accessed 1 May 2016]

27 Klapka, Sharon, 'The future of retail and commerce marketing'. Session presented at AdWeekXII, October 2015, New York, NY

28 Zen, Pola, 'How reviews helped Adore Me top the Inc. 500 list', *Yotpo*, 3 August 2015 [online] https://www.yotpo.com/blog/2015/08/03/how-adore-me-skyrocketed-growth-with-reviews/ [accessed 1 May 2016]

29 Klapka, Sharon, 'The future of retail and commerce marketing'. Session presented at AdWeekXII, October 2015, New York, NY.

30 Howe, Jeff (2008) Crowdsourcing, Crown Business

31 Tavakoli-Far, Nastaran. 'Beck, Arcade Fire and the music videos inviting fans in', *BBC*, 5 November 2013 [online] http://www.bbc.com/news/business-24762876 [accessed 1 May 2016]

32 Ehrlich, Brenna. 'Crowd-sourced Johnny Cash music video is a work of digital art', *Mashable*, 27 October 2010 [online] http://mashable.com/2010/10/27/johnny-cash-project/#4d8DZu9uhaq4 [accessed 1 May 2016]

33 Sloper, Gary, 'Why creative crowdsourcing is good for business', *Forbes*, 17 April 2014 [online] http://www.forbes.com/sites/centurylink/2014/04/17/why-creative-crowdsourcing-is-good-for-business/#7409b0fb1c4e [accessed 1 May 2016]

34 Howe, Jeff, 'The rise of crowdsourcing', *Wired*, 6 January 2006 [online] http://www.wired.com/2006/06/crowds/ [accessed 1 May 2016]

35 Surowiecki, James (2005) *The Wisdom of Crowds*, Anchor

36 Sloper, Gary, 'Why creative crowdsourcing is good for business', *Forbes*, 17 April 2014 [online] http://www.forbes.com/sites/centurylink/2014/04/17/why-creative-crowdsourcing-is-good-for-business/#7409b0fb1c4e [accessed 1 May 2016]

37 Plato, *The Apology, Phædo and Crito*, trans. by Benjamin Jowett, Vol. II, Part 1, The Harvard Classics, New York

38 Interview with Adore Me founder and CEO Morgan Hermand-Waiche. Personal interview, 5 October 2015

Next practice   10

Artificial intelligence fuels human imagination. From the early Jewish legend of the golem created like Adam from clay, to Mary Shelley's Frankenstein, our stories have reflected and captured society's fascination with creating intelligence because in that intelligence is the essence of being human.[1] From self-driving cars to robot dog companions, experiences that bring joy to the human experience are the subject of study (and commerce) for a handful of companies being gobbled up by technology and media businesses. Driving this fulfilment of our wildest creative imaginations is all the data that the 'big data' revolution has collected. The combination of commerce, creativity and data has fuelled the AI revolution that has been touted as the game changer in life and business. Not only will a person's home life change, but also the businesses that provide services are soon to be replaced (or drastically altered) by artificial intelligence. Until these machines become reality, however, AI is limited to its ability to corral and interrupt massive swatches of data. The challenge is to convert all this data into useful data. We must integrate the processes and outcomes of data, commerce and creativity, because the question of 'why' has been our imaginations. The remaining questions for us to solve are 'how' and 'what'. What has not been answered, and which only time and experience can define, is 'what's next?'. 'Next practice' requires the ability to see if our practices that exist now can handle what is coming ahead.[2] Many of the imagined possibilities for data and creativity in marketing are coming true or are near-term realities. The benefits that the combination of technology, process and user interaction can deliver through data are now becoming realized and are laying the groundwork for new ethical and technological breakthroughs.

10.1 Personalization part two

Personalization has been one of the big promises of the combinatory effects of data, technology and creativity. The ability to reach different consumers with different creative messages rather than having a single message that everyone sees is not just a media targeting revelation, but also a creative one that allows a brand to now target consumers (like teens) who may ultimately be different from decision makers (like parent purchasers) of products. The important line to toe is to create messaging and images that speak respectfully to consumers without appearing to know too much about them. Target's plight was infamously introduced when they began using their customer data to ascertain if someone was pregnant.[3] A combination of buying unscented lotion at 20 weeks and supplements of magnesium, zinc, and calcium at 12 weeks were among a few data points that predicted purchasing behaviours of baby care items. As a result, Target began to send circulars with coupons for pregnancy products to a young girl in high school, much to the chagrin of her father, who confronted Target about this seeming mistake. It wasn't a mistake. Some things are not meant to be discerned about customers.

Steven Spielberg's 2002 movie *Minority Report*, loosely based on a Philip K. Dick short story, is cited at advertising and marketing industry conferences the world over as an example of what's now possible thanks to the collision of data, tech and media.[4]

Personalized one-to-one marketing is a reality we are moving toward as marketers today face consumers with high expectations of relevance, individualism and relationship. From a technology perspective, this requires marketers to gain an actionable understanding of individual customers and an ability to treat people based on what they do (behaviours) and who they are (interests), rather than what they are (demographics).

CMOs are increasing spend in channels that support deep personalization such as e-mail and mobile, while decreasing spend on impersonal communication channels such as print, radio and direct mail.

Advances in personalization are based on two rapidly evolving technologies. First, we will continue to see increased sophistication of segmentation techniques. Micro-segments will be composed of individuals with commonality in their actions, not commonality in their demographic characteristics. Second, time-series analyses that recognize 'event-triggering' user needs (eg audiences go for a cookie break at 3pm each day or a family needs more toilet paper once a month) will play an increasingly important role in anticipating consumer behaviours.[5] This means that we will finally stop being served ads when we've already bought the product and instead move toward a system that can understand the need states before they occur. Time-series analysis will also let marketers see seasonality and trigger events that turn on and off customer need states.

10.2 Self-service data discovery and Q+A capabilities

Today's Business Intelligence (BI) market demonstrates a will and a need for B2B customers to have tools that make data discovery easier for analytic as well as non-analytic employees. From ETL (Extract, Transform and Load) processes for data to visualization techniques, there is a range of products and vendors that help with this process. Right now, we are seeing companies like Tableau, SAP, IBM, Trifacta and Actuate (OpenText) lead and shape the space of data and digital transformation for small and large enterprises to make it easier for users to extract insights from their data. The fusion of big data demands and self-service analytics will have a huge influence in the business world as data analysts increase their organizations' value.[6] While business intelligence has been around since the early 1990s, today's self-service models mean that non-analytic employees can ask questions and receive answers that are meaningful and readily understood by them. More importantly, the questions can be more expansive in scope because the intelligence behind the answers is not just limited to corporate data sets, but to the right mash-up of data sets to provide context to the answer. Companies like IBM have extended their artificial intelligence capabilities (such as IBM Watson) to provide a semantic layer and human-like interface to help deliver the insights in a form that expands beyond reporting.

10.3 The recognition of data equity in corporate value

'Data equity' is a term that describes the enterprise value that comes from investing in data capabilities. In the many interviews that have informed this book, an overwhelming majority of data programmes begin in marketing.[7]

Data equity is a forward-looking indicator of value, like other types of balance-sheet intangibles like 'brand equity' and 'technology equity'. As companies search for unique ways to uncover latent intelligence about their people, customers, operations and markets, the operational processes can contribute to lifting companies' overall ability to charge a premium or weather economic changes more easily. Data equity then becomes the link between an enterprise's data assets and processes and the overall market value for the company itself.

Of course, the impact to the bottom line is lagging in many implementations now. Only 37 per cent of senior leadership believe their current data implementations work. That's why, when looking at the ways in which core competencies of marketing are impacted, this book has chosen to focus on data and creativity to help translate that lag into real value for enterprises. Data equity requires companies to demonstrate how well they distil intellectual capital from their data.

Verizon's recent of acquisition of AOL demonstrates the commitment to more responsive discourse with the consumer. By connecting several of the largest multi-channel consumer touchpoints (specifically, TV viewership data through Verizon to digital viewership data to web properties like AOL, Huffington Post, Engadget and more) through the acquisition of AOL's advertising technology, Verizon now has the ability to understand, for the first time, the impact media and advertisers can have on consumer behaviour.[8] Most companies tracking and targeting users across devices can, at best, stitch together profiles of lookalikes, but not on a true user level. Verizon can track unique user sessions on their mobile phones, and, when people go online to pay their Verizon bill, the firm can connect that data to a cookie ID storing browser data. Because Verizon subscribers use the service to view video on their phones and through their TV set-top boxes, the company brings lots of additional behavioural video data to what AOL already has.

Verizon's data focus does not stop there. Location data helps provide context for consumer behaviour that advertisers did not at one point have. As a result of the combined data between Verizon Wireless and AOL, advertisers can now use location data generated by devices to determine demographic and other information about people who visit certain locations, and track their pathway to other locations. Data is anonymized, but can show the connection between visiting the grocery store and then the local gym. This type of information is vital to advertisers as they evaluate strategic marketing relationships, and also provides better data for AOL's ad targeting, optimization and measurement system. This new data set, called Precision Market Insights, can also help refine existing ad campaigns by providing more data for programmatic creative. By understanding the context of where people are coming from and going, creative can now integrate more meaningful messages like sharing healthy recipes on social media ads targeted per mobile device.

Location data is also pointing to a trend in user consumption behaviour that has, until now, only been anecdotal. Data shows that audiences consume data in places outside of work and home, and content consumption is now happening in shorter bursts of time. This means that there is a greater opportunity for creative work (social, digital, content, shows) to be different lengths, vertical viewing on phones rather than horizontal viewing, and even without sound. By understanding location, content can be relevant to where a consumer is and what they are doing.

Verizon's recent acquisition of Fleetomatics, Yahoo! and other data-driven businesses points the arrow to a broader Internet of Things (IoT) strategy. By owning an entirely connected ecosystem powered by data, the promise of smart living seems palpable. This vision, however, requires clarity and a hefty dose of governance.

10.4 Internet of Things (IoT) and bio data

By 2020, there are predicted to be 50 billion Internet of Things devices in the world that emit tons of data about consumers' behaviour and preferences. For example, Procter & Gamble Co. demonstrated in 2014 what it calls the 'world's first available interactive electric toothbrush'.[9] It links with a smartphone and records brushing habits, while an app gives mouth-care tips alongside news headlines. These devices can also save the data about when and how consumers use it and the conditions of the mouth, process images of the interiors, and potentially even make a dentist's appointment for the consumer. The important thing, however, is focusing on people's existing behaviour patterns and providing both a message and utility to deliver as a brand. Pushing advertisements of brands unrelated to the context and permission is not a wise choice. As the Internet of Things industry is still fast developing, technologies, entrepreneurs and marketers are still exploring consumer habits in the massive amounts of data they are creating.

One data source that is increasingly appearing in a marketer's toolbox is biodata.[10] Major data brokers like Acxiom and Experian collect thousands of pieces of information on nearly every US consumer to paint a detailed personality picture by tracking the websites we visit and the things we search for and buy. These companies often know sensitive things like our sexual preference or what illnesses we have. Now with wearable technology proliferating (it's estimated there will be 240 million devices sold by 2019), that profile's just going to get more detailed: information like our temperature, our mood, our motion and our biometrics can be used to understand a number of activities that are biophysical and personal.

10.5 Chatbots: a new frontier in customer service

Another buzzword you'll hear is 'Deep Learning'. Deep learning is actually a shortened referral name for 'Large Deep Neural Networks'.[11] Deep learning is a powerful model that combines anywhere from 20–30 neural networks to help process the model. A neural network is a computer system that is similar to human neural networks, which help us to perform complex functions collectively and in parallel with different systems – like breathing or chewing. The computer versions of neural networks acquire knowledge through learning and that learning is stored within the 'neuron' connections. One commonly used example is OCR (optical character recognition) software. OCR breaks the 'images' of words into smaller 'images' and that are translated from an 'image' to a binary format of 0s and 1s (ie data). This is how images can be digitalized and sent across networks. Those 0s and 1s are fed into a neural network to train it to make an association between the character image and the binary data.

In many ways, deep learning is considered the next wave of machine learning, but some refer to machine learning as 'supervised' learning whereas deep learning is often meant to also encompass 'unsupervised' learning. These neural networks, whether machine learning or deep learning, help solve more 'human' problems such as speech recognition, visual object recognition, and other language-related tasks like translation.

For marketers, this is an important concept as we consider that the internet now allows us to have customers via e-commerce who live in other countries and use different languages. Marketers, in the future, will want the ability to understand what they are saying regardless of language, tone and expression. Or we might want the ability to better understand what our target audience shares on visual social media like Instagram or Pinterest.

We may have technology partners who help us, but an understanding of their techniques goes a long way in understanding what they offer and how they are different from their competitors.

The good news is, most vendors (or internal data science analysts), have an array of machine learning APIs (application programming interfaces that are used by developers and data scientists to download and transform data) to help with this process. At the time of writing, the big four tech companies offer machine and deep learning APIs – IBM Watson, Amazon Machine Learning, Google Prediction and Microsoft Azure. There are also several smaller technology companies that offer recognition engines optimized for specific tasks – for example, Clarifai has a better ability than IBM Watson to identify abstract concepts like impressionist paintings or voice recognition powering Android phones. These machine learning algorithms allow marketers to provide tools to consumers so they can ask for what they want by picture (from hand-drawn to photographs). These algorithms can also help find related inventory based on attributes that the customer could not describe with words. This opens the door for better communication between marketers and consumers.

It is important to consider the factors of excellence for each data analysis technique to best evaluate its use for marketing purposes.

10.6 Smart Cities: new opportunities for marketing

Data and creativity can enable, at their core, a systematic process to problem solving beyond marketing and commerce challenges. Today, large urban centres like Houston, Miami, New York, Rio and Delhi are leveraging the analytic capabilities of data in combination with the creative ingenuity of urban planners, civil engineers and technologies as the world's urban population is set to double by 2050 (where roughly 80 per cent of the world's population will be in an urban environment).[12]

With this rapid growth ahead of us, we also have the ability to speak to cities on their state of health through low-power sensors, wireless networks, web and mobile-based applications that all speak in the language of data to provide information on traffic, pollution, sentiment, temperature, power, density and resource management. These Smart Cities are defined by their ability to operate along three dimensions:

- technology + data (infrastructure, architecture, open standards, innovative services);
- people + creativity (creative living, creativity, knowledge, innovation, education);
- process + institution (community, policy, regulation).

Smart Cities are also rich in opportunities for brands to provide utility to consumers that are brand effective. Initiatives like New York's Citi Bikes, Ireland's Dublinbikes, Barcelona's 'CityOS' strategies and Stockholm's Dark Fiber are focused on improving the urban experience.[13] This is done with creative and seamless partnership integration that can now be quantified. They are also consumer touchpoints that can generate rich data sets to better understand intention, friction points and behaviour. These initiatives are brilliant, effective and socially beneficial, and are credible ways in which brands can truly participate in the broader dialogue with consumers.

The sophistication of blending location-based technology with digital data enables out-of-home (OOH) to more effectively target consumers at a time when they are most receptive to those ads. According to Andy Stevens, senior vice president research and insights for Clear Channel Outdoor, the worlds of digital and OOH are radically different but are ripe for transformation through data:

> In digital we can get diverse audience insights. We can optimize in real time. But in OOH we have high impact. There is no ad-skipping. There is no 'below the fold'. Traditionally, in OOH it is hard to measure who is actually seeing that ad but we know there is a huge opportunity in data to change the industry.[14]

The creative and the targeting capabilities of OOH in connected cities are essentially partnerships between municipalities and marketers. Now, with behavioural insight tied to location, we can better understand the context and timing of need states to better feed the right message at the right time in the right place when the consumer has the right mindset to receive it.

By leveraging the current technology in the domain of Internet of Things and available personalization data, the vision of the smart city could be achieved. These technologies enable things, individuals, groups and services to share data in real time. Smart living can be facilitated by a personal data platform called HAT (Hub-of-all-Things) – think Amazon Echo, a hands-free speaker that is controlled by a consumer's voice. The HAT has the following functions:

1 Acquires personal data through internet-connected objects or services in the home and by pulling in social media data and transaction data from firms.

2 Stores personal data into a Hub-of-all-Things owned by the individual and only to be used with his or her explicit permission;

3 Converts disparate personal and Internet of Things data into a contextualized blueprint of how personal data of individual lives could be organized so that we can retrieve, use, visualize and analyse data to make better decisions.[15]

The Hub-of-All-Things construct places the individual within the context of the system's intelligence, ie based on a 'smart me' rather than a 'smart thing' philosophy.

10.7 Artificial intelligence

Traditionally speaking, computers have been used to enhance the human ability to carry out tasks. To date, we know this best as consumers when we see features like autocomplete and spell check. With machine learning, technology companies flip this model on its head and use humans to enhance the work of computers. The 'human in the loop' model is the premise from which machine learning will make the next leap in technology that supports the consumer experience. These leaps have application in personalization as well as natural language processing.

Natural language processing, otherwise known as NLP, will become more present in the future with the increased use of personal assistants such as Facebook's M, IBM Watson, Apple's Siri, and Amazon's Alexa. These 'human-like' interfaces (such as voice) are just beginning to scratch the surface. As this process unfolds, virtual personal assistants will become much more capable, and the growth of machine learning itself will accelerate as developers bridge the gap between human and digital language processing.

At the core of each of these technologies are optimized 'processes' that are waiting for humans to help make them smarter. The value, however, lies not so much in the process and algorithms in the software, but in the data needed to make them smarter. As *Wired* magazine writer, Cade Metz, shares, 'Google is giving away the other stuff, but keeping the data'.[16]

10.8 Privacy and identity, ethics, and transparency

Privacy is a major issue as we start to move into more personal data and greater insight generation based on the depth of data. Questions on access, sharing and usage of the data are just a few that marketers will encounter as we move toward the Internet of Things era.

The European Union has been leading the charge on what can be considered a global crackdown on commercial use of personal information, especially with their formal adoption of the General Data Protection Regulation in January 2016.[17] Originally authored in 2012, this regulation corrals the disparate laws of individual European countries into a more consistent set of rules. Specifically, it does the following:

> It broadens the definition of personal data, restricts use of data for profiling consumers, requires companies to give consumers details about how their information will be used and with whom it will be shared, and bolsters the so-called 'right to be forgotten' rules which would require companies and their partners to purge links to or replications of personal data.[18]

The proposal states that personal data includes 'name, an identification number, location data, online identifier or one or more factors specific to the physical, physiological, genetic, mental, economic, cultural or social identity of that person.'

It also states:

> Where personal data are processed for the purposes of direct marketing, the data subject should have the right to object to such processing, including profiling to the extent that it is related to such direct marketing, whether the initial or further processing, at any time and free of charge.[19]

That stance reflects differences in American and European attitudes towards data protection, and indeed to regulation in general. America has avoided overly prescriptive privacy legislation, believing that companies should generally regulate themselves.

While global companies have been preparing for this ruling, there are also now conflicting rulings in different regions that affect not only marketing and product teams' abilities to service clients, but also the ability of companies to fulfil their regulatory obligations for specific sector-governing bodies. Merck and Co, for example, cite that there are regulatory reasons why they have to keep data (for FDA approval or CDC support). The actual requirement to erase data on people can prove to be fundamentally problematic. Other categories, like financial services, also use consumer data to help evaluate risk and fraud. Without the ability to store data, it will not be possible to keep an accurate transactional record of those who might be using other people's data for deceptive purposes.[20]

Other countries' privacy rules will matter more. China and India will soon have more people online than Europe and America have citizens. China is focused on data privacy and security issues in part to promote the growth of China's e-commerce market and to also protect its government's interests. The guidelines of its Ministry of Industry and Information Technology (MIIT) do not provide a definition of 'sensitive data', or the specific guidelines by which privacy is defined. The laws also do not specify how individual consent to data practices should be obtained, nor do they elaborate on the types of measures that organizations should take when personal information is compromised.

10.9 Online and offline

Research indicates that 72 per cent of millennials research and shop their options online before going to a store or the mall.[21] So, despite the rising popularity of e-commerce, customers still value the physical retail experience. People don't want to choose between online and offline shopping. They want both. The debate and needs of marketers for data and creativity mirror this customer journey. We are still left with the need to do our jobs as marketers: create products and services that do a job and develop an emotional connection as the basis of a long-term (and loyal) relationship with customers. We now have the ability to do this with more precision and more heart than ever before, and the good news is, we can have both.

10.10 In summary

Marketing is changing radically, fuelled not only by the flood of data and technology, but also by new international labour forces and the prospect of new customers in emerging markets. This book examines in detail four major themes that help us define the term 'creative data' and the role of data in the creative development process: it offers a primer for the new terms and players relevant today, a way of thinking about problems, a method for designing a solution, and a process for working with teams and vendors.

As discussed in Chapter 2, this book discusses a process that focuses on testing a hypothesis about consumer behaviour and using a blended effort of creativity and data to test that hypotheses. Chapter 3 covers the language of data and deconstructs the process from marketing metric to analytic process to data-mining task. Chapter 4 challenges the marketer to think differently and shift their thinking from pitfall biases to useful frameworks to solve problems. Chapter 5 outlines a path to build an analytic group from one person into a relationship with other groups. Chapter 6 reviews the technology landscape and the external media, advertising and data partners who make the phrase 'right consumer in the right place at the right time' a real-time reality.

This book is for the industry, not the academic. Success is gauged by utility, not by novelty or complexity. Like creative professionals, analytical professionals know the power of a good edit. Upon finishing this book, the reader should be familiar with some of the methods and vendors available and have a deeper knowledge of what is possible. Yet, without the ability to communicate, it becomes difficult to understand the necessary allies and collaborators to use all available data. Marketers are expected to be polyglots who understand why consumers behave the way they do, the language of business, and what makes creative work emotionally inspiring. Now they must also understand the language of data and analytics and take the opportunity to speak with others about it, formally and informally. They must inspire their board members to support them; they must be curious seekers with a compass of practicality. Marketers must let everyone around them know that data is useful in the ever-present spirit of creativity.

Notes

1 Shelley, Mary J (ed Paul Hunter) (2012) *Frankenstein*, Second Norton Critical Edition, W. W. Norton & Company, New York

2 Sullivan, John Dr. 'Seeking out "next practices": the next generation of best practices', *Ere Media,* 26 June 2006 [online] http://www.eremedia.com/ere/seeking-out-next-practices-the-next-generation-of-best-practices/ [accessed 1 May 2016]

3 Duhigg, Charles, 'How companies learn your secrets', *New York Times*, 16 February 2012 [online] http://www.nytimes.com/2012/02/19/magazine/shopping-habits.html [accessed 1 May 2016]

4 Marshall, Jack, 'How has advertising lived up to "Minority Report"?', *Digiday*, 7 February 2014 [online] http://digiday.com/brands/advertising-really-like-minority-report/ [accessed 1 May 2016]

5 Angulo, Nataliam, '16 insiders weigh in on digital marketing in 2016', Marketing Drive, 22 December 2015 [online] http://www.marketingdive.com/news/16-insiders-weigh-in-on-digital-marketing-in-2016/411201/ [accessed 1 May 2016]

6 Harris, Derrick, 'The rise of self-service analytics – in 3 charts', Gigaom, 13 February 2015 [online] https://gigaom.com/2015/02/13/the-rise-of-self-service-analytics-in-3-charts/ [accessed 1 May 2016]

7 SAS, 'Data equity: unlocking the value of big data', 12 April 2012 [online] http://www.sas.com/offices/europe/uk/downloads/data-equity-cebr.pdf [accessed 1 May 2016]

8 Kaye, Kate, 'Behind all good ad-tech is data – and Verizon, AOL have lots of it', *AdAge*, 13 May 2015 [online] http://adage.com/article/datadriven-marketing/verizon-aol-pair-data-core/298607/ [accessed 1 May 2016]

9 Hu, Luna, 'Creativity in the Internet of Things era', *Holmes Report*, 26 June 2015 [online] http://www.holmesreport.com/sponsored/article/creativity-in-the-internet-of-things-era [accessed 1 May 2016]

10 Neal, Meghan, 'What happens to the data collected on us while we sleep', *Motherboard*, 19 January 2016 [online] http://motherboard.vice.com/read/what-happens-to-the-data-collected-on-us-while-we-sleep [accessed 1 May 2016]

11 Metz, Cade, 'Google open-sourcing TensorFlow shows AI's future is data', *Wired*, 16 November 2015 [online] http://www.wired.com/2015/11/google-open-sourcing-tensorflow-shows-ais-future-is-data-not-code/ [accessed 1 May 2016]

12 Singh, Sarwant, 'Smart cities – a $1.5 trillion market opportunity', Forbes, 19 June 2014 [online] http://www.forbes.com/sites/sarwantsingh/2014/06/19/smart-cities-a-1-5-trillion-market-opportunity/ [accessed 1 May 2016]

13 Wikipedia, 'Smart city' [online] https://en.wikipedia.org/wiki/Smart_city#Laguna_Croat.C3.A0 [accessed 1 May 2016]

14 Weisler, Charlene, 'The happy marriage of creative and data in out of home', Media Village, 3 December 2015 [online] https://www.mediavillage.com/article/at-last-the-happy-marriage-of-creative-and-data-in-out-of-home/ [accessed 1 May 2016]

15 Wakenshaw, Susan 'What is a 'smart' city?', *Hub of All Things*, 16 June 2015 [online] http://hubofallthings.com/Harriet/2015/06/what-is-a-smart-city/ [accessed 1 May 2016]

16 Metz, Cade, 'Google open-sourcing TensorFlow shows AI's future is data', *Wired*, 16 November 2015 [online] http://www.wired.com/2015/11/google-open-sourcing-tensorflow-shows-ais-future-is-data-not-code/ [accessed 1 May 2016]

17 Council of the European Union, 'Proposal for a regulation of the European Parliament and of the Council on the protection of individuals with regard to the processing of personal data and on the free movement of such data (General Data Protection Regulation)', 11 June 2015 [online] http://data.consilium.europa.eu/doc/document/ST-9565-2015-INIT/en/pdf [accessed 1 May 2016]

18 Kaye, Kate, 'New European privacy rules mean more complexity for data-hungry marketers', *AdAge*, 18 December 2015 [online] http://adage.com/article/datadriven-marketing/eu-privacy-rules-complexity-data-marketers/301854/ [accessed 1 May 2016]

19 Council of the European Union, 'Proposal for a regulation of the European Parliament and of the Council on the protection of individuals with regard to the processing of personal data and on the free movement of such data (General Data Protection Regulation)', 11 June 2015 [online] http://data.consilium.europa.eu/doc/document/ST-9565-2015-INIT/en/pdf [accessed 1 May 2016]

20 Kaye, Kate, 'New European privacy rules mean more complexity for data-hungry marketers', *AdAge*, 18 December 2015 [online] http://adage.com/article/datadriven-marketing/eu-privacy-rules-complexity-data-marketers/301854/ [accessed 1 May 2016]

21 Lewis, Robin, 'Millennials: double trouble for retail', *Forbes*, 30 April 2014 [online] http://www.forbes.com/sites/robinlewis/2014/04/30/millennials-double-trouble-for-retail/#1c8ca9ba4724 [accessed 1 May 2016]

INDEX

CPSIA information can be obtained
at www.ICGtesting.com
Printed in the USA
LVOW04s0717070717
540520LV00007B/14/P